3/07/2012

Caged

To Bangkok BJJ

Cameron Conaway

Caged

Memoirs of a Cage-Fighting Poet

Cameron Conaway

| Threed Press |

Please note that the publisher and author of this book are not responsible in any manner whatsoever for any injury that may result from practicing the techniques and/or following the instructions given within. Martial arts training can be dangerous—both to you and to others—if not practiced safely. If you're in doubt as to how to proceed or whether your practice is safe, consult with a trained martial arts teacher and/or nutritionist before beginning. Since the physical activities described herein may be too strenuous in nature for some readers, it is also essential that a physician be consulted prior to training.

This work is a memoir. While every effort was made to corroborate personal experience and emotional truth with actual truth, all human stories are subject to errors of omission, fact, or interpretation regardless of the best of intent. On rare occasions, details were altered to protect privacy, and composites were formed. Ages were estimated. Exaggeration and embellishment avoided. At no point was honesty sacrificed for creativity. Memory of the same event may differ from person to person. The author's subjects may remember things differently and he looks forward to learning of those memories. His intent was not to harm, defame, seek revenge or otherwise bring stress to others. *Caged* was written without malice or anger, and is the author's attempt to contribute to the most noble and ethical qualities in the creative nonfiction genre as found in graduate school workshops all over the world, and as written by Lee Gutkind, founder of the literary magazine *Creative Nonfiction*, and in Dinty W. Moore's *The Truth of the Matter*. The author believes the act of writing is ultimately about helping others through sharing inspiration, information and perspective.

Published by Threed Press

www.CameronConaway.com

Library of Congress Cataloging-in-Publication Data

ISBN-10: 0-615521-77-0
ISBN-13: 978-0-6155217-7-0
Library of Congress Control Number: 2011937043

First edition

14 13 12 11   10 9 8 7 6 5 4 3 2 1

Printed in the United States of America

Contents

For:

Mom
Nab
Maggie
the color red

"But his whole life was dominated by fear, the fear of failure and of weakness. It was deeper and more intimate than the fear of evil and capricious gods and of magic, the fear of the forest, and of the forces of nature, malevolent, red in tooth and claw. Okonkwo's fear was greater than these. It was not external but lay deep within himself. It was the fear of himself, lest he should be found to resemble his father."

– Chinua Achebe, Things Fall Apart

There was a time in this world when great poets were as revered and feared as great warriors. Both sat beside royalty. With one swift blow in combat, a warrior could end a man's life. With one wicked verse, a poet could ruin a man's life, even cause suicides by shattering reputations. Both were dangerous enough to kill the living, but a poet could kill the dead.

There was a time in this world when our greatest writers were our greatest fighters. They were endowed intellectually and physically and were weaponed with rhetoric and hands because they valued a holistic approach to developing the self. Those endeavoring to fully develop their mental and physical capacities were honorably called "renaissance men."

Today, we are forced into and rewarded by specializing—becoming a Shakespeare scholar or an interior designer, a painter or a wrestler, a politician or a cyclist. Diversity isn't respected much because it doesn't pay bills or help us acquire the material things that prove power. And poetry? Who reads poetry?

In the year 2011, there are fighters and there are writers and they are separate as can be. One bangs days away on heavybags, one bangs days away on keyboards. One taps their hands on blue mats to acknowledge defeat, one taps their pencils on tables as they craft sentences.

I didn't know either field's history. Nor did I strive for their fusion. I was just a boy wanting to remove the confusion that dripped from pain's wild roots, a boy who by ferociously pursuing instinct blossomed into a simple man.

The Power of Then: *Space for Reflections*
As you read, write here

CHAPTER 1

Across the Middle

Intro: Latin. Late 14c. "inward, to the inside."

Memoir: 1560–70; < F mémoire < L memoria; see memory

Makes sense to begin at earliest memory. What follows:
A matter of control. Finding connections in
memory's nonlinear snapshots. "Only connect!"

– E.M. Forster, *Howard's End*

With pistol's point pressed into my temple they led me halfway down the staircase. With boot in the small of my back they sent me tumbling down the rest. All for what? Because I was an eight-year-old boy who walked in on their orgy. A woman's tanned, sweat-glistened right thigh, several naked torsos and a Paul McCartney poster.

My father had brought me to Lordknowswhere, Pennsylvania, for a Super Bowl party. Cowboys vs. Bills. I liked Cowboys running back Emmitt Smith #22. My father liked alcohol whatever proof.

I stood only to walk to the kitchen to grab a bowl of cubed deer bologna— the kind with the chunks of cheddar cheese spread through it. Standing kept me eye level with genitals and asses, made me feel awkward, guilty when the drunks turned and stumbled over me. Even now I feel uncomfortable standing amongst those much shorter or taller. Sitting seems to generally level people out so presence doesn't take precedence over conversation. Words.

Smell: Beer on cat-hair-laced carpet.

With the kickoff to start the second half I accidentally kicked my father's beer over as I made my way from bologna chips-and-dip station to the floor in front of the television.

"Jesus Christ almighty, Cameron. Why don't you go play with the other kids upstairs?" This came after he said, "I oughta fan your ass for this," which he proceeded to do in front of the ten or so other adults in the smoke-hazed room.

It hurt a little, but he didn't embarrass me by pulling my jeans down. So I felt grateful, and like a complete fucking idiot for spilling his beer. *What is wrong with me? Why do I do stuff I don't mean to do like dropping snow cones or knocking over drinks? I must be retarded like he says.* I'd make "retard faces" in bathroom mirrors because it made me feel better knowing and seeing than not knowing and not seeing and getting beat regardless.

Two reasons I wasn't with the other kids:

(1) They weren't other kids. They all seemed to be at least 18.
(2) I liked Emmitt, that "smooth nigger" as the party people said.

After he fanned my ass, I sat down on a big circular plush red rug. It was halfway between the staircase (where the "other kids" were) and the couch where my father sat watching the game. Cross-legged, with a bowl of deer bologna in my lap, I felt safely dangerously alone. Safely because my father was *just right there.* Dangerously because the "other kids" were just right upstairs and my father was *just right there.*

What if they saw me sitting here like an idiot? Would they call me retarded? What if he saw me sitting here like an idiot—would I get my ass fanned again?

From couch: "Son of a bitch, there goes that Emmitt nigger," said the fat, bearded Punxsutawney Phil-looking man sitting beside my father. They rooted for the Bills because they said the Bills always get to the Super Bowl but just can't seem to win it. Plus Steelers fans hate the Cowboys.

From upstairs: "Go Emmitt go! Touchdown!"

I butt-scooted closer to the staircase, further from the couch.

From upstairs: "Best fuckin' back in the league baby!"

I full-out sprinted to the staircase before nerves settled in. *They like Emmitt too*, I thought. *I want to go tell them how the barber carved #22 in the back of my hair for last year's Super Bowl.*

Slowly, clutching the right handrail to stabilize my shaking legs, I made it to the top of the steps.

From room: "Yes! Yes! Fuck yes!"

Emmitt fans.

From me, while poking the door open: "Hey my mom let me get Em…"

"Get the fuck out of here. Someone get him the fuck out of here!"

Now, there were hands on my shoulders spinning me away to face the stairs. Then the cold metal slid slowly up, up, up past my cheekbone and settled against my temple. I couldn't think let alone speak. Tunnel vision. All I saw: the bright dance of light on a black pistol in a pasty hand—my father had this type of gun. All I heard: the high-pitched piercing hum of silence.

The force of the boot on my back whiplashed my neck and sent me hurdling down the staircase. My knees were brush-burned and bleeding when I finally reached the bottom.

From the kitchen: "Cam, your son just fell down the steps."

While walking towards me from the couch: "Christ Cameron, what is wrong with you? That's it, we're leaving as soon as this game's over!" He went back to the couch.

I sat down across the middle of the red rug. Then I adjusted myself so I was exactly halfway between them and him. *What is wrong with me?* I was obsessed with getting in the middle. I had no deer bologna bowl to occupy me. *Middles can be invisible,* I thought. *Like if I am directly exactly precisely between two things I can go invisible if I want.* Everybody was in the living room so I stood for awhile adjusting my feet by millimeters to find the direct exact precise center. Then I sat. Then I combed the carpet fibers with my fingers so they all faced away.

Log 1

Fibers: Think cheetah. They rest all day then explode after prey. This recruits and develops fast twitch fibers (Type II). These fibers are responsible for the explosive movements so vital for mixed martial arts (MMA) performance. Sprints, plyometrics, intense heavybag bursts, power cleans, clap pushups, clap pull-ups. Go hard then rest like the cheetah. Frequently training aerobically with long, slow distance runs actually converts more fibers to slow twitch. Not good. Cheetah train.

Individual	Percentage fast-twitch muscle fibre
Sedentary	45-55%
Distance runner	25%
Middle-distance runner	35%
Sprinter	84%
Cheetah	83% of the total number of fibres examined in the rear outer portion of the thigh (vastus lateralis), and nearly 61% of the calf (gastrocnemius) were comprised of fast-twitch fibres.

From: http://www.pponline.co.uk/encyc/speed-and-power-training-understanding-your-fast-twitch-muscles-will-boost-performance-41354

CHAPTER 2

The Prey Shapes
the Predator

Ducere: Latin. Late 14c. "to lead."

A wolf has a deer by the throat, but nothing yet has been ced-
ed, no energy yet surrendered or conquered or captured, and
the two are rolling around and wrestling, blood in the sand,
eyes bright in fury, and the deer is giving - in the moment - as
good as it is getting, kicking and lunging and grunting, stabbing with its antlers....
The prey, even in death, controls the predator by virtue of its
lower, more stable position in the food chain. If the wolf or
other predator is "too" successful, and consumes "too" much
energy, the base will sag or collapse, bringing low population
numbers of prey, and lean times.
The predator will have to bide its time and wait for the prey
to recover.
Waiting does not seem to us like a form of dominance.

– Rick Bass, The New Wolves

Sixteen years after the pistol incident and three years after I read *The New Wolves*, the quote still moves me by the suddenness of its raw intensity, by the way it reveals a lesson from the marrow of violence. Four ideas crucial to my personal development come from this quote: Fighting, Balance, Control, Waiting.

On Fighting

Fighting—be it war in muddy trenches, mixed martial arts contests inside a cage, arguments between spouses, intense contemplation, hair-pulling by children, dogfighting Michael Vick style or any other form of combat—is a word too often represented only by its physical manifestation. This results in the word sharing mind-space with other phrases and words like: slain soldiers, divorce, blood, violence, drugs, crime. It's no wonder then that the word carries negative energy in our consciousness. It's no wonder then that "cage-fighting" found itself banned time and again until—voila—Rick Blume (president and CEO of Battlecade, an extreme fighting organization that lasted only one year) morphed the term in 1995 to "mixed martial arts," a three-lettered acronym to share company with the NFL, NBA, MLB, and NHL.

All fighting forms have been nothing but positive for me in the long run. In the long run. In their infancy, they often caused tremendous pain, such as the time at Blue Knob Ski Resort when I was eleven or so. The trip was my father's attempt to show my sister (four years my junior) and me that his new wife and her son (about my sister's age) were cool. That we could all have some good ol' family fun together. Bless his heart. I do believe the man meant well. I believe he has always meant well. The problem was the consistent disconnect between what he meant and what actually happened.

This was my first ever attempt at gliding downhill on skis. After falling within the first ten yards, I got back to my feet and managed to accelerate my way down half the hill—about two hundred yards or so—before I really went down hard in sheer panic to avoid complete loss of control. My legs bent awkwardly behind me and the skis stuck deep into the snow. Both of my knees burned with the pain of pulled tendons. As my father skied to me I fought to free myself. I rolled, turned, and dug to no avail. He stood over me. I looked up to him. I reached my hand out to join his. He looked down on me.

"You're a pussy. Wah, wah," he said loudly as he pretended to wipe tears. "Look at little crybaby Cameron. Wah, wah."

"Help me, Dad," I mumbled quietly to quiet him, to try to lessen this growing scene.

"Get up, crybaby Cameron. Get up, you pussy." My hand hung empty. He poked at me with the spikes of his ski poles as though I were steak.

"Be a man, Cameron. Poor little, weak, crybaby Cammy. Stop crying and get up. Everybody is having a good time. Don't you dare ruin this by being a baby. Be a man."

"Help me, Dad!" I screamed desperately hard through tears.

He turned his back on me and skied on down the slope. He turned his back on me and I hated him for it.

Eventually I lowered my hand down to ease the pressure off of my knees. I closed my eyes hard to squeeze out the tears so I could see and suddenly I felt someone behind me digging a space around each ski, grabbing me under the armpits and lifting me upright. My legs tingled with the pins and needles of numbness, but I felt the blood rushing back. A stranger on a bright red snowboard asked if I was okay and I said yes and thanked her.

I saw my father cutting and gliding a quarter-mile down the slope. I struggled back up to the top, dragging the skis behind me, and spent my time in the warm log cabin ski lodge flipping through channels before stopping on a *Full House* rerun. All the characters on that show, even if they made the initial mistake of not supporting each other, would eventually apologize and become supportive. I wanted to be part of the Tanner family. Unreality cooled reality's burn.

> Sometimes a wolf might catch a young longhorn out on the range and, in biting at its flanks, castrate the animal; the calves who survived such excisions went on to become steers of prodigious size, growing horns far larger, and attaining more mass, than had they not been "cut." It is almost as if in failing to bring that male calf down, the wolves had instead given rise to something near-mythic, a steer they would never again be able to harass or injure.

My father metaphorically castrated me. The mental and at times physical pain he caused, along with my past insecurities and fears and the physical pain I brought upon myself by training to become a better mixed martial arts fighter, all of it was the wolf biting at the flanks. I was the young calf that could not be brought down, no matter how bad the times got. I may have been crying so hard I couldn't breathe after getting verbally harassed by my father—like the time before my 7th grade basketball game at the Building II Athletic Club where he called me the "son of a whore" in front of my mom, my best friends, and their parents. I may have been kicked square in the nose by a roundhouse after a two-hour-long practice session, a roundhouse that broke my nose a week before my first scheduled professional fight and caused me to withdraw, that staggered me backwards, made me see small flashes of white and yellow light and resulted in the biggest loss of blood I have ever endured; but I was never brought down. Depressed? Maybe. Unhappy? Yes. But not down. As a result, I grew, not anywhere in the realm of "near-mythic" proportions, but definitely strong enough so the onslaught of wolves I would face in the future "would never again be able to harass or injure" my newfound warrior spirit.

This is what fighting (in all of its oft-overlooked complexities) makes of me.

On Balance

"Newfound warrior spirit" sounds abstract, but it means I was learning more about my strengths and weaknesses and what I needed to do in my life to highlight those strengths and correct those weaknesses. It means that as I grew to be a stronger animal, I became more confident in how I handled the often-unexpected stressors in my life. Like any other animal, I learned I too had to live with the delicate nature of balance.

I believe everyone has a warrior spirit but I do not believe it is the same (or arises the same way) for everybody. My warrior spirit came from the realization that I must strive for balance between the mental and the physical. If I am stimulated mentally—by a new book, by a wonderfully rich conversation with a friend or family member, or by my own inner-reflections on past experiences—I must give myself a period of physical activity. For example, if I attended class all day then met with my mentor and former professor Todd Davis to discuss an essay I'd written, I couldn't go home and mull everything over. An overwhelming sensation of confusion would occur, and my mind would bounce from topic to topic without truly absorbing or digging deeper into new levels of thought. Instead, I had to get to the woods for a jog through the winding, wild trails at Canoe Creek State Park, wrap my hands and drop pounds of sweat into the concrete floors of the Altoona Boxing Club, or shoot baskets at a park until the moths gathered and circled tirelessly at the streetlight.

Physical stimulation for me has always been instinctive. When engaged in that Canoe Creek jog I did not think about any of the day's events. Instead, I was in tune with my body, I felt the leaves crackling under my feet, I heard the calls of birds and the scurrying of squirrels, I felt the sweat start to bead on my forehead and settle into my eyebrows. I felt my calves begin to burn during an uphill bend; I dodged branches as though they were oncoming punches and I lunged under balconies of leaves that hung over the trail as though I was shooting in for a takedown. I noticed the distinct smells of new patches of plants. I remembered the fallen tree about twenty minutes into the jog and whether I jumped over it with my left or right foot last time. I saw new piles of scat, wondered what the animals think of my smashing through their lush homes.

When I was at the Altoona Boxing Club training with the area's best professional boxer, Tom Wilt, I was focused solely on the accuracy of my gloves landing into the contoured grooves of those red-and-black Ringside mitts, on slipping and rolling with punches. I did not have to think "Okay, when he throws this left hook, I need to do this with my legs, then this with my hips so I can swivel back and counter with a straight right hand." Physicality in action is much too fast-paced for analysis. This is its beauty. When those mitts are flying at me I'm dodging and countering hard, feeling my power shoot up through my legs and then through the rotation of my hips before rising up into my back and exploding through the mitts. I heard the pop-pop-pop of a three-punch combination and it felt just as good as a compliment I'd received from a teacher earlier in the day. When the jog or the practice ended, then I could think back on how I could be doing this better or how I needed to work more on that. In the moment is in the moment.

There were times during my senior year, while pursuing a double major at Penn State Altoona, when classes or meetings lasted from seven in the morning until seven at night. Beginning at 7:15 P.M. I'd study lines for Euripides' Medea, the play in which I had the lead role in the coming months. There were times when that day extended into another day and extended into a week. Lacking time for physical exercise, I felt myself become antsy, restless, even a bit depressed. But eventually I knew there would be a time where I could focus on the physical, on the senses, a time when I could let that pendulum swing back the other way so it settled in the center.

Luckily for me, I'd grown up watching my single mom work sixteen-hour days so she could put store-brand rigatoni with sauce on the table for my sister and me. We looked forward to that meal every time she made it. It was warm and seemed to bring warmth into our conversation. We called the meal "rags," as in, "Hey Mom, can we have rags tonight?" We have no idea where the name came from but every time we said it we laughed. When I heard mom get the big plates out, I knew it was time for me to get the shaky cheese (Parmesan cheese) and forks for us three. Even when I was young I wanted to emulate the work mom put in to provide that meal. So from the time I could work I did. At fifteen, I tallied statistics at Vets Field for elementary flag football games—running sideline-to-sideline to make sure I saw exactly what happened and the jersey numbers of the players who made the play. Then I worked as a cook for the McDonald's along 25th Avenue, hefting large boxes from the freezer and slapping the quarter-pounders onto the grill for forty-three seconds, swatting the flies away at night so I could empty the grease trap so I could cook the burgers and fries that would fill it back up again.

McDonald's was physical and it was mindless. Pimples broke out all over my face because I worked hours bent over the stove from which the grease-steam rose. I skated easily across the floor in the grease that settled there. I felt only the burns on my hands, heard only the hiss of the grill press, smelled, oddly enough, only the mustard and ketchup, and tasted the Mc-Chicken sandwich (thanks to a fifty-percent employee discount) during each break.

Then, during the four years it took me to complete my undergraduate degrees, I worked as a produce associate at the Martin's Grocery Store across the street from McDonald's, specifically asking to "break down the trucks." This meant as an order came into our cooler—hundreds of pounds of fruits and vegetables on frozen wooden pallets—it was my job to transfer the products onto the carts for the other associates to take to the shelves. It was constant grunt-work, bending down at the knees and exploding upwards with heavy boxes of cabbage, climbing atop double-layered pallets to bring down the asparagus a customer wanted. It was a perfect way for me to make money, follow my mom's work ethic, and create balance between mental and physical stimulation. I don't find it ironic that one of my first poems in college was about my mom saving my life. When I look back, I see how she's saved my life in many other ways as well. For now, here's the poem I wrote that tells the story through the candy's perspective:

Lifesaver
I became
lodged,
stuck
through no fault
of my own
inside a dark
moist
warm
tube.
My color
dwindling,
a pressure
from below
so forceful,
ejected me
through the tube
and into
a dark room
with what looked
to be rows
of white chairs.
I flew
through
the air
onto a smooth
white
surface
where
I slid
losing
more
and more
of myself,
my flavor,
through
a red trail
of misuse. (2005)

Those four years in the produce department taught me the diversity of fresh food available (which served as a springboard into healthy eating) and the eccentricities of people. In high school I was shy, but in that produce department, though I often put my head down and finished the job, I became and remained interested in the human characters I encountered each day. It opened up the world to me, made me realize how different we all are as human beings and that different is okay, different is beautiful. From my boss who, when he wasn't imitating characters from Dave Chappell's show on Comedy Central, spoke primarily of professional wrestling, to the physically fit and often hilarious nearly-seventy-year-old co-worker who spoke of once watching a woman and donkey have intercourse, to the Italian restaurant owner who came storming in every Saturday morning: "Hey Camarone, you have any bigger egg-a-planta on di shelf?" to the obsessive compulsive woman who leafed through my newly stacked potato-and-apple counters every Friday evening for, no lie, hours without ever making a purchase—when I look back on it there is no place I would have rather been than with those people in that produce department. The lesson: Personalities come in as many colors as produce.

Not until years after my graduation from Penn State Altoona, when I began graduate school for creative writing at the University of Arizona and for the first time lived without the presence of my best friend, my mom, did I realize how sane that job had kept me, how important it was for me to always maintain an awareness of how far my pendulum swung to each side so I could best balance it in the center.

On Control

I'd learned that balance in the center meant controlling two variables. First, controlling the awareness that balance was necessary for my happiness. Second, controlling the steps that kept that balance in place. It's the same steps a psychologist might give to their client—first recognizing and admitting the problem so one can best master how to solve it.

But it took me a long time to learn about the self-control that would keep me in balance. The way I became aware imbalance could occur was something I stumbled upon. In high school I'd kept a workout journal, discussing how my body felt, what exercises I completed, what weights I used and how many repetitions I performed on a given lift. Still, sometimes days would pass where I had excellent workouts at the gym or the woods but for some reason did not want to record them.

Maintaining the journal became a chore. I'd crack it open to see that my last entry was two weeks ago—I'd faked an illness to get out of going to school for three or four days during that stretch. Maybe being called a pussy by my father bubbled back up to the surface. Whatever the reason, I felt I wasn't writing consistently in the journal because I was a weak person. I hated myself for being weak and I'd scribble notes in the journal like, "just keep fucking writing" and "stop being a little bitch." I used hostile notes against myself that were eerily parallel to the words my father used against me. To achieve anything, I needed an opponent. If there wasn't one then I stepped in against myself.

Nonetheless I kept failing. But I gradually noticed that when I had a great day at school (which was rare) I'd also have my best workouts at the gym. I didn't enjoy reading or math or science or writing, but loved the feeling that arose from completing a project I was nervous about. I loved finishing. And it was on those days I mastered some project or test I'd been dreading for weeks that I'd attack whatever physical activity I did later in the day with feverish intensity. Curious, I began pouring over my journals and noticing the dates I made prominent by drawing all sorts of stars and exclamation marks—my way of calling attention to great workouts among the mediocre. Through this process I found, in a vague way I couldn't yet fully comprehend, a correlation between finishing something for school and a killer workout.

The correlation was opaque at the time. I didn't fully understand that mental stimulation, and more exactly, self-control, could lead to more rewarding physical stimulation, which could lead to happiness. But I saw something about how mental happiness—even in brief bouts—meant something positive for my workouts.

Days when I spoke a lot (rare) to a girl I liked meant better workouts. Chicken-patty or cheese-steak hoagie days (my two favorites) meant better workouts. Days when my mom, sister, and I ate rags and watched a sitcom together meant better workouts. Days I bought flowers for a girl on Valentine's day, told my grandmother and my grandfather on my mom's side that I loved them, was social with friends after school, or performed random acts of kindness, like shoveling an elderly neighbor's driveway, meant better workouts.

During my senior year at Penn State Altoona, I realized that so much of my success physically over the years—those exclamation-days in my journals dating all the way back to high school—were a result of factors I could control.

Finding correlation was one thing, a thing I still believe was as much luck as anything else, but controlling knowledge of myself was a whole other arena.

I began cracking open books much more frequently, not so much to actually learn but because I knew if I did I would have a better workout and feel a euphoric state of happiness before bed rather than the tossing and turning that came from my constant contemplation on the painful events in my past. Over time my reasons for learning changed. Those words I may have merely glanced over became sought-after and mulled-over poems by Sharon Olds or Ted Kooser, essays by Ernest Hemingway or Raymond Carver or biographies of my favorite fighters. I became just as engaged in the mental as I did the physical, and I began two separate journals. In one, I detailed my diet and workouts and in the other I detailed my moods and thoughts. While at the University of Arizona, I combined them into a single journal because I realized how related the two seemingly opposing sides were. More often than not, I had the power to control (or at least influence) how I felt, learned, trained, and, in turn, how happy I could be. *Holy shit*, I remember thinking to myself, *I've read about this in quotes, but can I actually control my happiness regardless of what happens beyond my control?*

Of course, there's a lot we can't control. It was during this time my mom called to say Bo, our beagle, died at the age of fourteen. Suddenly I began to dream about death. In one dream, my grandparents and I were hiking at Sabino Canyon in Tucson. Pap slipped and tumbled down head over heels to the bottom. When I looked down from the top his body was about the length of a fingernail, his head was smoothly severed from his neck and resting face down beside him. His shiny black hair glistened in the sunlight. "Gram, we need to get down there to help Pap," I said. "We will not," she coldly replied. "If we find him I won't be able to collect the insurance money on his death." I grabbed two fists full of her brown, permed hair and launched her over the edge. She landed the exact same way Pap did. Her body pressed identically onto Pap's body and her head landed face down on his. I woke in a sweat, scared shitless.

In another dream, my mom and my stepdad Bob (who I call Nab) were on their way home from a Pittsburgh Steelers game. Just as they pulled out of

Heinz Field, a brown UPS truck crashed into their Jeep, killing them both. I could see clumps of mom's hair stuck in the dashboard. I panicked and wanted to call her but couldn't because she was dead. I rang and rang her phone to let her know of the news, that I was broken, that I needed help. I woke feeling as though I would come home at semester's end to an empty house. A house of death.

Then, in real life, my younger sister Courtney's best friend, Jessalyn, a girl whose vibrant, high-spirited personality had made me smile each day I worked with her while at Martin's Grocery Store, died in a car accident. I struggled to sleep the night I heard about her death, not so much because I felt sickened by the sudden loss of someone so filled with constant life, as by the thought she was watching me. I felt as though she was trying to tell me through the silent desert air to give to people as she did—with smiling eyes and contagious enthusiasm. I realized that night I admired her naturally radiating contagiousness so much there was a sliver of jealousy inside of me. I wanted to impact people the way she had. *Begin now*, I told myself. Fire doesn't always slowly burn itself out. Sometimes it's doused with water and gone as quickly as its flames danced.

One month later I went through a difficult breakup with a woman I'd dated even prior to graduate school, then I became mysteriously ill with something that ripped fifteen pounds from my frame in the first three days and left me too weak, quite often, to make it to the bathroom in time. When I sneezed, I shit. When I farted, I sharted. It was terrifying to lose control of my body, the vehicle I most felt in control of—the instrument I trained and sharpened and tried to be as ultra-aware-of as possible. I feared I had come down with a rare, incurable disease. That after my death I'd be a poster-child for this newfound disease, stories told about it by Sanjay Gupta on CNN specials. And here I was, alone in Arizona, 2,000 miles away from home. And it was here where, as in the ski lodge after I'd fallen on that slope as a child, I turned to shows like the *Fresh Prince of Bel-Air*, *Full House*, and *Home Improvement*, shows where any problem at all could be solved within twenty-three minutes. It wasn't a dire disease, but it was salmonella.

Some two months after learning of Jessalyn's death, and while salmonella swept any and everything out of my stomach, my sadness, fragile heart, and weakened spirit were swept away. It all began through AOL Instant Messenger (*welcome to the 21st century*, I told myself) where I established the foundation of a relationship with a woman I'd known in high school. Maggie. Back in high school everyone thought she was perfect for me but we never developed a relationship due to my shy, insecure nature, her drive to play elite-level soccer, and my drive to become a world-class fighter.

As I was beginning graduate school she was finishing up her physical education and health teaching licensures at West Virginia University. Enter Nerdom: One day her screen name appeared on my buddy list. Part of me had always been interested in her as a person, even if just for the surface attributes I knew of her: a beautiful woman with a killer instinct on the soccer field. Our online profiles contained the same two quotes by German philosopher Friedrich Nietzsche.

(1) *The most spiritual men, as the strongest, find their happiness where others would find their destruction: in the labyrinth, in hardness against themselves and others, in experiments. Their joy is self-conquest. Difficult tasks are a privilege to them; to play with burdens that crush others, a recreation. They are the most venerable kind of man: that does not preclude their being the most cheerful and the kindliest.*

(2) *The most spiritual human beings, assuming they are the most courageous, also experience by far the most painful tragedies: but it is precisely for this reason that they honor life, because it brings against them its most formidable weapons.*

I sent her a message jokingly asking if she stole those quotes from me. She wrote back, "Haha. I sure did," and it began. When we moved from Instant Messaging to phone calls our conversations often ended around the four-hour mark. We were both recently hurt by relationships, both actively committed to *not dating* for a long, long time and both harboring and trying to learn lessons from past pains that spanned the gamut from eating disorders and reconstructed knees to verbal, psychological and physical abuse. We were hurt but we bared all, wobbly fighters still swinging. Years have passed. We wobble no more. We're now living together in Bangkok, Thailand.

When we first began speaking, my journal exploded. I found the other fifty percent of myself for which I was willing to wait a lifetime. This threw all the plans I'd made in haste for a loop. As much as I thought I controlled the intricacies of life, I learned so much was still a mystery to be accepted and welcomed rather than aggressively unraveled. Simultaneously, I found myself unable to control anything, from something so fundamental as a bowel movement to something so lucid as love. The juxtaposition heightened and reinforced the lesson. So much could not be controlled by anything other than patience. So much of control was the opposite quality I imagined it to be. So much of control is not authoritative action (as the male culture often suggests) but mindful waiting.

Waiting does not seem to us like a form of dominance.

On Waiting

Waiting is where my quest for learning currently resides. It is the fourth and final and most difficult part for me to accept.

Those closest to me told me to be patient with the production of this book. But even patience has weaknesses. I've been threatened with a lawsuit, a lawsuit that made the book publisher I'd worked with for over a year in preparation cancel the contract at the last second (as the book was released for pre-order) for fear of the finances it would take to fend off the suer. In the meantime, I've watched as the literary book industry has disintegrated over the years. So I gave in to the kicking and lunging and grunting. Despite the best intentions of those mentors in my life, I don't believe they ever understood the connection between my health and the creation of this book. *Caged* called out to me like a child, not for its own selfish sake, but because it was the balance-maker for the hours of hiking, running, sparring, swimming, weight-lifting and yoga to prepare my body for the physical demands of MMA. *Caged* called out to me because it knew for me to continue to live (to learn) I had to feed it. To live meant feeding my former self to my current self.

Sometimes the best lessons I learned in life were when actions were not taken—when my father did not reach down to help me up, when the journal was not written in, when the roundhouse kick was not dodged or defended. But to continue being patient, to continue letting the threats or the industry delay this book into oblivion would have been a slap in the face to all writers and artists everywhere. I asked myself and others millions of questions, but in the end it came down to this: *What is a world in which writers get threatened and then blocked from sharing the stories that most shaped them?* It wasn't one I wanted to live in, so I took the steps needed to go for it. Sometimes we can and need to be our own wolves.

Here is *Caged*, presented to you with all the purposeful ambiguity of its title. The obvious: the physical structure where MMA bouts take place. My thoughts toward that cage are like the cycle of seasons. My feelings change gradually, brushing against one another until their colors fade and become solidified as one like the leaves of autumn.

A second meaning of *Caged* is the sense of isolation I felt for the duration of this quest - from the writing, the seeking of a publisher, the landing of a publisher, the cancelling of a contract and the stigma a writer carries when they have to present a book to financially-scared publishers with a preface that says, "By the way, if you like what is to come, you'll need to know there is someone who says they will be 'relentless' in their pursuit of not letting this get published." Loneliness comes "from being unable to communicate the things that seem important to oneself," said Carl Jung, one of the most influential thinkers on psychology. I found myself unable to communicate both my story and why I chose the various roles with which I increasingly began to define myself: a man, a mixed martial artist, an actor, a poet instead of the potential financial security of a businessman despite my difficulties caused by lack of money.

I reflected on the inmates in solitary confinement I saw during class prison tours when I was a Criminal Justice major. I realized that some people are literally caged, that even people unincarcerated could be caged. I was one of these people. One of many. The imprisoned living.

Then, while I was the Poet-in-Residence at the University of Arizona and was teaching poetry to young women detainees at a juvenile detention center, I realized that the idea of being caged in multiple dimensions was a consistent theme throughout their poems.

From those experiences grew the belief that every decision made in life first *had to be* caged—had to be contained in a small area to block out other ideas. But, just like the spaces between prison bars, there had to be spaces in these decision-cages too. These spaces, I came to believe, were what allowed people to view the idea while also being able to contain it. The spaces between the bars were just as important as the bars themselves.

I began trying to cage every aspect of my life. Every bite was thought about and questioned. Every breath controlled and regulated. Every movement researched. The way I was living was an unnatural state that became natural. It combined my reckless dream-reaching, my mind's meticulousness, and the vigor of a young adult who now knew the importance of distance—not just of landing a jab or hook or uppercut—but of an event and the emotions tied to that event. Of truth-seeking.

In short, I created a mind-version similar to what enclosed those inmates, a sort of mind-space where thoughts (some worthy and some worthless) could swirl around without a place to exit, could meet each other with the hopes of finding a connection despite (and possibly as a result of) their unconcealed differences.

The ideas were caged in my mind, at times rattling bars and at times playing quietly in the corner, but always, in some way, engaged. I didn't have a choice but to listen. I shit quicker so I could watch an extra few minutes of fighting instructional DVD's so I could get an edge over my opponent. I felt guilty just hanging out because it was time I could be shadowboxing or reading a new poet. I became obsessed with learning. And obsession's shadow draped over every minute of my life. I lived in a prison of productivity.

Still another meaning to *Caged* comes from sharing the same name as my father. In a *New York Times* article titled, "Where's His Right Hook?" by Maureen Dowd, Barack Obama states:

> Somebody said that every man is either trying to live up
> to his father's expectations or trying to make up for his
> father's mistakes. And in some ways, when your father's not
> there, you're doing both. You try to live up to the expecta-
> tions of somebody who's not present to tell you that you've
> done a good job, but you're also trying to make up for the
> mistakes that partially led to his absence.

I never knew what my father expected of me. I did not see it in his eyes, nor his actions or words. So I fabricated them. I pushed myself harder in everything I attempted. Without clear expectations, I decided I had to be the best in everything I did. *He would want that*, I told myself. My father had been a martial artist in his youth. He worked at the Altoona Hospital as an orderly for many years before he moved into the criminal justice field and began a career as a correctional officer at a medium security prison. This was what I knew he achieved, and I believed any father would want his son to have better, to do better.

One thing already in print: In August 2009 *Cameron Conaway* was in the Altoona Mirror newspaper under "Police Reports" for an altercation he had with a Best Buy employee. Wasn't me. Caged by name.

Perhaps what cut me the deepest is that he was absent for the most important moments in my life—the ones I remember, the ones I've become defined by. He never met a woman I dated, never watched me fight, never served as a role model when puberty was shaping my body, never saw me graduate from Penn State Altoona or from the University of Arizona, never offered advice when my mind was reaching for values to define what it meant to be a man.

Instead, I picked up qualities from other people—from legendary martial artists Ken Shamrock and Bruce Lee; the attributes I admired in my mom; from mentors and professors Todd Davis, Guy McPherson, and Steve Sherrill; from Martin Luther King Jr. and the 14th Dalai Lama; from my grandfather Ken Leonard and from my stepfather Nab, to name a few. This is how I began assembling pieces to the puzzle of myself, and I am still working towards its never-completion.

The piecing together has shown me that there is a primality to the arts of fighting and writing to which I'm incredibly attracted. We know through many written accounts and artworks of the time that pankration, an Ancient Greek word meaning "all powers," made its first appearance as a sport in the Greek Olympic games of 648 B.C. Pankration was an ultimate fighting discipline involving every known way to physically beat another man without weapons. Particularly popular among Spartans, contests involved punching, kicking, limb twisting and strangling. The only recognized fouls were biting and gouging. A contest ended when one of the fighters acknowledged defeat.

Pankration filled the niche of a total contest in a way boxing and wrestling could not. As is the case today, most reports from Ancient Greece indicate that no-holds-barred fights were often finished on the ground through takedowns, chokes, punches, elbows, or joint locks. There were no weight divisions, no time limits, and only two age groups: men and boys. Referees were armed with stout rods or switches to enforce the rules.

The contest usually continued uninterrupted until one of the combatants was submitted, which was often signaled by the submitted contestant raising his index finger. In today's MMA, fighters who wish to give up often tap the mat or their opponent's body three times. This is called tapping out.[1] Like

---

1 In MMA terms, "Tap" or "Tap-out" refers to submitting either physically by tapping the mat or the opponent three consecutive times, or verbally by saying "no" or some other fight-ending phrase when the referee asks if you want to continue.

today's MMA referees, pankration referees had the right to declare a draw or stop a contest under certain conditions and award the victory to one of the two athletes.

The majority of the Greek warriors who served under Alexander the Great during his invasion of India in 326 B.C. studied, practiced, and implemented the techniques of pankration. Arrichion, Dioxxipus, and Polydamos were big-name fighters forever linked with their unbeatable prowess as pankratiast practitioners. Some records report that when humans were no longer a big enough challenge, they fought lions. Even Hercules is reported to have been a pankratiast. But like any sport popular enough to have the names of its participants remembered or to stake its place in the Olympics, we also know it developed for long periods of time prior to its official introduction.

Perhaps it began with small circles of friends who wrestled around and eventually came to figure out—maybe even by accident—that this move choked somebody unconscious while a slight variation of that same move only annoyed. How many hundreds or thousands of years had the skills and techniques been evolving? Nobody knows. Can we assume humans have been engaged in some form of hand-to-hand combat since we first understood what it takes to survive and wanted to secure food, shelter, water, fire, and mates? When we realized we had the ability to physically hurt each other? I can't help but wonder when we became curious about how to improve upon those abilities. I assume that we've been fighting since the beginning of time. Today, the catchphrase is "Mixed Martial Arts"—the discipline of how two, external-weaponless bodies can most effectively attack and defend. MMA will continue to evolve as our knowledge of the human body continues to evolve.

The roots of communication are every bit as difficult to pin down. Maybe it began the first time two people looked at each other, or, maybe it began when one person communicated with their own body—engaging in all of their senses—realizing they could see their movements, could touch themselves and feel it, could produce a sound and hear it. The Egyptians are generally thought to have originated writing, with the Sumerians as another possibility. What began as nonverbal gestures may have escalated into sounds, into drawings, into evidence of a Greek alphabet system that we've found chiseled into stone dating back to at least the fifth century B.C.

Fighting and writing are of the body and the mind. As fighting requires the body to be crafted into a lethal weapon and paired with the mind to learn and express, so writing requires the mind to be crafted into an organizational, associative treasure trove of experiences and thoughts before being paired with the body—the hand and an instrument—to express. This is why I chose (or something or someone greater than myself drew me) to embrace both art forms. But how did that choice come about?

What draws us to what we love and what allows us to continue that love, or, conversely, lets that love burn out? Chance occurrences surely matter. When I was thirteen-years-old, for instance, I was captivated by an Ultimate Fighting Championship (UFC) video cover that stuck out from a shelf as I was walking to the porn section at Family Video. But why did that move me? Was it because I was in a bad mood that day and subconsciously craved violence? Was it because when I was a little kid I saw my father's karate trophies atop the television set? Was it because I was fascinated when he demonstrated martial arts kicks, in part, because when I tried to do them myself I fell down? Was it because martial arts flicks were occasionally on the television at home and the heroes, the great men, were all great fighters? It is amazing how what we're drawn to can grow from minor childhood experiences and blossom into lifelong loves. What's just as amazing is that those moments build and are stored somewhere in our brain and may not exhibit themselves or have the spark they need to catch fire until much later in life. If ever.

Caged is a book that swoops as a hawk into the waters of perspective. Many hawk-swoops end without captured prey, with only new water droplets on their talons. Like the hawk, I seek the meat below the surface. There will be blood.

Log 2

Surface. The fighter whose body looks better—more muscular and more "ripped"—does not necessarily move better, is not necessarily stronger or more conditioned, is not necessarily the better fighter. What you see is often not what you get. This is the "all show, no go" principle. Everyone wants a six-pack of abs, but they often neglect the more important transverse abdominals (TA) for the showy rectus abdominals. The TA is the deepest and arguably most important abdominal muscle when it comes to human performance, but it's too far below the surface to make us look much better when we're in our swimsuits. The TA provides spinal and trunk support by creating intra-abdominal pressure to become an internal weight belt of sorts. (Tip: Do not wear a weight belt. If you need a weight belt it's because your TA is weak. Training with a weight belt will train your body not to rely on its own built-in weight belt. Then, when you're out lifting something heavy and don't have your weight belt near, you might blow out your back, or worse.) It also assists in the respiratory process. Imagine you are pulling your belly button into your spine or focus on what your abdomen does during defecation. This is the TA. Planks are one exercise that hit this area. To perform a plank, get in the top of a pushup position, but instead of holding your weight on your hands, bend your elbows and rest on your forearms while keeping your knees, stomach and chest all stabilized and off the ground. Hold the position for a designated time. Rest. Repeat.

CHAPTER 3

Fighting in Phone Booths

Close quarters combat. Read it again. Listen to the 1-2-2 syllable-beat like rain on a roof. Hear how the alliterative beginning of each word drags across the phrase like a metal dog leash across linoleum.

I've been in love with close quarters combat fighting since I rented a UFC video featuring Ken Shamrock when I was thirteen. Recently, I've realized my pursuit of poetry is also based on a love of close quarters.

Efficiency in small spaces, secure places.

Launching missiles over oceans doesn't interest me. Nor does pulling a pistol and firing from yards away. I'm not interested in rambling writers who splash sporadic red herrings for the sake of lengthening their novel. Nor do I like magazines interrupting a story with an advertisement then directing me to the page where I can finish.

Feeling my opponent's chest rise against mine interests me, as does seeing his temples pulse when he clenches down into his mouthpiece and drives his shoulder into my face. I'm interested in poets who pack more sounds, images, and experiences into a single stanza than all the songs on a pop-music station over the course of weeks.

I'm interested in how the best Brazilian Jiu-Jitsu fighters put themselves in the optimal alignment to break their opponents' bones. I'm interested in how the best poets decide where to break lines to create dual meanings.

I'm interested in being the best I can be in the squared-circle of a ring and on a squared piece of paper.

Enclosure brings intimacy.
Enclosure brings vulnerability.

Fighting in close quarters combat allows me to know my opponent and myself. I see how only his left eye squints when he throws a straight right hand. I see the "RIP Mom" tattoo on his shoulder. I feel nothing during the heat of battle: the ultimate feeling. I hear his voice through wordlessness. I know what he smells like when dry, when sweat-slick.

Fighters meet each other enclosed in a small space so we can best engage each other's senses. We speak through our minds and bodies. We speak a silent conversation surrounded by a packed arena of thousands.

Writing is close quarters combat too. How can I best convey aspects of my life and share it with others in the most efficient, practical manner possible? How can I get my words to resonate with a reader—through silent conversation—in the confines of a book, on the confines of one page, then the next, and the next? How can I best use your precious time? How can I show myself as intimately as possible? How can I stand before you in silent symbols with open palms?

Before each round ends, the sound of sticks signals ten seconds left. Fighters pick up the pace with hopes of stealing or securing the round in the judges' eyes.

Replace round with chapter. The writer tries to finish each section with power—enticing readers to turn the page.

The abilities of a fighter reside in the body and are not exhibited until released by training or competition. Fighters do not throw crisp knee-strikes as they clock in for another day of work. They do not roll for a kneebar while cutting the grass. But those who train carry the benefits everywhere.

As long as a book is closed, it says nothing. When opened, a well-written book bursts into the mind's ear with honed sounds and creates crystal-clear images in the mind's eye. It can contain it all: mystery, inspiration, history, rhythm, misery, life. Those who read carry the benefits everywhere.

What I love most about editing writing is taking a sentence of fifteen words and trimming it to nine while stating the same information, only better.

I look forward to when I'm low on a bottle of vitamin D capsules because it means I can open a new bottle and try to fill it with what exists from the old bottle.

I try to fit as many hard-boiled eggs as possible into the Tupperware container so long as the lid still fits securely.

I often wonder if a machine could be developed to tell athletes exactly how much and what kind of food to eat to recover from workouts without over- or under-eating.

I've wrestled at 135 pounds, fought in MMA at 145 and 155 pounds, and bulked up and grappled at close to 180 pounds. I often wonder where I am most efficient, at what weight I have optimal levels of strength, cardio, flexibility, and agility. How can I be my pound-for-pound best? I'm still searching for answers.

In The Land of Poetry and Fighting, Efficiency rules the throne. I try to live here, so I shave my head because hair is dead and dead is inefficient.

I'm drawn to fighting because the best fighters use the least energy to complete a maneuver—knowledge of leverage, body mechanics, spatial relations. Elite fighters perform the same maneuver I do, but move less. They use space purposefully, and when they take space from me (controlling my hips for example) I do not get it back. They are space misers.

I'm drawn to poetry because the best poets use the least space to show the most story—knowledge of language sensitivity, thought-capturing, spatial relations. Elite poets use space purposefully. Here's one brief lesson:

The cancer-spotted
decrepit

    old man

reluctantly rolled onto his back

took a shallow breath

smiled to his loved ones and finally
laughed.

Did you anticipate death, or the word after "finally" to be "died?" Even if for a fraction of a millisecond? The half-second of white space as your eyes moved from the right-hand side of the page back to the left gave you the time to anticipate.

The poetry tactic of allowing one line of poetry to flow into the next without punctuation impeding is called "Enjambment." It's from a French word loosely meaning "running lines." Poets, like fighters, both reap the benefits of roadwork.

The best poets use the same letters I do, but use less space, fewer pages, fewer words, and less of the reader's time. Their works remain immortal, inhabiting not only our libraries, but our speech in the form of references, puns, and life lessons. I try not to worry for whom the bell tolls. I know it tolls for all.

In the Land of Poets and Fighters, those revered as gods are the masters that no longer have to think before they act. Through disciplined practice, their skills are exhibited instinctually.

As famed BJJ fighter and instructor, Saulo Ribeiro, once said, "If you think, you are late; if you are late, you use muscle; if you use muscle, you get tired; if you tire, you die."

Fighting and writing's deepest layers of beauty lie not only in the physical and mental realms of what we know, but also as an incognizable instinct, a realm we will never fully know but will forever feel.

CHAPTER 4

Bending Steel

The divorce counselors said they wouldn't record my statements. Days later they replayed them to my father. With his left hand he beat them back into me.

I was about eleven years old at the time and when my father drove I usually felt safe. If he lost his temper while behind the wheel he couldn't hit me. Only smash the coffee cup off the dash. He picked me up from the corner bus stop on 25th Avenue, (my mom, sister, and I lived in a bisque-colored house with brown trim directly in the middle of this block) to take me back to his house, a fifteen-minute drive. Fueled by my disobedience—sharing my negative feelings about him to others, counselors or not—it was here when what I thought was a *definite couldn't* became a *possible can*, when he first tried to crack me while driving.

The speed limit was twenty-five. On the passenger side to my right was my house. On the driver's side to the left, Fairview Park, where I spent my days playing basketball until mom's yell of "Cam-rin!" from the front porch signaled dinner.

The way he held the steering wheel as though preparing for a bench press—arms extended, elbows locked, white knuckled—served both as a way to temper his anger so he wouldn't hit me and, this time, as my cue. While he was driving I pushed up the lock with my elbow, slowly, so he couldn't tell. Then I ripped off my seatbelt, pulled the handle, bumped the door open with my right knee and hurled my body and Ninja Turtles lunchbox from the Dodge Dakota. I skidded on my knees across the asphalt, rolled up onto the curb, dizzily raced home, slammed open the gate, burst through the door to our house, closed it, locked it and sat scared-still against it, gasping and tucking my head into my knees to be as small as I could. My father pounded that door for fifteen minutes and the vibrations thumped into my back, bounced the tears from my cheeks and into the blood from my brush-burned knees and down they dripped along my hairless shins. I thought of the time at the ski slope, of getting upstairs to my room and of praying to a god I wasn't sure I believed in to please not let his pounding break the windows of the door. My mind strayed, my body stayed.

Several months after the divorce, I was court-ordered to spend the weekends at my father's new house (actually the house of his second wife), with his wife and her son (about three year my junior) from a previous marriage.

To make me feel comfortable and happy during our weekend hours together, he placed an adjustable basketball rim into the black pavement in the backyard. At first, the rim was seven feet high and he would play one-on-one with me. I loved it, the time together. But after a few weeks he turned away from me and spent the weekends doing yard work or running errands. Sometimes, I pretended to play against him. More often though, I turned to someone more consistent: Chicago Bulls small forward Scottie Pippen. Scottie was my favorite basketball player, and through my imagination I could be him or play against him or be on his team anytime I wanted. Looking back, it was as though my father's fuel over his court victory wore off when he realized he had won not just a victory over my mother, but the grand prize: some rights to the complexities of raising a child while already involved in complex and stressful legalities and relationships. As we grew apart, my imagination blossomed. I'd use a broomstick and raise the rim six inches every six months—I kept track of the days on a wall calendar. When the rim reached the regulation height of ten feet, I seemed to have reached young adulthood. In a way, that rim raised me as I raised it.

This particular summer day, "The Reignman" Shawn Kemp of the Seattle Supersonics gave Scottie a battle down in the post because of his greater size and strength. It was tied nine-to-nine, win by two to eleven, and I had to pee.

I threw open the glass sliding door, making sure to quickly shut it behind me so Ruby, the scarred, beaten, cinnamon-colored, racing champion greyhound (now rescued) couldn't use her elegant long strides to squeeze past. With each stomp across the hardwood floor, the inner jellyfish-sting of needing to pee worsened. As I shoved the bathroom door open I saw father's bare ass crack like a skinned three-fourths eaten apple, bent over. His wife stood with her back to me. "Dad?" I said, as he yanked his khaki shorts up, silver belt buckle clanging. "I'm giving your father an allergy shot," his wife said. "Get out and close the door, Cameron."

I followed directions, especially because I was frightened. I'd felt my father's silver belt buckle against the bone of my hip before. Still, fear can't contain curiosity. Through the door I asked, "Dad, why don't you take pills for your allergies like me?"

"Don't work," he said, his muffled voice came from low to the ground and was evidence that he had reassumed the hike-the-football position. I heard the creak of the faucet handle, and ran like Ruby before the sound of rushing water forced the pee from me. Outside, I hid behind an oak tree and went there. Scottie slashed to the basket, Kemp flagrant foul! Scottie received two free throws from behind the chalk line and next possession. He was a lifetime sixty-seven percent free throw shooter so I had about a two-in-three chance to go up by one. I purposely missed the second free throw for the excitement of a buzzer-beater. A reason to smile.

***

My father's basement featured a bench press, free-weight plates, hexagonal dumbbells, and small green rubber dumbbells for me. Mounted on the television set and on top of the Nintendo console were dust-covered karate trophies from his youth, including the "Most Sit-ups in Class," his personal favorite. He posted pictures of bodybuilders from *Flex Magazine* on the wall for motivation. And he taught me 21's. "Sit down," he said, as he unfolded two steel chairs. He placed a forty-five-pound dumbbell in front of the chair he sat in and a fifteen-pound dumbbell in front of the chair he wanted me to sit in. "Here's the deal. The first seven reps will be full reps, then the next seven will be partial reps at the bottom, then the final seven reps will be partial reps at the top like this." He wore a tank top and when he demonstrated each repetition the perfect ball of his bicep peaked higher and higher. When he concentrated intensely or when he was hurt or when he smiled—it was always the same face. It always looked like a smile. I'm not sure which emotion he was expressing this time, but when he looked at me looking at his bicep and said, "Someday you'll have what I have," I felt like the heir to his throne.

My father was my king. "Who am I?" he'd frequently ask me. "My Dad," I'd say. "No," he'd say. Who am I?" "My king, my lord," I'd respond.

I pumped my arms hard that day to impress him. I grimaced and pushed through the burn. There were lessons and metaphors in this moment that I didn't understand at the time—about the benefits of gritting through tough times, how developing strength often means the breaking down of something, how strength *needs* weakness—that continue to shape my mind and body. Looking back, I don't find it ironic that one of our greatest bonding experiences included bodily pain.

Days later, Scottie beat Shawn in the backyard and I ran into the house to grab some water. From the basement, I heard my father's bellows interspersed between the thunderously loud whips and chains and the infectious "psycho-somatic addict insane" lyrics of Prodigy's song "Breathe." I went down the first two steps to peek at him. I sung along under my breath, "psycho-automatic attikasane." His hands were covered in chalk as he positioned his body under the bar for a bench press. There were a couple of forty-five-pound plates on each side and when he lowered the bar it dropped fast, bounced off his chest and trembled as it slowly rose. The steel bar began to bend and I saw my father scream as the music blasted loud and blurred his sound, as the familiar veins bulged from his forehead and neck. He racked the bar and pounded his bare pecs like a gorilla. A line of chalk streamed nipple to nipple from the bar. In tune with "Firestarter" by Prodigy, my father ran to the white canvas Everlast heavybag hanging from a swivel chain. He launched looping gloveless hooks with each hand. Old and fresh patches of blood splattered the bag—as if Jackson Pollock had rolled up a rough draft canvas and filled it with t-shirts. The old stains were such a deep brown I never recognized them as blood until I saw my father's knuckles swing back in a flash of red. The bag swung on the swivel and made the house shake. I even heard it while Scottie lit it up in the backyard. "Training for the Toughman!" he said, masking his startled embarrassment when he spotted me spying in awe through the handrail bars at the top of the steps.

The Toughman fights were held at Altoona's Jaffa Mosque—an early 1900s building hosting anything from banquets and weddings to the annual circus and professional wrestling. The punches thrown were sloppy and circular, rather than the crisply linear blows I noticed when my father ordered pay-per-view professional boxing. I loved to watch the fighters and my father had no problem ordering now that he was living in this new house. A couple times though, after a couple beers and my pleas to watch prizefights, he said,

"There shouldn't be a price-tag to watch two black guys beat the shit out of each other." I remember laughing. I was a young son too blinded with jealousy and awe regarding the virtues of a "man" I saw in my father to think alternatives to his thoughts existed. "Shut up and go to sleep." "These chips are better with this salsa." "Your grandpap's a lazy welfare bum and doesn't love you." "Clean your plate." "Your mother's a lunatic." "There shouldn't be a price-tag to watch two black guys beat the shit out of each other." They often registered as truths to me. Unquestioned truths.

Now, as I sat with his friends from work in the musty air of the mosque and waited for him to enter the ring, blood and pain came from my chewed fingernails. Finally, the announcer hollered, "Here he is folks—Cameron 'The Cobra' Conaway!" He hadn't seriously trained in any martial arts since his youth, but here he was, "The Cobra," perhaps the announcer created alliteration on the fly. My father fought a tall, gangly, praying mantis-like man. This man's punches were strong and linear. They reached my father's face while his own circular, sweeping hooks were still in their windup phase. Mantis gradually trapped my father in the corner and the announcer yelled, "Gitem, Gitem, Gitem, Gitem!" Some fans responded with whistles, but what I remember most was the loudening and lengthening sound of their collective buzz. And I remember teeth. I remember looking up at all the adults and seeing many teeth. They must have been happy.

Round one ended; I tasted the battery flavor of my blood from a ripped hangnail. Round two began. My father looked like a helicopter's rotors when he missed, then, one landed. A left and he is left-handed. Mantis man's nose began to leak blood.

The fight went on, but my father helicoptered haphazardly the rest of the round. Round three began and it was another linearity vs. circularity war. My father's rotors were spinning less often and with less speed while the mantis landed five, six, seven unanswered shots and my father went down and stayed down for the ten count.

I cried then ran towards him then cried, too shaken up to do both at once. He was lying on the ring's canvas. During one of my fragmented sprints the security guards grabbed me and turned me away from the ring when I cried out for my battered father.

A few fights later the promoter asked my father to compete in the next round because he had broken the mantis's nose when the one helicopter punch landed. He said no. The damage was done. To both of us. He was hurt, tired, and sore. And I had just watched another man beat the shit out of my father, my dad, my king, my lord.

The memory of his unconscious, crumpled heap of a body, limbs splayed awkwardly like a dead deer while people cheered abruptly changed how I viewed the world. My father was human enough to be knocked unconscious, human enough to bleed. The words he said, too, must be human enough to bleed.

As the weekends at my father's new house grew habitual, I became closer to Ruby. She quivered with fear when anyone came near her. She often slept in corners, so the protection of walls surrounded her on as many sides as possible. Although I had a bunk bed with my sister, I'd often sleep on the floor beside Ruby, resting my head along her muscular thighs. I wanted her to see my gentleness, to forget her past and trust again. Dogs offer an unadulterated spirit, an inexplicable openness no matter how closed they seem. When I slept beside her, I couldn't help but remember some experiences I'd had with my father and other animals.

One time he found a turtle along the road and claimed it could be a great pet, "just like a dog." So he locked it in our yard and brought over the cordless power drill from the shed. He drilled through the turtle's shell while explaining over the abrasive sounds, "he doesn't feel a thing. This is what his shell is for." Turtle shell dust clouded my vision, but I saw legs flapping and thrashing. My father looped a piece of yarn about twenty feet long through the hole in the shell and handed me the other end. "Walk it," he said, heading back into the house. I stood there for what seemed like hours, urging Raphael to move, to glide his yellow belly across the cement walkway. He didn't move. A week later my father said he'd found Raphael up on Wopsononock Avenue. A car had struck him. He said something about turtle soup. I felt crushed but laughed because my father laughed.

I was in love with all animals. I could connect with them better than people, who seemed untrustworthy like the counselors. So when the sign at the zoo read: "Don't Feed The Monkeys" and my father unwrapped a piece of Juicy Fruit gum, paced around chewing it, then threw it into the monkey cage, I watched in horror as the curious little monkey whose wiener resembled the shape of a number two pencil grabbed the gum and ran. It became matted in his forearm hair. Eventually he worked it out. Then he ate it. Then he choked and hacked like my grandpa (my father's father) before cancer killed him—my first experience with human death. I felt crushed but laughed because my father laughed.

Two Years after the Engine Shop Closed

He had chiseled cheekbones, forearms
of sinew and vein, a life spent grasping spikes,

breathing blackness. White walls, linens, sheets
the color of the gown he wore that day in the hospital.

He was nothing but clavicle. Cheekbones so sharp
nobody kissed or touched his face. The casket

was black, the color everybody wore the day he died.
I stayed under the trees in the shadows. A priest, dressed

in black with a white collar, said my grandfather was proud
of me. I ran, out from the shadows, leaves like brittle bones

beneath my feet. (2006)

Prior to the divorce, mom decided it would be best if my father moved out
so they could have some time and space to think about things. He lived for
a year or two in a house by himself and we got along very well during this
time. Shortly after he moved into this house he bought an albino boa constrictor and an iguana named, cleverly, Iggy. He'd put the constrictor around
his neck. One time, when he let Iggy roam the house, the iguana wriggled
free and ran under the refrigerator. My father reached under to pull him
out and got whipped by his tail. Iggy came running out, hissing, whipped
my ankles and then ran back under the fridge. When my father grabbed
Iggy's tail and began pulling him out, the whole tail came off. The bloody tail
bounced around as high as the kitchen cabinets, independent of its owner,
spraying blood and pasty goop. I felt crushed but acted pissed because my
father was pissed.

So now I befriended Ruby. *Maybe she trembled because my father mistreat-
ed her*, I thought. As time passed, I refused to go to his house because of the
way I was treated and the court system penalized my mom with a large fine.

When this happened she was held in a phrase I'd become all too familiar with, "Contempt of Court." It happened more than once. Shortly after one of these occasions I finally gave in and let him take me back to his house so mom didn't have to pay another fine. During the quiet drive to his house, he said a car had hit Ruby. The driver thought she was a deer. I felt crushed but could act sad because my father was sad.

The last time I was at my father's house was one week after my birthday. I was thirteen or so. He had picked my sister and me up at home in the Dodge Dakota and began raging about something that happened the previous weekend when I was at his house. Those familiar veins bulged from his neck. He shouted that I hadn't thanked his new wife for the birthday presents she'd given me. My mom taught me manners and I followed them without fault. Situations like this seemed to arise often, situations forcing him to choose between his wife and me, or between her son and me. I had attended divorce counseling sessions called "Children in the Middle." But as I reflect, it seems as though he was in even more muddled middles.

One time her son tackled my sister Courtney out in the snow while we were building a snowman. He pounded on her with fists as hard as he could and was yelling curse words and spitting in her face. I tackled him off of her and did the same thing to him he did to her. Of course, he said I'd punched him in the face even though I didn't and I was disciplined severely.

"If I punched him in the face," I protested, "he'd be bleeding everywhere like you were at the Toughman." I was about two months into boxing lessons and overly confident.

"Very funny, tough guy Cammy. Get in your room. I don't want to hear another word."

For my birthday present, my father's wife had wrapped each candle or figurine (I can't remember which) on the cake with cash. That was big-time money and I'd never seen anything like it. Stunned, I thanked her repeatedly. I'd probably received gifts worth that much before, but never did I see that much actual cash. A few days after my birthday I flashed back to the boy at school who told me that her father might be convicted of stealing money. I had no idea how or why or really what "convicted" meant at the time, but it didn't sound good. It wasn't until years later that I learned that he was ordered to have his medical license revoked due to Medicaid fraud.

When I saw the twenty-dollar bills on the cake I started some mental multiplication. This money could be given to mom. That's what made me excited. So when my father asked what I was going to buy with the money I remember, for the first time in my life, struggling to fake a smile. I remember thinking that while my father was always talking about refurbishing the in-ground pool and buying a brand new hot tub, mom would use money to buy us rags. At the time, I wasn't mature enough to see the full complexity of how money and gifts could be used as a ploy to buy forgiveness, support and love. But I felt something weird, something wrong about how it was the times when I was most hurt that I was given toys or money.

In that Dodge Dakota, my protests were overpowered by my father's anger. I knew he didn't believe me or didn't remember or wanted to show his wife he would fight for her no matter the reason, no matter the opponent, no matter the truth.

During the fifteen-minute ride, Courtney, though four years my junior, stuck up for me. He reached into the back seat and tried to crack her with his right hand. After this verbal assault that lasted from our home to his, we trembled in the stilled silence as we exited the truck. I pushed the front seat forward to help Courtney out but he pushed me out of the way and grabbed her, lifted her out of the truck, smacked her butt then heaved her little body through the air. She smashed into the electric garage door with a sickening thud and he grabbed her coat to launch her again. This time I was the one who snapped.

"I did say thank you, you steroid fucker!" I exploded toward him to protect my sister and to hit him, hurt him, kill him. I ran at him because I was tired of running from myself, pretending to be NBA superstars instead of seeking, discovering, and wearing my own jersey. I ran at him because I was tired of feeling like what he said I was: a "retard" and a "pussy." But when I got within a foot—father pinning Courtney to the ground with his right hand—I ate a left backhand across my face that sent me stumbling. I realized I didn't have a chance, so I ran, I ran away from him as fast as I possibly could.

I ran until I reached the pro shop of the golf course across the street, pretended to look at the black and blue high-top socks and again tasted the battery flavor of blood. The manager came up and asked if I needed help. "Yes, no, just looking, sir." During the run to the shop I'd rolled my ankle in a putting green divot. It felt as numb as my face from my father's blow. I went to the counter and asked to use the phone, called home to mom. My nineteen-year-old future stepbrother Bobby said he'd come to get me. Years later he says he was scared to death. Says he told himself if my father came close to the car to attack him he had made his mind up that he would run him over. The thought of coming home after a weekend with my father always felt good. But not this time. Until Bobby arrived, I prayed to a god I didn't know I believed in that my father wouldn't find me. I prayed to a god I didn't know I believed in that my sister was okay. I prayed to a god I didn't know I believed in to forgive me for leaving her, I should have fought and died for her, taken as many backhands as he could give. Instead, I sat by a bargain bin of socks and watched the window with the intensity only fear can summon. I saw that Dodge Dakota peel out and move in the wrong direction, looking for me.

Divorce

The boy runs, arms brushing
against his windbreaker
as if saying "wish-wish-wish"
through closely cropped grass
passing men wearing khaki pants,
white polo shirts. His left ankle buckles
on a putting green divot. Ankle, numb
as his left cheek moments ago.
He reaches the Pro shop
sucking air like a cichlid,
"Can I help you with something?"
"Just looking sir," decorum out of instinct.
He browses through the black
and blue high-top socks, bites his lip,
tastes the familiar salty-warmth.
He limps to the counter, asks
"Can I use the phone please?"
watches the window like a cartoon. (2005)

Bobby arrived and I ran into the car. Fear of being seen and for my sister's health made my open-field sprint sluggish. I paused in the direct exact precise center between the pro shop and Bobby's car. Only this time there were no carpet fibers to comb to preoccupy my mind. I was torn in half by my own halves. To act or not to act. I acted and ate a backhand. My sister. Where was she? Was she bleeding? Could we pick her up or was she with my father?

"Cameron, let's go man. C'mon," Bobby said. I got in the car.

"That fucking fucker, Bobby. He's a cunt ass cocksucking pussy ass steroided bitch. I'm going to murder him. While he's sleeping I'm going to fucking murder him and that fucking fat-ass pig-faced whore he calls a wife. I swear to god, Bobby, I swear to god I'm actually going to take life. I want to fucking see him covered in his own goddamn blood. And I'll kill that fucking kid too. Spoiled fucking brat. I want this to be a massacre. Dad's a fucking pussy with all his lies about his steroid injections being allergy shots and all his weapons and all his beer and shit. He's an alcoholic scumbag prick and I'm going to fucking end it all. Put me in prison the rest of my life, go ahead. Put me in fucking prison. I don't give a shit. I don't give two shits. It'll be fucking worth it when I see him dead."

I was crying and cursing so hard I had to gasp for breath. The quiet and shy son who was used as a pawn piece, who just had to take whatever the system and his father dished out had just snapped. But the tears didn't cool my rage. I sat smoldering. Bobby didn't say a word. He nodded and seemed to understand something about me I never knew he did. I never felt crazy during my rant. And I never felt he felt I was crazy. Maybe our year together playing video games, basketball, and watching every Bruce Lee movie ever made gave us an understanding of each other. Or maybe I was saying what he was feeling.

Most martial arts movies are about one thing: revenge. A bad guy kills a good guy's loved one and the good guy trains and goes on a rampage. A good brother is tortured by a corrupt drug lord and the sister trains and goes on a rampage. A young son tired of abuse snaps when his sister is thrown against a garage door and he trains and goes on a rampage.

On the passenger side floor there was a metal handheld training device that is used to develop greater grip strength. I squeezed it with both hands while I cried and shook with murder in my blood. I realized how easily its steel could bend, realized how things that were sturdy and tough and unbreakable might not be. Like him. I thought about my father's wife possibly pumping him full of steroids so he could bend steel. So he could look the part of toughness he lacked on the inside. I knew I'd never know for sure about the steroid use, but I also knew that not all truths in the world come with receipts and documentation.

When Bobby and I pulled into the driveway of home, mom and Nab came running out to see how I was. Mom was crying and hugged me and I shrugged her off. She was crying for my safety, my sister, for the terribleness of the whole situation. I was crying because I wanted to kill and couldn't.

"Get the fuck out of my face. I'm calling him. I'm calling that steroid fucker. He still has Courtney. Get the fuck away from me. Where's the fucking phone?"

"Cameron, just try to calm down." Mom said more. Everybody said more. I heard their sounds but not their words. White rage.

I dialed his number.

Ring. Ring.

"What do you want you fucking bitch?" He must have seen our number on his caller ID and thought it was my mom.

"What do I fucking want? I want a fucking father not a pussy bitch like you who has his slut wife pump him full of steroids. You're a fucking pussy and I'm going to kill you someday. Mark my fucking words, Dad. I. Am. Going. To…"

"Oh little Cammy is so tough when he runs away and hides behind a phone."

"Don't you fucking interrupt me. Listen to me you cocksucking fucking scumbag you are going to die. I am going to fucking kill you because you aren't a father you're a college-money stealing, little-girl beating, whore-fucking, steroid-using little bitch. You're not my dad. You are going to die soon asshole. I'm going to fucking murder you, you fucker."

I slammed the phone down because I was out of breath and didn't want to give him an opening to fill the silence. I was angry, aside from the obvious, that my rage and crying and lack of breath and racing heart made all my words slur together as though they were one. I wanted him to understand me, to know I meant every word I said. I haven't talked to my father since. The last words I said to him were, "I'm going to fucking murder you, you fucker."

I feel no regrets for this. I look back at the tiny young boy still years away from puberty and feel only pride that he stood up for himself. The curse words were words I'd heard everyday at the playground where I'd go to play basketball. I never said them before, let alone like that, and I couldn't believe how easily they all strung together. During a recent phone call with award-winning Canadian Playwright Brad Fraser, he told me:

"A man isn't a man until he stands up to his father. It doesn't have to be a negative situation. There are men I've met who are in their forties and are working the jobs their father told them to work, who are running the family company and unhappy as hell. They have no idea who they are or what they want or even what they value in life. They are little clones of their father and they're miserable. When a man stands up to his father he becomes a man."

I became a man at age thirteen.

It took years for me to fully internalize that my father's actions were choices. He lost me, his first-born son, the person he named after himself. I've replaced images of his karate trophies with my own trophies from MMA; his high school diploma with my college degrees in Criminal Justice (the field he works in), English (communication: something he naively thought a basketball rim could provide for his son) and Creative Writing (my vehicle, like his Dodge Dakota, that will forever provide me a chance to speak without fear). How ironic is all of this? How purposeful? I have no idea. But perhaps I'll be fortunate enough to replace myself with a child whose name will not bear my father's scars, whose name will not be a constant reminder of wrongs he or she wants to right.

Log 3

Righting wrongs. In terms of neural adaptation to physical training, it has been said that it may take 300-500 repetitions to create a new movement pattern, and 3,000-5,000 repetitions just to unlearn a bad habit or faulty movement pattern. The take-home message: Technique and form must always come first. Otherwise you're not only wasting time, you're burying yourself alive.

CHAPTER 5

Watching Me

Yesterday I discovered a bowl of plums in the icebox
that had sat there forgotten for a month, and I tossed
the plums one by one into the icy grass near the woods
where I've seen deer. A dozen dusky purple plums, past
their prime: an offering. And this afternoon when I go
out to look, the frozen grass is bare, and I am filled with
a joy I can't get to the bottom of.

– Abigail Thomas, A Day in the Life. Catching Days Blog.

I'm settled and comfortable and in love with Charlottesville, Virginia. Nothing watches me now. No matter where I was, something watched me. I can't remember not being watched. Whether I was writing in a library or barbell-lunging at Gold's Gym, when I was given a vibrating pen for my 13th birthday and discovered the thrill of masturbation, when I'd grade my college student's essays to background sounds of Mozart and the trickle-drops of the coffee pot on Sunday evenings. When I stepped onto the yellow school bus in ninth grade, a little boy with a big backpack.

Each day I stepped onto the bus I'd push PLAY on my Walkman to Track 2 on rapper Ja Rule's "336" CD. A two-minute song that opens:

Are you a figment of my imagination?
Or am I one of yours?

And the refrain:

Are ya watching me?
They be watching, niggas they be watching, keep watching
Keep watching me
Now don't look down
Are ya watching me?
They be watching, bitches they be watching, keep watching
Keep watching me
Now don't look down
Who's watching me?

"Niggas" did not mean African Americans called a derogatory name. It meant people to me—all people. All eyes of the other kids on the bus who watched me until I sat.

"Bitches" did not mean some bad-acting women or a female dog. It meant morally weak people—cowards who would rather watch and judge than do and be.

The "keep watching" meant not, as insinuated in the song, for others to watch my future glory, but was my way of saying, "keep watching me, go on, watch all you want. I don't care." It made me feel I was confronting the watchful spirits that hung from me like wet blankets. Confronting them directly, though with faux confidence.

The reason in my superstitious mind?

Because these spirits aren't lyre-stroking good-natured angels. They watch and wait for me to screw up so they can send their Zeus-bolts of negative aura into my life.

Examples of my crazy magical thinking:

If I eat junk food all day, a family member may be diagnosed with cancer within the month.

If I watch porn to masturbate rather than using thoughts from my mind, my frail, sick grandmother may be forced to endure a miserable, sleepless night.

If I procrastinate rather than returning grades to my Johns Hopkins Center for Talented Youth students promptly, I may get the flu the following week.

If I lazily spend hours watching a reality TV show, my sister may get in a serious car accident.

If I don't push myself at the gym, the chance a rapist gets hold of my mother increases.

It was all a game of chance. Whatever watched me dealt the cards based solely on my actions or inactions. But, it's not that way. Not anymore.

I fought back. I realized the decisions these spirits wanted me to make, like eating healthy, were good for me. They wanted me to avoid temptations, to avoid the easy way out. They wanted me to realize the benefits that can come from delaying gratification. They wanted me to learn lessons from discomfort. This wasn't a time to exhibit control by being mindfully patient. This was a good fight to fight. So I fought back by constantly eating healthy, challenging my mind with good books and my body with rigorous exercise. These spirits may be a long-gone ancestor, some indecipherable aura, or, more likely, a product of the accepted beliefs around me. Regardless, I believed that they respected my fight enough to grant me some positive things:

My fiancée.
A relatively happy, unharmed family.
A stable career where I can help bring about beneficial change in the world.

Whatever watched watches no longer. Maybe it was all part of the spiritual process that most everyone goes through, the one that usually ends in the adoption of actually believing in supernatural ideas or of a religion. My personal process made a rational agnostic out of me. But, I'm grateful I went through the phase. I'd have accomplished little without it. Maybe these ideas or spirits are just part of my conscience, maybe I've beat them back often enough that they've gone dormant. Maybe they'll go varicella zoster on me and since I've knocked-out chicken pox they'll return and strike as shingles.

The Patience of Varicella Zoster

So cleverly coward
it attacks the young.
Swirling van Gogh skies
erupt in unitchable itches.
Sleepless nights,
not Starry Nights.
Then it's gone,
until sixty years later,

it strikes again,
like a match –
rather,
like a hammer,
into a nail,
into a shingle. (2005)

My former fear of some unknowable, fabricated myth has granted me the distance needed to see how other myths control the culture that surrounds me. When I freed myself from the cage of this "watching me" myth, I realized so many people around me are also caged by myths. (I admit, I am undoubtedly still owned by myths that I'm unable to see. My point is that it's important to try to see myths for what they are, and to try to see them for what they are means we first need to bring awareness to them. My point is that great benefits can come just from trying.) Newtonian physics has been trumped by quantum physics, but some scientists can't let go and are caged by their beliefs of the latter. Other people are caged by memories. They may have had a bad experience with a particular race when they were young, and, years later, they allow that memory to taint their view of an entire race. Myths can be useful and pragmatic, but also factually wrong at the same time.

All religious books contain some sort of motivational and inspirational stories. The danger is when we view these books as being *the only truth*, as being different than any other book on the shelves at Barnes & Noble. When this happens, we give up our backs and allow religious myths to apply the rear naked choke to our minds. Some people need religion—they use it as a crutch to lead moral lives. If this prevents these people from becoming hedonistic, then the myth has worked. But at no point should we forget that myths are myths. We can't let myths become our reality.

For whatever reason—films like Bill Maher's *Religulous* or books like Christopher Hitchen's *The Portable Atheist*—there is a rise in consciousness and therefore acceptance that most everything in the Christian bible (and other religious texts) had already been written about. A few examples:

In 1280 B.C. the Egyptian Book of the Dead speaks of a dude named Horus who was born to a virgin, baptized in a river, walked on water, had twelve disciples, was crucified and resurrected three days later.

Krishna, 1000 years before Christ, a carpenter born of a virgin and baptized in a river.

Mithra, 600 years before Christ, born on Dec 25, performed miracles, was resurrected.

Many of the moral and philosophical beliefs in the Christian bible are nearly identical to those of Lao Tzu (about 500 years before Christ), Socrates (about 400 years before Christ) and Plato (about 300 years before Christ).

Might these examples also be myths? Absolutely. Whether religious stories are plagiarized products of earlier fables and religions, simply borrowed and amalgamated from these various sources, or even completely made-up stories which align with older made-up stories, it's the way human beings have fully believed in these texts, not simply as fictional stories from which to learn great lessons, but as absolute truths that has been the cause of perhaps more innocent people being murdered than any other idea in human history. It's too bad war gets all the attention; it's too bad the plant is easier to see than the root.

I'd believed in the myth that whatever watched me really existed. It was scary, and at times dangerous, to believe in something unreal because it forced me to push myself too far. But it was normal in the small town where I was born. Most everyone believed in stories that were likely not true. They (and I include myself here) even went to see these stories reinacted on Easter and Christmas. I've fought it and I'm hopefully free of it, but there were certainly positives from being under its spell. Dogma can cage us if we're not careful or if we're vulnerable, and sources of dogma may include art, science, and other aspects of culture. But religion usually trumps all.

Religious books are the most tremendously successful and inspiring books of all time. Millions of people around the world live good, generous, and pious lives with the help of them. Millions of others, though, take a different route or simply can't separate life from fiction. They believe ancient myths are absolute truths and they cast their political votes by these "truths," they even shame and set flame to homes of those who don't believe in these "truths." Some strap themselves with bombs and fly airplanes into buildings. They take whatever book they have that is deemed "religious" and they consider themselves "Pro Life" because of it, or they believe virgins will await them after death, or they see homosexuals as the scum of the earth, or they believe God will take care of and infinitely, divinely, beautifully replenish the environment as we mine and dump and pump and pollute at will. They take this book and, when they are voted into office because of their belief in it, they use it to (mis)shape our country, and, in turn, the entire world. How do I know? Because like every other human I've asked myself how I am here and why I am here and I've felt the pull to simply make shit up. Much of religion grew from an honest attempt to understand these fundamental questions. Much of religion grew from a difficult, good-intentioned, thoughtful process called "Making Shit Up." Unfortunately, even honesty can't turn shit to wine. So what happens when people take shit from others and fully believe it? Some good shit, sure. But not always. And regardless, it's still shit.

Why aren't readers of Stephanie Meyer's *Twilight* books traveling (and calling it a "mission") to third-world countries and murdering people who don't believe in vampires? Because they realize her book is fictional. It's fake. Only crazy people would believe otherwise. This doesn't mean fiction can't contain elements of reality. But when people say they had a feeling that "Jesus saved them," what does this mean? What if they never previously heard of Jesus? Would they have ever said this? Would they still have seen his face in pieces of toast? What if the stories instead used the name Orangutan? Would people say, "I felt saved by Orangutan?" At the least, these missionaries often assume they know something "divine" and that they are doing good in the world by sharing it with (or forcing it on) others. This too may be good-intentioned, but it's sad. A better exchange would be for the "third-worlders" to show the missionaries how to plant seeds. Real ones.

In our quest for economic growth we've built billions of buildings and we went to "third-world" countries and "helped" them by doing the same. We said we wanted "to save" those "barbarians" who planted their own crops and raised their own sustainable plots of land. Who's laughing now? Probably the few "unsaved" (those who were still allowed to keep that same plot of land) when they hear news that people in America want to go back in time and live "sustainably" like them. It's cool when fashion recycles itself, it's not cool when sustainable living does because it means there was (and is as I write) a period of absolute and possibly irreversible destruction.

Honestly, I've cried and been motivated by the story of Christ. For years of my life I wore W.W.J.D? bracelets. I've taken good life lessons from religious books and as I prepare for a trip to Thailand I'm excited to visit the Buddhist temples to learn from the monks. I share this not to sound preachy, but to hopefully influence others to see the benefits of embarking on a similar journey of liberated (cage-free, USDA organic, free-range) thinking.

A significant portion of my life has been spent trying to recognize and then cut through bullshit. Now, I'm interested in societal truths. At times, this may mean bushwhacking through dense, controversial subject matter. I don't like to do it, but I feel that I have to. Sound missionary-istic? The search for truths is the search for self. If this were a self-help group now would be the time where I'd stand up and say: I'm Cameron Conaway, and I'm a radical rationalist.

> This is my simple religion. There is no need for temples; no need for complicated philosophy. Our own brain, our own heart is our temple; the philosophy is kindness.
> – Dalai Lama

This preamble leads to MMA, in particular to a February 2010 New York Times article by R.M. Schneiderman titled: "Flock Is Now a Fight Team in Some Ministries." In short, the article highlights the rising fusion of MMA and Jesus Christ's teachings in order to tap (pun intended) into the male 18-34-year-old bracket—which many pastors say is increasingly absent from churches because churches have become more amenable to women and children. So, pastors must evolve (pun definitely intended) with the times, the times that state: UFC 100 was the top selling pay-per-view event of 2009. Rather than relying on fear from fables to increase some church's unfortunately truer trinity of Attendance = Revenue = Power, pastors are relying on the realist of fears: the fear of the fight and its attractiveness to young males who are trying to prove themselves.

I walk a thin line of contradiction.

On one hand, there is nothing more primal than fighting. It helped me develop respect, determination, and a healthy and moral body and mind. Perhaps this reality balances Jonah-living-in-a-whale stories, balances the inspiration that can come from even the most imaginative, fantastical of fictions. Perhaps the real and the unreal could combine to create stronger bodies and minds, better brothers, husbands, fathers.

Or:

Perhaps this fusion will only perpetuate the antiquated and dangerous dogma that continues to drag America and the world into its scum:

"The man should be the overall leader of the household," said Ryan Dobson, a pastor and fan of mixed martial arts. Ryan is the son of James Dobson, the founder of Focus on the Family, a prominent evangelical group that donates money to, among others, those who support the belief that homosexuality is preventable and treatable.

There's even a popular MMA clothing line started by former Mighty Morphin Power Ranger Jason David Frank called "Jesus Didn't Tap." If Jesus did tap, would it have mattered? And what's wrong with tapping? It signals you've been beat by a superior fighter. If you never tapped, you'd never be able to train let alone compete because your body would be a rubble of broken bones and torn ligaments. The story of Jesus's crucifixion is powerful and brings me to tears for its act of assertive passivity, of sacrifice. Besides, even if Jesus wanted to tap, his hands were nailed to a cross. And if he verbally tapped by saying, "stop," I doubt a referee would have stepped in.

I think Jesus was a very wise man who inspired others. He's awesome. Greedy people preaching him for green paper and power are not.

I've believed in some crazy things. I've believed that whatever watched me would send little black specks of impurity or evil or weakness pumping through my blood due to something I ate or said or thought or did not do. The way to clear the specks was to cleanse somehow—a bath, a workout. Now, I cleanse because it makes me feel healthy—not because self-developed myths force me to. I take care of myself because it allows me to better care for and give to others, because it means I won't add to the national debt built on resource wars and the bodies of those with preventable diseases. Yesterday, I stretched and breathed deeply and dropped sweat into the ever-darkening sauna room wood at Gold's Gym.

Minutes after I entered the sauna, a man who looked to be thirty-five walked in. He wore a white t-shirt with a red UFC logo emblazoned across the front. Rob Zombie blasted from his headphones. *No problem. Cool dude getting pumped and primed for a good workout.* Then he began boxing the wooden walls with his bare hands. *Arrogant, awkward, uncoordinated movements. Just a few weeks of MMA lessons under his belt.* He continued the bare-knuckle pounding and I saw his fists flail back with the red of blood.

Suddenly I was seeing my father pounding on the front door after I jumped out of his Dodge Dakota at twenty-five miles per hour, ran home, and locked him out. I remembered how he screamed, "Open up!"

Open what up? The door leading to my past? A conversation between us

instead of your monosyllabisms? Open up about emotions? About girls I like?
Open up my squinted-from-crying eyes to see the monster you are? Open what
up, Dad? So much more needs opened up between us besides this fucking door.

I came back to the present. What are you punching? Why put your fists
into walls? What is missing inside you? What are your fists moving for? To
be surrounded by sexy women? To drive a BMW? To have all eyes watching
you?

I asked myself these questions as the man in the sauna continued pounding and moving in the same green way I've watched hundreds of others do
in equally strange places. Fighting filled big holes in my life. It always taught
me many new things about myself—I didn't want to fault the guy because
I'd been there. But I wondered what his story was. Did he have daddy issues too? Was he lacking confidence? What did he gain when he punched
wooden walls with bare and bloody hands? Did he believe he deserved
pain? Maybe he cheated on his wife, maybe he slapped his kid, maybe he
lived a life of drugs and felt guilty. And rather than trying to live the rest
of his life morally, he decided to inflict pain onto himself the way his father might have when he was little. Or maybe pain made him feel alive in
a world he viewed numbly. He kept pounding. I kept pulsating deeper into
my hamstring stretch. He pounded harder, faster, louder. I stretched harder,
deeper, pain. He pounded. He pounded. My blood is half my father's blood.
He pounded. He pounded. I pulled. He pounded. I pulled. He left. I relaxed.

After years of questioning myself, I've learned that there were times when
I've felt forced by internal and external forces to hate myself, and that because I hated myself I deserved to endure pain now and again. I saw this
hate in the man in the sauna. I wanted to say something but didn't know
what. As he pounded away, a quote came to me from environmentalist Derrick Jensen's *Endgame*:

> Premise Fourteen: …we are individually and collectively
> enculturated to hate life, hate the natural world, hate the wild,
> hate wild animals, hate women, hate children, hate our bod-
> ies, hate and fear our emotions, hate ourselves. If we did not
> hate the world, we could not allow it to be destroyed before
> our eyes. If we did not hate ourselves, we could not allow our
> homes—and our bodies—to be poisoned.

I grabbed my keys and went home to write, to try to slow down life in order to capture and share the complexities and idiosyncrasies that make it so damn beautiful.

I write because when those plum-purple age spots come and I go I want my story to continue to help others. I want it to sustain others when they need sustenance. I want others to know where I've been, how I marched through, of, and among this world and this reality. How I believed in bullshit at points in my life but worked hard to be rid of it. I want others to know me so they can know themselves and I want to know others so I can know me. I want others to know that real childhood scars heal, but not when band-aids replace self-reflection.

Oxidation   yellows

books   wrinkles

plums   stops

hearts.

Sometimes what keeps us alive
eats us alive. (2009)

Log 4

Sunrise Alive Shake

12oz water

2 scoops protein powder blend. Recovery, limits cortisol, steady amino stream.

½ cup wild blueberries (frozen). Highest total antioxidant capacity of any fruit.

½ cup organic spinach (frozen). Natural form of ALA, alkalinize.

3 tbsp olive oil (extra virgin first cold press). Anti-inflammatory, joint/heart health.

1 tbsp cinnamon. Regulates blood sugar, lowers LDL, cognitive function.

1 tbsp cocoa powder. Blood flow, lowers BP, antioxidant.

1 tbsp green tea leaves. EGCG, antioxidant, improves hdl/ldl ratio, caffeine.

½ tsp pure creatine powder. Brain function, muscle work capacity.

CHAPTER 6

Crime and Astonishment

This is the mental portrait I paint of my father when I'm in grad school in Arizona. And I will forever be and never be him.

Thick black steel-toed boots and long bold steps. Keys to everywhere are attached to left hip and brush against pants and cling against belt clip—a reminder, a metaphor, of power. A man who looks at the ground in convenience stores, at sporting events. A man who looks away while talking to you. This man now walks with a lone rooster's postured confidence. He reaches for every bit of his five-foot nine-inch frame. He looks through bars and into eyes. He smirks, then those thick black steel-toed boots take more long bold steps. He finds only humor in the inmate with nightmares who pisses himself, the inmate with no teeth, the inmate who checks out Walt Whitman's *Leaves of Grass* while others do clap pushups.

He's a correctional officer at a medium security prison.
I'm a creative writing teacher in an all-female juvenile detention center.
He gives the finger while driving to any kid with long hair and tattoos.
Mine: Stars on chest, WARRIOR on stomach. Tohono O'odham maze on back.
He throws nickels hard at homeless people to hurt them.
I encourage my students to invoke knowledge from the soil of their past.
He cries in laughter at the inmate with a limp and stutter.
I cry for the young girl who saw police pictures of her mom in a gutter.

We are unbelievably similar. The insecurity of our smallness. Our lack of confidence when we speak. Our facial features. Our interest in martial arts.

Our speech patterns. Our soft side. DNA and personal history trapped us both into what and who we have become. But he is left-handed to my right. He has green eyes to my brown. He's continued a cycle I've spent my life trying to break.

Many mornings—first grade through fifth grade—he'd wait with me at my bus stop regardless of the weather. He'd make sure I was warm and equipped with sharp pencils, my schoolbooks, and an eraser. We often stood in silence; silence filled with more words than this paragraph. And when that bus would round the corner, half a mile away, turn in front of Pizza Hut and head towards us, he'd lean his body to see it and I would mimic his action. He'd say, "There it is, about damn time," and I'd pull my book-bag tighter to my body and get ready. He'd get down in front of me on his knee to make sure my coat was zippered up. The man loved me deeply. He'd look into my eyes and ask what I was going to do.

"I'm not gonna take shit," I'd say. He'd smile and pat me on the back.
"Right. Don't take shit from anybody. You don't, do you?"
"Dad, I don't."
"Are you sure?"
"I don't take shit, Dad."
"Good."

He'd stand with his hands in his pockets as I got on the bus. When I looked back, he'd be walking towards the house, head down.

I am not sure why this is one of the few moments I remember of him caring about me, or, rather, showing care for me. Maybe I've expunged most memories of him in order to move on with my life, to let go of the hatred I harbored as a teenager, the bitterness I felt as he completely missed out on some of my life's first real successes. Maybe I can't remember the good moments because the bad overpowered them, or because all the good occurred when I was young. Whatever the reason, today is my last day teaching in the Pima County Juvenile Detention Center in Tucson, Arizona, before I graduate from the University of Arizona's MFA Creative Writing Program and head back east. Today is the day I find myself thinking of him again. Well, of the parts of him in me that always will be.

The young women I work with at the detention center inspire me in myriad ways. Most were dealt a bad hand in life: savagely losing a parent, or two, in a drug-deal gone awry, suicide, abandonment, deportation. Yet most are strong enough to admit in writing the mistakes they'd made. Many have even admitted to me that they believe it's harder to have a parent be alive yet not in your life than it is to actually have a parent be dead.

Today they wrote about the mishaps that led to their confinement, who was hurt most by those mishaps and what they need to do to right their wrongs when they leave the detention center. They wrote of drug addictions, of joining local gangs because they wanted a family, of breaking into homes for drug money, food money, material things, of cutting another human being with a steak knife.

During a discussion about trust, many were brutally honest enough to say, "I don't trust myself in certain situations." Not only can they speak of their personal issues, they can write them down on a piece of paper, one of the most physical forms of self-actualization. These young women tell their stories through tears, without fear of judgment. They are open and honest and willing to be vulnerable. They have many of the unique qualities that make for a great teacher.

As I left the detention center today, I sat in my car and thought of their words. Then I saw a hat in the backseat that I borrowed from Nab that read "Moose" across the front, a members-only bar chain with locations all throughout the United States. *Moose*, I thought. Then my mind bounced back to the lessons these young women in the detention taught me. *Moose could stand for Move On Or Start Eroding.*

Once we dip into our past enough to reflect on our decisions, the decisions of others, on emotions and the lessons we can learn, we must "Move On Or Start Eroding." If these girls defined themselves only by the few experiences that led to their incarceration, as others do of them, they would be bound for a depressed life. But most are able to move on. Most are able to roll around in their mistakes, cover themselves in the mud of it, then let that mud exfoliate them so they can begin new. After reflection comes change and after change comes a new self-definition. They no longer define themselves as gangbangers, or drug addicts, or thieves. And I should no longer define myself as the son of a father who couldn't or hasn't or wouldn't or wasn't.

These young women have shown me that we all struggle in our own ways and we must remember that lesson especially during times of crisis. All of our stories are worth telling - not simply the worst or the best of the lot. In the moment we are hurting the most, other people all across the world are hurting badly too. I am part of the web of humanity. Someone may hold the door for me as I walk into a bookstore to buy writing from an author long-gone. From the present moment of someone holding a door, to picking up work by a writer who wrote hundreds or even thousands of years ago, I'm part of humanity and will never be alone no matter how alone I feel.

Dwelling on my father's actions or his lack of actions would serve no purpose to me anymore. I've tapped so deeply into all of my feelings about them I feel I've exhausted the topic. Now was the time to "Move On Or Start Eroding." M.O.O.S.E. time. Corny as it sounds, I wore the Moose hat for the nine-mile drive back to my house in Tucson.

As I walked in the door I saw I had a voicemail from an old friend who had finally met her father for the first time. He had left her when she was too young to remember him. She sounded excited and said she knew I'd be interested in hearing how it went because she knew a little about my own father issues. I was interested, but I was also drained on the topic because of the constant thinking and writing I'd been doing on it and I knew she'd ask about my father. I believed that now had to be my M.O.O.S.E. time, my time to plant my foot and take that first step forward. I didn't call her back. I feared it would sidetrack my personal growth. I felt guilty. Still do. We'll have a good, long talk soon my friend. Here's my apology for not receiving your words when you were most excited to share them.

While in the sky somewhere over Arizona en route back to Altoona, I reflected on the parts of my journey that led me into the desert in the first place. In 2002, with graduation from Altoona Area High School fast approaching, it came time to select a major for college. To attend college or not wasn't a choice; both mom and I wanted me to be the first in the family to attain a college degree and access doors otherwise closed. I was torn between physical therapy and criminal justice, so I applied to Saint Francis University in Loretto, Pennsylvania, for physical therapy and to Penn State Altoona, a.k.a. "Next-Door U," for a degree in criminal justice. Saint Francis said my SAT results were too low, but Penn State Altoona said yes.

The choice was made for me. Although physical therapy felt right and I loved every aspect of physical training, I wasn't accepted. Even if I was, I began to feel pain of the type physical therapy couldn't mend. Societal pain. To put it bluntly: I hated people who did bad things. I mean hated. I hated people who were offensive to women, who hurt children, who stole, who did drugs, who did anything I deemed as wrong or gave other people "shit." It tormented me that I wasn't making a difference. I wanted all of these people behind bars. A criminal justice degree would give me that chance.

I could be a hero. I could, no, I *would*, work for the Federal Bureau of Investigation and obliterate all bad people. I wasn't aware enough to care about the lives and stories behind their moments of criminality. Their life experiences didn't matter and their problems and struggles didn't matter, these things didn't even cross my radar. What mattered was they were screw-ups and should be imprisoned for life. No second chances. Plus, it was the field my father worked in, and due to my lack of confidence in myself and in him, I thought: If he can work in this field, so can I.

Two years into the program, I found I'd changed thanks to having award-winning professors like Criminal Justice and Sociology guru Dr. Edward Day. Of course, it took disciplined work on my end to make sense of every single thing I was learning, but it was the exposure to the brilliant and open-minded faculty and staff at Penn State Altoona that lit the fuse to change my life for the better. I realized most incarcerated people weren't screw-ups, they screwed-up. A big difference. Stories began to matter to me. And these realizations applied directly to my thoughts about my father. He wasn't the terrible, evil man I once thought he was. He wasn't even a screw-up. He was a good man who wasn't dealt a great hand of cards by his own family, a good man who simply didn't have the tools, a good man who made mistakes, a good man who had screwed-up and lost a relationship with his son. At his core, he was and is a good man.

Although my interest in and knowledge about the sociological aspects within the criminal justice field deepened, I branched away from the inadvertently influential path carved by my father. Through broad class choices, I explored my own interests, carved my own path. Like forearm veins, my interests spread in different directions and eventually led to the hands, to writing.

Years later, a month after receiving my Master of Fine Arts degree from the University of Arizona, I pondered on how my father's absence affected me and how his own father's crudeness must have affected him. Father's Day came and went that week, and it served as impetus for me to find closure. I literally put my Moose hat on, as those incarcerated young women would have laughingly encouraged me to do, and I wrote a letter.

Dear Father:

We live in a small town so I'm sure you've heard about my accomplishments, but you don't know how influential your absence has been on me. That's why I decided to write this letter. Let me be honest, most memories I have of you are negative. But, this has been good for me. I've used those experiences to shape the kind of man, husband and father that I hope to be. I will make many mistakes, but I will accept and value the lessons those mistakes offer. I will be upset when I am let down, but I will give second chances. I will embrace the sacrifice necessary to sustain a long, loving marriage and a positive relationship with my children. I will first seek to understand and then will thoughtfully communicate my emotions with those I love. I will continue developing as an individual so I can best provide emotional, physical, and mental support as a partner.

When I trained for fights, studied lines for a play, equations for a statistics class or even when I began teaching in Arizona, I constantly thought of how I felt you turned your back on me and this drove me to tap into deeper levels of motivation—levels that propelled me above my peers in nearly everything I attempted. Though you haven't been around, the negative influence you've had on me turned out to be incredibly positive, leading to the most rewarding moments of my life. Though I haven't seen you in over twelve years, you've continued to raise me, continued to be a father. And though I will never forget the times you belittled me, the havoc your anger caused and the times you simply weren't there, I forgive you. I understand part of how you raised me was a result of how you were raised. I understand humans are inherently fallible. I sure am. But I know you are a good man, and I forgive you.

I cannot forget though. I've learned too much from our past to ever want to forget. I'm currently writing a memoir in which I've extracted many lessons and much self-understanding from our experiences or lack of experiences. I'm writing to tell you everything that has happened between us has been like fighting—the short-term pain of training is excruciating—but the feeling of achieving dreams, of learning the practicality of hard work, consistency, and overcoming fears is priceless. I do not know what I'd be without the pain you caused, but I know I wouldn't be nearly as happy as I am right now. I'm as confident and strong as I've ever been. I hope that brings you happiness.

In continuing with honesty, I don't want to see you and I don't want a relationship with you right now. Nab is the father I want the relationship with. I'm surrounded by wonderful families, friends, and have the toughest, most beautiful, most inspiring woman I've ever met in my life as a fiancée.

My purpose of writing is twofold:

(1) If you feel a load on your shoulders from "failing" your first-born son, I want to remove that load. Promise me you'll not judge yourself too harshly.

(2) I've felt over the years I've been the one to blame for your unhappiness at work, in your current marriage, in your life. Courtney tells me you cry sometimes over thoughts of me. I want you to know I'm happy and that I'm balanced and conditioned enough to remain this way. That's all a father should want. Please let that bring a calming energy to your soul.

You've provided me with everything I'll ever need to be curious, grateful, humble, and successful in this world. For that, I love you.

~Cameron

CHAPTER 7

Whenerya Doin That Chokin?

Gram is in the Intensive Care Unit on the eighth floor at the Altoona Hospital as I write. She is undergoing dialysis while she sleeps and I am sitting in a chair beside her bed. The plastic tubes that come from the grotesque animal body of the ventilator distort her face. They pull hard, fish-hook her at the side of her mouth. She looks more like the baby sand shark my fiancée once removed a hook from on the pier in Emerald Isle, North Carolina, than the woman who helped raise me, than the woman she was two days ago. I'm torn between how much time to spend with her and how much time to spend writing. It shouldn't be a difficult decision, but images of her are fresh in my mind and if I don't get them written down now I fear I won't get them at all.

Pap and I seem to re-bond over her hospital bed. My college years pulled us apart a bit, but when we talk now, we talk as adults and it's always a jolt because I still see him making peanut butter-and-jelly sandwiches to put in my lunchbox before elementary school.

Dear Papadeas

You buttered each side
of the bread
before putting the peanut butter
and jelly on.
Why your PB and J's
were so good has always
been a mystery to me

until now.
The smell of those sandwiches
lasted all day in my lunchbox.

I can still remember
mom dropping me off before work.
You rocked me on your chair
until we had to go.
You used to cook mac and cheese
for dinner when mom worked late.
Still to this day
I can't eat
mac and cheese
unless mom makes it like you. (2004)

I bring up "Peak Oil" today and among the mechanistic whistles and chirps we speak about why the government hides so much from the people it is meant to serve. He brings up Roswell, New Mexico. "It's arrogant of us humans to think we are the only form of life out there," he says. "They live among us, Cam." The word "live" brushes abrasively against my ears and somehow finds a way to the pit of stomach.

I'm reminded of how, years ago, Nab's father made it through a quadruple bypass and recovered enough to resume his intense workouts at the gym a few months later.

A Question of Heart

Imprinted on hospital linens, a shroud
covers the coffinbed where he lies,
post quadruple bypass, four veins
stripped from his legs strung to his heart
where blood is forced in great gasps. Hours
after slicing sternum, the doctor walks in
with a stuffed bear. *Clutch the bear*
to your chest. Nostrils flare with the labor,
each breath an effort, and with every inhalation

the bear undulates with the rhythm,
straddles the bridge of bone, gives
life to the fingers of a man. (2006)

Gram and Pap's fiftieth wedding anniversary is less than three months away. Pap wants to renew their vows. He mentions that he might want to get the man who performed my mom's wedding to come to the hospital. Soon.

I go back into the hospital. Gram's new face is burning into my brain. Now, three more tubes are taped down to her carotid artery and each tube has a syringe filled with some medication and each syringe dangles awkwardly against the side of her face. She barely moves. The nurses let the sedative wear off some today so they could check her true vital signs. Off her sedatives she struggles just to change positions, to move her body a mere two inches to the left. It hurts to watch her hurt, her struggle. The snake-like hiss of the ventilator doesn't fade to the background or become tolerable like most consistent noise eventually does. Instead, it remains front and center. Ostentatious. Breath. She can wave her arm and even nod when the sedatives really wear off. If her brown eyes are open, they have a blank stare that looks through you, looks into everything you've ever done in your life. Gram waves for Pap to come closer. He walks to her and runs the back of his hand tenderly across her forehead and into the now-emerging grayed roots she's hidden so well over the years. He smiles.

"What do you need, Connie? A big steak?"
She shakes her head no.
"A bowl of rocky road ice cream?"
No. The corner of her lip wants to smile.
I say, "How about a big bottle of water, Grammity Gram?"
She enthusiastically nods her head yes.

She's not allowed much water, but the nurses let Pap wet her lips with a small green sponge on the end of a plastic stick. He dips it in water and rubs it gently along her lips.

"There you go honey," he says softly. "Bet that feels good."
She nods her head yes.
"Can you open your mouth for me and bite down a little bit?"

She opens her mouth, bites hard onto the sponge of water.

The wrinkles of Pap's smile catch his tears, "Christ Connie, I didn't say eat the damn thing."

Gram's eyes crinkle. She's smiling at her man with her eyes, with every faculty she can summon.

Mom is working at the hospital today. She swings by to check on Gram every hour or so. On one trip, mom motioned me to come out into the hallway. She said she had a dream of Gram's face. Gram was walking towards her, able-bodied, but with each step her face became more contorted, more like a Wes Craven horror movie character and less of what mom remembered.

Kidney failure, diseased and spotted lungs, breast cancer, and a heart filled with love and stents, but unable to recover from the triple bypass several years ago have laid her low. At sixty-six she's sharp and witty, with Internet friends from all over the world. Hours before they took her to ICU she was cracking jokes about the stylish holes in my sisters' jeans. She asked what I was doing. I told her I recently purchased some mats to put in the garage so I could train BJJ. The last words she said to me before she entered her current state of unawareness and before "I love you":

"Whenerya doin that chokin?"

What she meant was, "What time are you leaving to go train BJJ?" She was genuinely interested despite her innocent ignorance. She smiled hard after she said it, the kind of smile where her cheeks rise up to close her eyes. She was proud of what I accomplished, no matter what it was, no matter her lack of understanding. And I'm proud of her warrior spirit, how she's handled herself in this crippled state. I'm proud when I say, "Gram, I got a teaching spot. I'm the professor you always said I would be," and I see her muster a slight crinkle of a smile in the corner of her eyes.

I'm proud when I put my hands in her tied-down-to-the-bed hands, and I feel all she can give: a soft squeeze. A squeeze that says, "In this weakness comes my most immense form of courage and strength. Feel it, take it, spread it." She gave her all even when her all wasn't much. That squeeze brings tears to my eyes and I instantly want to curl into her lap for a nap like when I was little. I can barely reciprocate her squeeze because the slightest movement of her fingers was enough to Jell-O my knees with awe and love. There is a novel in her squeeze.

What I know: She led me back into the soul of this memoir even though I feel guilty for not being with her or Pap for every minute they're in the hospital.

On my drive home this night I thought of Ted Kooser's poem titled, *At the Cancer Clinic*. It's the poem that made me know without doubt I wanted to be a poet.

At the Cancer Clinic

She is being helped toward the open door
that leads to the examining rooms
by two young women I take to be her sisters.
Each bends to the weight of an arm
and steps with the straight, tough bearing
of courage. At what must seem to be
a great distance, a nurse holds the door,
smiling and calling encouragement.
How patient she is in the crisp white sails
of her clothes. The sick woman
peers from under her funny knit cap
to watch each foot swing scuffing forward
and take its turn under her weight.
There is no restlessness or impatience
or anger anywhere in sight. Grace
fills the clean mold of this moment
and all the shuffling magazines grow still.

from Delights & Shadows, Copper Canyon Press
Port Townsend, WA (2004)

Your courageous strength when you were most weak made my shuffling feet grow still, Gram. I'm trying to understand life and share it. This is fighting. This is writing. This is me. Keep fighting and I'll keep writing, Grammers. I love you.

And after those two agonizing weeks, amazing and wonderful news: Gram recovered, went home, and began a Facebook account.

Log 5

Recovery. Low-intensity active recovery activities (like light hiking) encourage blood flow that delivers precious nutrients to and helps remove lactic acid from muscles while also reducing accumulated blood lactate. This process speeds muscle recovery. Use active recovery immediately following intense workouts and/or on off days.

CHAPTER 8

Fairview

Fair:
Not stormy or foul; Fine
Sufficient but not ample; Adequate
Superficially pleasing; Specious

– Merriam-Webster Dictionary

The cage from the baseball field and 25th Avenue were all that separated Fairview Park from the home of my first thirteen years. It was in this home that ten-year-old me moved my bones to enthusiastic personal trainer Tony Little's abdominal exercise videotapes. He'd say: *Move it! You can do it!* and I'd respond with whimpered exhalations as my abs warmed then proceeded to burn my voice cold. I didn't know why I was doing these tapes everyday after school; I only knew that working myself until it hurt was how I would become good at anything or strong like the teenagers at Fairview. Being the best was all about *pushing yourself* and *no pain, no gain* and *how bad do you want it?* and *the best go that extra mile.* Well, at least that's what I vaguely remember basketball players of the Chicago Bulls saying as they won a single-season record seventy-two games during the 1995-96 season.

So I tried to crunch my way to greatness. The Bulls served as inspiration for the first half of Tony's video and "The Undertaker," a World Wresting Federation (WWF) professional wrestler, served as inspiration for the other half. If he could sit up as though exiting a coffin after getting the flying elbow from the top turnbuckle by "The Heartbreak Kid" Shawn Michaels, surely

I could sit up in the comfort of my room, back against plush carpet with a poster on my door of the Bulls' Michael Jordan flying through the air from the free-throw line coming into view when I turned my body to perform the "oblique squeeze." *You can do it!*

The grass at Fairview's baseball field was mowed but not cared for like an actual baseball field. The white foul lines were noticeable only with a squint. The basketball court was paved but not level and one rim was half a foot higher than the other. Actually, the rims were doubled, one rim fused on top of the other, to last longer if people dunked. (For whatever reason, when the ball hit the double rims it would bounce off twice as hard as if it had bounced off a single rim. This meant a missed shot would cause the ball to roll all the way down the hill and into the baseball field.) We neighborhood kids chipped in our small change to replace the nets when they frayed. The jungle gym set had the basics and glistened with graffiti. Overall, it was a park. It was a fair park.

I learned many lessons at Fairview. The first was that I was a runt, a midget, a short stack, puny, weak, probably had a small dick, and should stay on the swing-set with a coloring book while the men played basketball. I learned of my smallness through words before I felt it on the court.

When I had the chance to play, I'd battle down in the post with the big kids—they laughed and forearmed my back so hard to secure position that I felt my neck whiplash. They got rebounds seemingly in the clouds but I'd get my fair share (sufficient but not ample) if a ball ricocheted and made it to the ground. But, for all I lacked, I still had some confidence in my handles. For years, every time the older kids would let me play, I'd get my hands on the ball and get a few good dribbles in before they took it away—either man-handling it or reaching in and batting it. When I shot (which was rare) I was swatted to a chorus of "take that shit back to yo mom's house, pee wee." And the ball, usually my ball, reinforced this statement as it rolled down into the baseball field and crept its way closer to my home, the place where I slept with it clutched tight to my chest under the blankets each night. Its eyes were SPALDING. And I'd always make sure SPALDING faced the doorway so it could see and alert me if somebody tried to break in.

The home had a garage and therefore a place for motivational posters and workout charts. While mom worked her long days the car was gone which meant the garage was all mine. I would spend hours each day, from third grade through eighth grade, working on ball-handling drills to censored

Tupac songs, pretending to shoot at a real rim and not be blocked. We had a rim attached to the outside of the garage and then, then! I was able to shoot and shoot and shoot (albeit at a seven-foot rim) without the pressure of looming large men around me. Then, then! a birthday would roll around and I would get a small basketball rim to hang on my bedroom door. My imagination soared when I had my own rims. I could be as good as I wanted, could be who I wanted, where I wanted. I could be Michael Jordan at Madison Square Garden and slice to the rack or BJ Armstrong and stand in the corner and shoot the three. I could be Charles Barkley and back down a weaker defender or Hakeem Olajuwon and work my pivot-foot feints before hitting a jump hook. I could be more than one of these players in a matter of seconds, interchanging personalities in a two-on-two game.

When I was too tired to continue a game in my room after a long day at Fairview, I'd gather all my wrestling figures and the miniature ring where their matches took place. I'd get a fresh sheet of paper and print the header: Pay-Per-View. Then I'd create matches for the event, listing my least favorite wrestlers first and progressing until the main bout. There was drama; some wrestlers backstabbed their tag-team partners. Others sided with a corrupt manager or stole another wrestler's girlfriend. The main event was usually some sort of freak show. It'd be "The Ultimate Warrior" or Bret Hart against whatever action figure I could scrounge up—Spiderman, The Incredible Hulk, or all thirty other wrestlers. Matches began with my favorite wrestlers taking a serious beating, battling back, getting flattened again, then, in breathtaking fashion, pulling out the victory. While I played, I kept up a commentary like the T.V. announcers about their exhaustion, the maneuvers they were performing, their sweat, their heart.

> "What a clothesline by the Big Boss Man! Folks, the Warrior
> is down. Good God almighty, I don't know if he can get back
> up. The Warrior is grabbing the ropes! He's shaking the ropes!
> The Big Boss Man is shaking too! The fans are going wild!"

Once, I even played tackle football with these Fairview behemoths. My anxiety waiting for the first time I was tackled or had to try to tackle was one of the most frightening moments in my life up to that point. To cope with my nervousness, I unconsciously snapped my fingers over and over for hours. Halfway through our game I noticed the flesh of my thumbs and middle fingers was rubbed raw, large pus-filled blisters had formed on all four digits and it all stung like hell. I climbed the cage that encircled the baseball field where we played and fled to Bev's house (our next door neighbor with the yippy Yorkshire Terrier) since my mom was at work. Bev was a wonderfully calming older woman who worked at the Altoona Hospital with my parents. I asked her for a band-aid and she fixed me right up—first pouring peroxide over each wound. She asked me what happened. I told her I did it playing video games too much. It still hurts me that I lied to her to hide, what, that I was scared? Where in my life might I have learned to mask fear? Hmm....

That was the end of football for me. Mid-way through the game I had intercepted a pass, and even though I got smashed shortly after, I had my claim to fame.

Miraculously, I started to become everyone's number one pick at the playground. At first, I thought it was because of that interception. Because I got the chance to play more, I'd stay at Fairview longer and longer and this meant I used my bedroom rim less and less. The players would line up to shoot for captains and to see who got first dibs. As a way to show machismo and get a laugh from the women who watched, the captain would pick me first as if to say, "I can win with this thing. That's how confident I am." "This thing," of course, was me, and I'd leave with pebbles and dirt embedded in the brush burns on my knees. I'd leave with a stiff neck and sore lower back from trying to get rebounds. I'd leave with fingernails bitten down to the quick. But, I'd never leave until mom's yell of "Cam-rin" carried across 25th Avenue, the cage, and the baseball field before it landed in my ears.

I learned about drugs at Fairview Park too. I learned about a white powder that was sniffed off the black seat of the swings. I noticed how everybody who sniffed wiped their nose immediately after as though it were wet or itchy. I noticed how those who sniffed would run flapping their arms like birds and interrupting our basketball game. They'd come over to the next swing where I was and push me too hard until I got scared. I learned of the sweet smell of a cigarette that was different from my mom's. I noticed how the smokers lounged in the cedar chips like my pet gerbils at night, how their pupils would get so large that I couldn't tell where they were looking. How, when a car drove past, they'd all curl up in the tubular sliding board (also like my gerbils in their cardboard toilet paper rolls). I learned about filled lower lips and how most of the girls seemed to like guys that put stuff in there and could play basketball with it in there. I noticed how they'd spit on the court and how my ball would smell good when I got home, so good it made me salivate. I noticed too how they had yellow bottom teeth.

They were generous in their offerings to me but I was always too afraid to try. It wasn't just that I recalled mom's talks about how drugs are bad or that I knew they'd destroy my body. I was just flat-out afraid. And I think the names I was called actually helped me say no. I turned their frequent offerings down easily because it was only fitting the stereotypes they cast upon me. Saying no wasn't a big deal because I wasn't known for toughness. I was a pussy who cried and bit his lower lip to hold back tears when I got knocked over and brush-burned. A pussy saying no to drugs, well, was damn near expected.

I was thirteen when we moved away and Fairview Park became a memory. I was never old enough to get good enough (or physically developed enough) to be the best player there, but I was there long enough to see the dramatic difference I felt in myself when I could get two dribbles in before they took it, then three, then four, then make a pass to another person. In other words, I tasted a different drug. A drug called progress.

Log 6

Journal Entry
Progress. Deadlift Progression for Maximum Effort Day:
Bodyweight = 150lbs

10 minute walk on treadmill
2 sets of 20 reps with 45lb bar
1 set of 10 reps with 135lbs
1 set of 5 reps with 225lbs
2 sets of 2 reps with 315lbs
1 set of 1 rep with 385lbs
1 set of 1 rep with 405lbs
1 set of 1 rep with 450lbs ← -All-time personal record!
15 minute cool down (breathing and stretching) in sauna

Life is like the deadlift. The majority of time is spent progressing towards something that either may never happen at all or, if it does happen, will only last a second. I must maintain awareness about how the deadlift trains muscles from the foot to the jaw and everything in between—core, grip, bones, confidence. It will help me with take-downs and even help me avoid back problems later in life. All these writing classes may never get me a book deal. But they are training me to communicate better, to better appreciate the smaller things in life. The goal may be to deadlift 3X my bodyweight and to be a suc-cessful writer, but I can't lose sight of the benefits acquired through-out the progression. I pumped my fist and let out some sort of wild, joyous roar after the deadlift. But while in the sauna I thought, "Now what?" I hate that I have to keep pursuing something. I hate that I'm not happy unless I'm tangibly making progress: Increasing the weight I can lift or the number of poems I get accepted for publication. As much as I know I'm supposed to "focus on the journey, not the desti-nation" and "just be," I can't. I try so damn hard but I just can't. Will I ever be able to change?

CHAPTER 9

Those Damn Shiny Gold Men

They were there for the first thirteen years of my life. I still remember their smooth, golden bodies lined up one after another on top of my father's television set—karate trophies each with an identical shiny gold man on top locked in a kicking position. It still surprises me how influential they were. And I'm still not sure why.

Was I drawn to the trophies because they were in such a prominent position? Was it my character, shaped by past experiences or genetics that was drawn to those trophies? Would I have studied the martial arts if they hadn't been there? Why wasn't I drawn to the prominent mounted deer or bear heads on the wall? Why did the stillness of their faces and eyes not feel real to me? They were nothing more than old, abandoned, dust-collecting sculptures. What about the framed photographs and paintings of wolves, sunsets, oceans, and mountains? What about the pictures duct-taped to the wall from bodybuilding magazines?

How much, exactly, did those shiny gold men change the course of my life? Tiger Woods was exposed to golf at an early age and became a phenomenon. Parents in Brazil expose their children at an early age to BJJ and they become monsters on the mat. Bill Gates had a rare opportunity while still a child to play on a computer (for free!) and look what he became. The Beatles, so early in their career, had an opportunity to play in front of an audience for eight hours a day while in Hamburg from 1960-1962. Sure, they worked harder than other bands, but they were granted a rare opportunity to do so. So much depends upon what we have access to as youngsters, so much depends upon capitalizing on rarities.

so much depends
upon

a red wheel
barrow

glazed with rain
water

beside the white
chickens.

Still, there is an unknown of what draws us to those things. When asked, "How many teenagers in the world had unlimited free computer access time in the early seventies?" Bill Gates said, "If there were fifty, I'd be stunned!"

I was raised with access to a television set and video games and I spent a lot of time with both. But when people ask how I got involved in the martial arts, I'm constantly coming back to those damn shiny gold men. I could say physical stature insecurity, that I was sitting the bench a lot during the basketball season, that I wanted to protect myself, but those facts, while true, feel superficial. Rather than insecurity, maybe I wanted immortality. Maybe I wanted to be dipped in gold and remembered.

I often recall a quote from Pulitzer Prize-winning writer Donald Murray when I begin to write as a way to find answers.

Writers write to learn, to explore, to discover, to hear themselves saying what they do not expect to say. Words are the symbols for what we learn. They allow us to play with information, to make connections and patterns, to put together and take apart and put together again, to see what experience means. In other words, to think . . . Writing is the most disciplined form of thinking.

Today, I feel I owe part of my life to BJJ. Here's its brief history (one account of many) from Rickson Gracie's website (Rickson.com). Rickson is perhaps the man who most embodies the art.

Jiu-Jitsu, which means "gentle art," is the oldest form of martial art. It originated in India more than 2000 years before Christ. It was created by monks who could not use any type of weapons to defend their lives against barbarian attacks. It spread through China, and eventually took root and was elaborated on in Japan where it became the first martial art style. The samurai clans in Japan adopted Jiu-Jitsu as their own traditional style to defeat an opponent regardless if the situation was striking, throwing, or grappling. With the passing years, they split the techniques and developed other martial arts styles such as judo, aikido, karate, etc.

In 1914, Japanese Jiu-Jitsu champion Esai Maeda migrated to Brazil, where he was instrumental in establishing a Japanese immigrant community. His efforts were aided by Gastão Gracie, a Brazilian scholar and politician of Scottish descent. As an expression of his gratitude for Gracie's assistance, Maeda taught the Brazilian's oldest son Carlos the essential secrets of the ancient martial arts' technique. Carlos taught Maeda's techniques to his four brothers, and in 1925 they opened the first Jiu-Jitsu academy in Brazil. For the Gracie brothers, teaching the art was more than an occupation. It was their passion.

One of the brothers, Helio Gracie, paid special interest to the use of the techniques. Helio, being of small frame, light in weight (only 135 pounds), and frail in health, was 16 when he began learning Jiu-Jitsu. Being unable to participate in classes, he would sit and watch his older brother teach every day. One day when Carlos was unable to make it to class, Helio was asked to instruct. Because of his size and stature, he began to work with and adapt the basic rules of Jiu-Jitsu. He introduced the application of leverage to the art, making it possible for a smaller opponent to defeat a larger one. He began experimenting, modifying and enhancing the basic techniques to make them effective for a person regardless of his or her stature. Thus began the

development of a new and more effective art: Gracie Jiu-Jitsu.
   Helio's skills eventually enabled him to beat some of the world's greatest fighters. Helio's feats include the longest fight in recorded history - 3 hours and 45 minutes, nonstop - and the historic match against Masahiko Kimura, who was probably the greatest fighter Japan ever produced. Now in his 90's, Helio Gracie still teaches and is widely recognized as a living legend. Helio's quest became today's Gracie Jiu-Jitsu, a martial art that is continuously evolving as a result of input from practitioners throughout the world.

The art of BJJ gave me the confidence that I could not only protect myself and those close to me, but gently kick the shit out of somebody if need be. In turn, this confidence in physicality gave me the confidence to pursue other endeavors: deepening my education, taking the lead role in a campus play, writing and publishing and even allowing myself to be vulnerable enough to be in a committed relationship with a woman.

I owe much of my personal success and inner happiness to this art. I believe if I hadn't pursued it, hadn't both surfed along the wave of confidence that came from tapping out a man twice my size as well as being controlled and utterly dominated by a man much smaller than I, I wouldn't have believed in the pursuit of things. Learning how the slightest, subtlest shift of the hips can completely make or break a move made me see minute details of a leaf, of a smile, of the religious beliefs of another culture. I began to see the trees of the forest, which was a great first step considering that I didn't yet fully believe in the forest.

I learned that it was healthy to lose and to rebound. In BJJ, a sparring fighter is always on the verge of winning or losing a position or the match. A win could mean moving into half guard (a position where a fighter is on their back, but has both of their legs wrapped around one of their opponents' legs) after being side-mounted (a position where the fighter that is flat on their back allows the fighter on top to cross their body—if a camera is looking down the position of the fighters would look like a plus sign). Through this constant series of winning and losing or *almost* winning and *almost* losing, I came to respect trying, or, metaphorically, to enjoy the journey and not just the destination. I came to respect and trust other men I trained with after I lost the respect and trust for my father. These men beat me not with raging backhands, closed minds, and crippling words but with technique and grace, with artistry and empathy. They beat me and helped me up, showed me what I did wrong, what they did right. They encouraged me, essentially, to continue along the path even though consistently losing is the norm for a novice – the only way to get better.

I learned the benefits that can come from being uncomfortable. As a smaller fighter, I often relied on flexibility to ward off attacks from bigger, stronger, or more technical fighters. Often I was crunched into a pretzel on my back, chin touching chest, knees beside ears. I learned that if I could just find a way to be comfortable with discomfort, to breathe and think and relax rather than panic, I could wear an opponent down, find an opening, or at the least, avoid getting into an even more uncomfortable position.

The application to real life came when I began admitting what I didn't know, and began asking questions. I'd always been shy because I didn't want to sound stupid. Now, I began to enjoy asking questions and engaging others in conversation. The discomfort washed away and I began to be able to think during conversation of ways to deepen the topic, of ways to remember what I heard. I believe this is the reason I became good friends with several of my professors at Penn State.

In short, BJJ is one reason I succeeded as an undergraduate and went on to graduate school. Just as a series of maneuvers brush against and blend into the next, I feel the art has intertwined so deeply with my life that I no longer see the influence of its individual parts on me. BJJ's effect on me is like sunshine, the 3,000–20,000 IU of vitamin D after only 10–15 minutes of exposure, absorbing silently into the body to reduce disease risks and improve overall health—it's with me even though I can't see or feel it. This art, regardless of my proficiency in it, pulsates some sort of sunshine vitamin into each beat of my heart.

I learned to value consistency. Training daily is the best way to retain the sensitivity of body movement and of technique in BJJ. After several days, let alone weeks or months without practice, my body responds less intuitively to the demands of the art—I forget moves I drilled for three hours several weeks ago. But if the moves didn't stick in my brain, the value of consistency sure did. I applied this to school. I kept up with studying—even just a little bit each day—so the information was always fresh and was easier to digest in small pieces. In my junior year in college, I really began to excel using this style. I'd break my day into small hourly pieces, devoting each segment to a particular subject matter. This worked much better than trying to read a series of fifty William Blake poems at the beginning of the week for the discussion at the end of the week.

Consistency infused my relationships as well. I began to keep in touch more frequently with friends and professors and as a result, found the deepest and most enriching human connections of my life. This act led me to Instant Message a woman I hadn't spoken to since high school graduation nearly five years earlier. Our relationship blossomed despite her living in Morgantown, West Virginia, while I was in Tucson. I consistently wrote her letters and e-mails, replayed in my mind things we talked about, and brainstormed questions I could ask her. In short, the consistency I learned from BJJ is a reason why I've found the woman I'm going to spend the rest of my life with.

I learned to be diverse. BJJ requires more physical attributes and subtleties than any other sport I've played. It entails brute strength, explosive power, aerobic endurance, high levels of total-body flexibility, absolute relaxation, and control of the breath, sometimes all at the same time. I concentrated on improving one attribute of BJJ in each training session and found that my workouts became much less boring as a result. They were always different, made new. Also, the diversity of styles and positions made me strive to be well rounded. I didn't want to only be a bottom player (often on my back) or a top player (often putting my opponent on their back). I wanted to learn both, to be able to see the benefits of each. I realized that I could never be a specialist in BJJ or in life.

I wanted to learn how to act, how to write better, how to work out smarter, how to landscape, how to speak a different language, how to view films as works of art rather than sheer entertainment, how to eat better, how to dance, how to give and accept love, how to raise a family, how to repair a toilet or a PlayStation 2 or a lamp. I wanted to be a Renaissance man and encourage others to do the same. Diversity on the mat reinforced the value of diversity in life. I could never be the specialist that Ph.D. programs encouraged me to become by studying, for example, only Eighteenth Century British literature. This was the primary reason sixteen English Ph.D. programs rejected me after I received my MFA degree from Arizona. I studied literature from all ethnic groups across all periods of time. Well-roundedness hurt me when it came to pursuing a Ph.D., but BJJ allowed me to accept and then value this aspect of myself.

The basis for improvement in BJJ occurs when each teammate and instructor essentially says, "Here is a more effective way to put my body at a mechanical disadvantage."

We live in a society with rerun NutriSystem commercials advertising, "Pizza, burgers, pot roast... Real food, for real men!" The assumption here is that if a man skips a pot roast for grilled salmon and a side of broccoli his manhood is up for debate. What is a real man, and why does this definition depend upon him loving pizza, burgers and Ford F-150's? Action movies with Vin Diesel's single emotion of anger and main activity saving weak women are still blockbuster hits. Lebron James, an icon of the NBA, storms out of the arena without so much as a handshake to the players on the team that eliminated him from the playoffs. "I'm competitive," is the excuse he gave in a later press conference. How oddly beautiful it is then to be in a class where I am learning the most efficient ways to break limbs and choke people unconscious without the slightest bit of ego, where an instructor cries with joy when he hands a new belt color to a deserving student, where men routinely and every second in our world right now, are giving up, then smiling in defeat. Ultimate vulnerability. That's manly.

I learned that the phrase "never give up" is a crock of shit. In BJJ, not giving up could leave you broken-boned or unconscious and unable to continue training. Instead, you learn there are perfectly acceptable times to give up, that the decision is not always weakness, but wisdom. It took experiences and reflections for this lesson to kick in, for me to see that the "never give up" philosophy can lead to many problems. It kept me in hurtful relationships, kept me working jobs that made me miserable. It kept me holding grudges and kept me from seeing other political, societal or religious perspectives. It caged me.

Around this time, graduate school MFA rejection letters came pouring in. First: Notre Dame, Iowa State, Iowa, Florida...then twelve more. Finally my acceptance letter from Arizona came when my family's dogs Chloe, Bo, and Pharaoh barked madly at the mailman and woke me from my depressed slumber. I saw how my rejection-letter-induced depression was silly. Sure, I went zero for sixteen, but just as in BJJ, sometimes you can be utterly dominated but latch a slick submission onto your opponent late in the fight if you can weather the early storm. And even if I went zero for seventeen, there's plenty to learn from suffering a dominant defeat. Of course, there isn't a definitive set of rules about when or when not to give up. But I know if I step back and actively reflect on a situation, I can finally decide which is more appropriate. Giving up is always an option, but not always a failure.

Fight enthusiast and comedian Joe Rogan once commented during a UFC event that the martial arts—because of MMA—are evolving faster than at any point in history. In less than twenty years, people have been able to discover which martial arts are the most effective in a combative contest that is as close to a hand-to-hand fight to the death as possible. Prior to the UFC in 1993 and extending back hundreds, even thousands of years, martial artists of different styles either were not allowed (a taboo) or were unable (because of location and lack of transportation) to use their style against another style. Bruce Lee is often credited as the first martial artist to bring martial arts cross-training into the mainstream. He studied many forms, keeping what worked for him from each style and discarding what did not.

The recent physical evolution in the martial arts seems to be bringing with it a newfound respect for the undeniable yet unquantifiable qualities of the martial arts. Many young fighters who are initially gung-ho about competing in MMA end up quitting, quite soon, finding that adding to the win column is often not a deep enough well of incentives to sustain the rigorous physical, mental, and spiritual demands of practicing and living a variety of martial arts.

I still don't know precisely what drew me into the martial arts. It could have been those shiny gold men, it could have been the first UFC video I rented, it could have been…anything. But I know what the journey I'm on has made of me, and I know that the fighters who are remaining successful, remaining happy, are those like Lyoto Machida, Renzo Gracie, and Frank Shamrock—fighters who would live by the martial arts even if they didn't provide a paycheck or a trophy with a gold man on top.

I'm comfortable admitting I do not know how I became interested in the martial arts just as I'm comfortable admitting I do not know if I'll be given another day on this earth. Why strive for bookends? Stories do not change, only the lives they live in do.

CHAPTER 10

Mind Margins:
A Pre-Debut Prose Poem

Date: January 21, 2006
Time: 7:00 P.M. to 8:21 P.M.
Location: Lifetime Pavilion, Columbus, Ohio

7:00 P.M.

Doors open to fans. Hum sound intensifies. Cyprian honeybee mob around lone Oriental hornet—asphyxiation. Public Address mumbles inaudibly. Marilyn Manson's *The Beautiful People*. Smack of insteps and gloved knuckles into Thai pads. Exhalations from three-strike combinations range from ahh-ahh-ahh to shh-shh-shh. Nothing is shh right now. Nothing is quite. Nothing is quiet.

7:15 P.M.

Beer fills their plastic cups. Bubbles rise in the hands of many. Blood pressure rises in the bodies of few. Stadium lights create warmth on flesh of many. Reach the cold temperature on the insides of few. Sweat without warmth. Warmth yet teeth chatter. Stiff joints won't lubricate despite movement. Locked knees. Hands twitch subtly.

7:30 P.M.

See opponent. See opponent's tattoos. Skull and crossbones. Needle bit our flesh. His name is Clint. Like Eastwood. Looks Dirty not Hairy. Beanie casts

shadow over my eyes. Must hide fire until I burn him. Public Address introduces ring card whore's strip club affiliation and porno for sale. Hidden fire
from eyes fills my stomach.

7:45 P.M.

Porcelain is cold on cold ass. Abdominal contraction. Burn. Dairy Queen
ice cream machine consistency. Wipe. Look. Find red. Burn. Wipe. Look.
Find red. Door reads: For good time call erased number. From stall to right:
Somebody's gonna get fucked up tonight, Dave. From stall to left: Hell yeah,
those fighters and those bitches.

8:00 P.M.

Wade through crowd to dressing room. They part for me like in movies.
Penis retreats from fear. Cup on. Thigh goosebumps from satin Thai shorts.
Erect nipples, shirt off. Stomach feels a hollow twenty-six inches from shit.
Bare feet on carpet feels stable. Bounce up and down. Feel chest follow.
Honeybee's hum. Announcer introduces Clint.

8:08 P.M.

Cue Rob Zombie *Dragula* with opening lines: *Dead I am the one, Extermi-
nating son. Slipping through the trees, strangling the breeze.* Hum becomes
alcohol-induced screams and kick-his-asses. Strangle: to kill by stopping
the breath in any manner. See: *Mata leão.* See: Lion Killer. See: Rear Naked
Choke. Bouncing but feel nothing but heart beating.

8:18 P.M.

My name. Feel nothing but hear DMX before rampway: *I got blood on my
hands and there's no remorse. I got blood on my dick cuz I fucked a corpse. I'm
a nasty nigga when u pass me nigga look me in my eyes. Tell me to my fuckin
face that u ready to die.*

8:21 P.M.

Are you ready? Are you ready? Let's get it on! Ceremonious glove touch as we've done since 648 B.C. says artwork on bowls and earth walls. Bounce. Smack of insteps and gloved knuckles. Find red. Wade through. Until I burn him. Feel nothing but. Nothing is quite. Nothing is quiet. Somebody's gonna get fucked up tonight.

CHAPTER 11

Caged-Part One

8:21 P.M.

When we touched gloves I felt the energy of his body. The enigma he had been became human. This was his first weakness, his transformation from a question, a mystery, into nothing more than flesh and blood. I could only punch through the specter of an enigma. Flesh and blood I could crush. His tattoos told me he was a boy who wanted to hide behind a skull and cross-bones, a boy afraid of his own fear. But I knew well the way the needle had bitten his skin, the way he'd clenched his teeth to keep from wincing. I could see the pierced holes in his nose and ears, even his nipples. This was a disguise he never wanted to discard. This was the costume I would have to tear from him to win my debut fight. As we did the ceremonial glove touch that dates back to gladiators thousands of years before us, as we carved our place along the ancient continuum of hand-to-hand combat, I realized I had the ability to destroy him. Any weakness I could expose would let me end his life with my bare hands.

If it weren't for the rules. If it weren't for the referee.

When I was thirteen my father and I severed our ties. The ties were frayed shoelaces at that point. To make conversation short, I tell people he left my mom, sister, and me. But left is loaded like a left hook. What I mean is that he was no longer a father. What I mean is I only remember a few occasions of him ever showing affection or concern. What I mean is most loving acts are captured in old videos and photographs and not in my memory. What I mean is this: he left us long before he left. What I mean is when mom could no longer burn the loose shoelace frays smooth with a lighter she filed for divorce.

He fought hard for custody, perhaps not for the sake of my sister and me, but to drive a stake through my mom and reinflate his shattered ego. He threatened us kids never to say anything bad about him in front of the divorce judges, filled our impressionable young minds with phrases like "Your mom is a psycho lunatic" and "She's too crazy to raise you" and followed it up by giving us twenty-dollar bills or taking us to Toys R Us. A seductive candy that Courtney, four years my junior—a nine-year-old pigtailed little girl—was more apt to chew on.

He used alcohol and weight training to combat what must have been a torrent of negative emotions—the times are few when he was without beer or barbell. And violence. He used violence.

My body was still frail, just starting its own fight with puberty, when I saw my father hurl my sister against the garage door, when I flew at him with all my might and ate a backhand. What was I supposed to do? What was left except to make sure my mom and sister were safe? I slept each night only after I knew they were asleep. I checked the locks repeatedly, got out from the warmth of bed at the slightest sound and often sat on the porch alone at night. I watched the cars on 25th Avenue glide by so seemingly sure of their direction, so unlike me. Watched moths flicker around the road's lone streetlight in their consistently, chaotically-organized way. Watched the silhouettes of teenagers at Fairview Park and listened to their laughter. I heard the wind and hated it because it meant I couldn't listen to the silence of our front and back door knobs. Safety.

The porch and I met like this a few times a month over the course of years. Our relationship sharpened my senses. This wasn't a leisurely or passive act. To me, this watching and listening was a matter of life and death. Not because mom was weak—she stands 5'3" but has a thick-boned athletic frame from her teenage years as a sprinter and from the demands of her supportive service job at the Altoona Hospital. Her days are still spent pushing and pulling people on litters or in wheelchairs, delivering the dead to the morgue, lifting and delivering hospital equipment to any one of the fourteen floors, and performing emergency CPR when a code is called.

But sleep meant vulnerability and vulnerability meant the potential for danger. I knew mom was tough. I was in pursuit of my own toughness. I was doing what I thought a man should do. With my father gone I was the man of the house. Looking back, I realized I desperately longed for a father figure.

I found him at Family Video. Like many teenaged boys, I wanted to see what was in the special video section, the one enclosed by thin drywall with the signs "Must be 18 or older to enter." I thought what I wanted was pictures of slick breasts and asses covered in oil. I edged towards the entry, glancing every few steps over my shoulder toward the clerk. He seemed uninterested in my guilt, preoccupied with actual customers. Before I reached the porn though, I saw a VHS video case featuring a muscular man in black spandex shorts, blood coming from his nose and glistening his bronzed, squared chest. His hair was wet with sweat. He was fatigued but ready to go on. This wasn't what I came in for, but I had to have it. In bold yellow letters it announced *The Ultimate Fighting Championship*. And in the lower right-hand corner it read *Unrated: Contains Violent Material*. The clerk called my mom for permission.

"It's called the Ultimate Fighting Championship: The Brawl in Buffalo," he said. "Yes, here he is." He handed the phone to me.

"Hey mom, I wanted to rent this video. Martial arts guys fight each other. Can I get it?" In a tone conveying allowance but not full acceptance, she said I could and I soon found my new father: Ken Shamrock. "The World's Most Dangerous Man."

I walked hurriedly home (about one mile) and popped the VHS tape into the player. The person who had rented the tape before me must not have rewound it. All of a sudden, famed boxing announcer Michael Buffer announced the fighters.

"He is the Russian National Judo Champion, the World Sambo Champion, 'The Russian Bear,' O-leg Tak-ta-rov!"

Ken paced in his corner, eyes closed, calm but with an underlying intensity. A leopard.

"He is the defending UFC Superfight Champion. The Master of the Octagon. He is, "Ken Sham-rock!"

They fought for thirty-three consecutive minutes and the result was a draw. Back in 1995, the UFC did not have a scoring system or judges. Although they used the tagline "There are no rules!" in the early 1990s, they did operate with a few. There was no biting or eye-gouging, and they frowned on (but allowed) techniques such as hair pulling, headbutting, groin strikes, and fish-hooking (where a fighter inserts his hand into the mouth of another fighter and attempts to split his cheek open). If a fighter didn't tap-out, get knocked out, or get put in a position where he could not at all defend himself against strikes, the fight went on. One thirty-minute round plus an overtime period.

I later learned from *Beyond the Lion's Den*, the sequel to Ken's memoir *Inside the Lion's Den*, that Ken and Oleg were actually friends. Ken was training him. But Ken knew Oleg wouldn't tap-out. And Ken didn't want to knock him out. Here's an excerpt from the book.

> In addition to being his friend, I was also trying to get him into Pancrase [an MMA organization in Japan, Ken was the champion there too] and if I broke his leg it would be a while before he could recover and he needed the money. I figured my best chance of winning without seriously hurting him was to beat on him with punches... If I could open a cut and get him to start pouring blood, I could get a referee stoppage. It might not have been the best plan going into a fight, but considering the options it seemed like the best option available. And it turned out fine. I battered him around for the duration of the match, the bout was declared a draw and when Oleg recovered he went on to fight in Pancrase.

Post-fight, Ken raised Oleg's hand. Bleeding, they hugged and smiled. This was what they loved to do. It wasn't a fight in the way I had thought of the word "fight." It was better: a contest, a game, a sport. And Ken, although he was stacked with muscle and appeared ferocious, was down to earth, respectful, gentle, articulate. I felt like he was everything I wasn't, he was everything I wanted to be. This mix of qualities, strength in body and mind, opened my eyes. I didn't have to be one or the other. With Ken Shamrock as my model of inspiration, I could be both. *No, I would be both.*

Prior to discovering Ken, I'd played basketball throughout my youth and into junior high. Unfortunately, politics—nonexistent on the playground— were rampant in the more formal setting of school-based teams and leagues. The guys whose parents schmoozed the coach played more. Simple as that.

As I watched my best friends' moms and dads inch their asses closer and closer to the coaching staff—each inch seemingly an extra minute of playing time for their child—I grappled with whether to open my mouth for what was fair or to shut up so my best friends could be happy. It wasn't a matter of my happiness versus their happiness. If I spoke up and they were benched and I played, I'd not only jeopardize friendships, but I'd feel the awkward weight of guilt for the duration of my precious minutes on the court.

As was my custom then and still is my custom now, I kept company with quiet passivity, hoping my actions, not my spoken words, would pay off. As I sat on the bench, I edited then hummed lyrics to "Bullet with Butterfly Wings" by the Smashing Pumpkins.

The original lyrics: Despite all my rage, I am still just a rat in a cage
My edited lyrics: Despite my long range, I am still just a rat in a cage

The song's title perfectly described how I felt. I felt the silent storm of a bullet inside me. But my voice was muted, as though something beautifully acquiescent inside me told me to be still. Years later, I unraveled the conundrum. These two ideas, painfully stretching me damn near to my breaking point, weren't so antithetical. One was a result of my fighter spirit, the other a manifestation of my writer spirit. The former wanted action; the latter wanted to sit back and stealthily observe. I didn't have such insight then, I just figured my pain was because I was a shy little boy too afraid to speak up for himself.

Thanks in large part to sparks struck by Ken Shamrock, I quit playing basketball for Keith Junior High School midway through the eighth grade season. During that season, Coach always told me to sit directly beside him so he could put me in when the guards committed their turnovers, but I purposely sat humming *Despite my long range* to myself at the end of the bench, away from Coach, away from the team. This space stood for what I wanted: the ability to control my own outcome, to compete at my own discretion, to be able to blame myself and only myself.

Just before I quit, Coach pulled me aside and showed me the team stats—points, assists, steals, rebounds, blocks. "As a sixth man you lead the team in more categories than any other player," he pointed out. I'm not sure why he told me this other than to boost my confidence, so I continued my complacency. It worked. I spent a few more games on the bench beside him. "Sub!"

he'd yell to the ref when he wanted me in the game. But instead of substitute, I couldn't help but think of submission, the MMA and the dictionary definition.

MMA: Submission: a fighter may admit defeat during a match by a tap on the opponent's body or mat/floor or by a verbal announcement.

Dictionary: Submission: characterized by tendencies to yield to the will or authority of others, usually involves a stronger, more dominant personality coercing a weaker, more passive personality.

Even though I was mostly a benchwarmer, my father came to many of my basketball games - even if it meant he sat by himself because of the awkwardness between he and my mom. As a young dude, I loved seeing him there but also took it for granted. *He was supposed to be there.* As an adult, I see it was yet another example of his quiet love for me, another example of how he's a good man at his core.

My mom made every one of my basketball games despite how she worked shift after shift. She cheered me—going from intense excitement filled with clapping and "Go Cameron" to her tight-lipped worry when she thought I might be hurt. Although I knew the hours she logged at work were for Courtney and me, although I could see how quickly her white work shoes became scuffed and worn-out, seeing her in the bleachers smiling at every single game regardless of whether I played hit me viscerally. Without a word, they both showed me lessons about love and parenting and life that stick with me to this day.

I either cried or was pissed after every basketball game. So when I told mom I wanted to quit, she asked me to think about it for a few days and if I still felt that way to tell Coach. I still felt that way, and when I found Coach in the hallway during school I knew it was my time to take action.

"Coach," I said quietly. I felt my lip quivering and my eyes begin to itch. "I'm not going to finish the season. I'm not having fun and there are other things I want to do."

"Cameron, just stick it out for me and the team. Finish the year. We need you."

My tears came out. "Yeah, okay," I said. "I will." Guilt may have made me answer differently, but it didn't change my actions. And rather than come to him again, I avoided him when I saw him in the hallways. I made sure he never saw me. I stopped going to practices and games. When he pulled me aside a week later in the cafeteria and asked if I was okay, I told him I was sorry. I looked down to the ground and said, "I just can't do it anymore." He didn't say another word. He turned and walked away and I felt like I had just let down the entire world.

A few days later, mom bought me Ken Shamrock's memoir *Inside the Lion's Den* and I read about his journey from foster home to foster home. A troubled, often homeless young boy, Ken endured. When he was hungry, he stole candy bars from gas stations. When he was tired, he'd find a place out of the rain to sleep—under bridges, with friends, wherever. His pent-up rage was often worked out through his body, pushing through hundreds of repetitions of body-weight squats until the burn in his thighs turned to numbness.

When Ken was fourteen, a man named Bob Shamrock rescued him by serving as a foster father. Bob fostered hundreds of other young boys[1] over the course of his lifetime, taking them under his wing and offering a second chance to those who made a few poor decisions or mistakes or were dealt a bad card. Shortly after Bob took Ken into his home and officially adopted him, Ken replaced his original last name of Kilpatrick with the luck and strength associated with Shamrock.

Ken was fourteen when Bob rescued him. I was fourteen when Ken's memoir rescued me.

I carefully cut Ken's pictures from *Inside the Lion's Den* and taped them to the ceiling above my bed. I called every martial arts school in Altoona and surrounding cities, but they all focused on the traditional, outdated, and ineffective "flashy" martial arts. By "flashy" I mean those that looked cool but weren't practical for an actual fight. Ken, who lived in Susandale, California, often won his fights with a submission—a choke or joint-lock— but in Altoona, a small former railroad town, there was not a submission grappling school let alone an MMA school. All MMA fights begin with

---

1 One of those boys was Frank Juarez. Frank, following in Ken's footsteps, changed his name to Frank Shamrock and went on to become the reigning UFC Middleweight Champion (1997-1999). When Ken's time came and past, as it abruptly does for all fighters, Frank became the athlete and person I most wanted to emulate. He continued the evolution of a "mixed" martial artist and is considered by many to be one of the pioneers for cross-training in multiple martial arts and realizing the conditioning component for MMA.

the combatants standing, so I decided to take the most basic approach to developing myself as a fighter. I began training at the Altoona Boxing Club.

A former barbershop turned free-to-the-public boxing gym, the A.B.C. was founded by Johnny Robertson, a man whose mission was similar to Bob Shamrock's. Johnny was in his mid sixties, stood 5'4", with frazzled gray hair, a smashed nose, a bulging belly of muscle, and cauliflower ears. He reminded me of a muscled-up version of Mick, Rocky Balboa's trainer in the Rocky movies. He founded the club and kept the gym free of charge because he knew from his own experience how exercise and a nurturing mentor could change the lives of struggling, lower-income youth. To this day the boxing club is still free and he charges only one dollar for his "Robertson Fitness Camp classes." And if even that's too expensive you're still welcome to join and drop sweat alongside other members. "I just wanted to keep kids off the streets," he told me once. "And it's worked."

The A.B.C. featured several duct-taped heavybags, an unused toilet against a white paint-chipped wall and the smell of warm sweat and leather. This was where I learned the fundamentals of how to fight while standing. Like Ken, I began to work through my frustrations by pushing, pushing, pushing my body to limits beyond where I thought it could go. I grew stronger. My shoulders burned as I held three-pound dumbbells at chin-level and threw punches for three-minute rounds. My calves burned as I skipped rope. My abs burned as I sat back then up then twisted then back again with the medicine ball whose medicine tasted bad going down but worked wonders for core stability and for the transferring of punching power when sparring. I'd walk into the gym as an enraged and scared shitless young man and I'd walk out with a euphoria that tucked me into bed at night. It would wear off the following morning. Still, each time I stepped onto the bloodstained blue canvas, each time I hooked my thumb through Everlast wraps I grew as a fighter and man.

The transition from the hardwood to the squared circle was not seamless. At times, between the ages of thirteen and twenty-two, I'd abandon the boxing club for months and spend my time lifting weights or playing pickup basketball. I'd always come back to the A.B.C. though. I'd miss the way my fists would dance on the heavybags in rhythm to the rap music. I'd miss the exhaustion. I'd miss lacing up those Everlast wraps and feeling like I was going to war against myself. However, when I was thirteen and had consecutively trained for three months, I signed up for the Golden Gloves boxing tournament for juniors (aged eight to sixteen) in Pittsburgh, a city with a reputation for developing world-class boxers. Former Golden Glove winners included Muhammad Ali, Joe Frazier, Mike Tyson, Floyd Mayweather Jr., Evander Holyfield, and George Foreman. The week before the competition I turned fourteen.

The smoky, dimly lit arena and the energized, alcohol-drinking crowd cemented my feet to the ground and glued my hands to my ears. The air was so thick that two inhalations felt like one. Nerves prevented me from throwing a proper punch without stumbling around like a drunk. Worse, I was like a person naturally uncoordinated and then drunk. I'd thrown thousands of these same punches in the gym. But now I choked. I wanted to grapple my opponent to the canvas like Ken would, but boxing compared to MMA is like checkers compared to chess. I was quickly outclassed, pelted into the corner like the lone survivor in a game of grade school dodgeball. Punches kept coming. The wind was knocked out of me. I couldn't move even though Johnny screamed at me to circle out of the corner.

Since I had quit basketball a year earlier, each punch my opponent landed further reinforced the idea that I was a quitter, that I didn't have the heart to be an athlete let alone a fighter. It was a nightmare and I was blind. I couldn't see, literally. I had been hit so many times and from so many angles that the headgear spun around and covered my face. My opponent kept slugging and slugging. He couldn't see the eyes he watered, the nose he bludgeoned. I heard the *ch-ch-ch* of the ten-seconds-left sticks. This is often when most fighters try to impress the judges. Not me. The sound meant only that I had to take punches to the face for ten more seconds. A blow across the temple made my legs wobble and I almost fell. A pounding metal sound. Saved by the bell. Now I truly understood the meaning of that old cliché. Though *the ref stepped in and stopped the fight* should have been the cliché that happened.

Johnny ducked under the ropes and came into the ring. He didn't believe in setting stools down so fighters could sit. "Sends a message of weakness." Instead, he grabbed me by the shoulders and stood me upright in the same corner where I was just beat on. He looked me in the eyes.

"Do you want to continue?" he asked quietly. I couldn't answer. Didn't want to let down a man who had so much faith in me.

"Cameron. Yes or no?"

I couldn't take any more, but I couldn't bring myself to say it. Johnny tossed the referee the white towel that signals surrender. I was ashamed. He, my mom, and my stepdad had driven two hours to watch this and I remembered all the time they spent driving me to practice, the money spent to buy me boxing shoes. I felt like a colossal waste of their energy, like a waste of a person.

Then Johnny said, "You did good, Cameron. He's had a ton of fights. First one's the worst. You got it out of the way. I'm proud of you." That was the first and last time I competed as a boxer. It took years to sink in, but that miserable night in Pittsburgh I won what I wanted to win. The respect of a man I respected.

Months later, I was a freshman at Altoona Area High School. I found myself in a place where the self-conscious mixes with the rush of hormones and where physical development ranges widely. I became enamored with the vascular bodybuilders on magazine covers, the ones who had the gorgeous, half-naked women caressing their bulging biceps.

That would never be me. I've always been small. I looked like I was ten, was only an inch above five feet and my 105-pound frame made me insecure to say the least. I gulped down protein shakes bought with the money I made flipping burgers at McDonald's. I hit the weights and avoided cardio at all costs (because cardio would burn precious calories) in an attempt to make up for what I wasn't given naturally. My confidence began to build alongside my body. I taped a picture of Ken Shamrock inside of my locker. I also had a six-inch WWF action figure of him I found for two dollars when a toy store went out of business. They were constant reminders to endure then overcome then succeed. The action figure had bendable legs, so I sat him in the upper portion of my locker and imagined he'd come to life *Indian-in-the-Cupboard*-style when the locker closed.

A friend of mine, along with his whole family, had black belts in Tang Soo Do and owned a dojo chain just outside of Altoona. I tried this art with them for four months. Kicks were flicked out and meant to be landed to the stomach or face with the twenty-six weak bones of the foot rather than launched Muay Thai-style (often into the thighs of the legs) so the thick tibia could both inflict and withstand the damage. Hands were often held at the waist rather than along the sides of the head like in boxing. There was no grappling component whatsoever. The sport component was called "point-fighting." The premise was this: whoever could land a clean shot (regardless of how weak) against their opponent would get one point. As soon as one fighter landed a shot and received a point the bout was stopped, the fighters would break and they would do it all over again. The competitors were talented, no doubt, but were perhaps better suited for impersonating kangaroos than fighting no-holds-barred.

It was not effective in an actual combat situation. Not only could I see this, but it was also proven time and again in many of the sport's premier organizations, including the UFC. Taekwondo fighters (similar to Tang Soo Do and karate) danced around and eventually a grappler closed the distance, took the taekwondo fighter to the mat and smashed him with elbows and punches or tapped him out with a submission hold. Or, the taekwondo fighter would dance around, flick a kick, break bones in his own foot, then be knocked out by a boxer's punch. Some members in his family spoke of Tang Soo Do to me and to loyally paying customers as though it was the end-all and be-all of self-defense and real fighting, but I believed there was more, better, although I felt powerless to be the change I wished to see. This knowledge embittered me. When they spoke, I'd bite my tongue to the point of pain. This too served as a reminder: Altoona had many martial arts academies, just not practical ones that mattered much in an actual fight.

On the other hand, wrestling was a style that mattered. Fighters with strong wrestling pedigrees were able to use positional dominance and their superior physical conditioning to take the fight to the ground, get a top position and use a technique called "ground and pound"—meaning they were able to bring their opponents to the mat before raining down punches. This often resulted in a referee stoppage because of a cut or because the opponent could not defend himself against the onslaught.

I joined the wrestling team as a senior. But I had the MMA mindset. *Well, this move wouldn't work because I could get choked* or *Why isn't this armlock allowed?* Something still fascinated me about Ken Shamrock making champion fighters cry uncle with ankle-locks. Often he didn't even throw a strike, instead using his agility, conditioning and knowledge of leverage to make his opponents submit to his grappling holds. It was such a humane way to end a fight with so few rules, both fighters walking away completely unharmed.[2]

The grappling-dominant style that Ken used had many variations and went by many names. But the best pure practitioner of it in the UFC was not Ken Shamrock. It was a string-bean of a man named Royce Gracie. Royce called his style Brazilian Jiu-Jitsu. Whereas Ken was possibly the first truly "mixed" martial artist—versatile and skilled at using strikes and grappling as well as his sheer physicality—Royce was pure grappling technique, pure leverage, pure patience, pure BJJ. This style had not yet appeared outside of Brazil, so the martial arts world watched in awe as this scrawny man strangled and armbarred (an armlock that hyperextends the elbow joint) and dominated their heroes. Royce Gracie proved that BJJ was the world's most effective form of fighting. Period.

I loved this style of fighting. Gentle yet devastating. Beautiful yet practical. It was what I was and what I could not be: a quiet, complex thinker with swift, decisive actions.

Literally translated to mean "the gentle art," jiu-jitsu focuses on using energy displacement and leverage to prey on the places human beings are most vulnerable: the neck and joints. The application of these strategies, imported from BJJ to MMA, was the work of Royce Gracie and his legendary family. Many other members of the Gracie family wanted to (and could have) been the one to prove BJJ's effectiveness on the world stage. But, Helio, the elder of all, chose Royce.

Due to Royce's success in the UFC and the accompanying demand from others to learn BJJ, the family opened dozens of Gracie Jiu-Jitsu academies throughout the world. Today, Gracie BJJ academies or BJJ academies influenced by the Gracie family, number in the thousands. The most renowned BJJ academy for MMA fighter development is the Renzo Gracie Academy in midtown Manhattan.

I still had a bigtime itch to learn, to redeem myself through MMA. When I look back I wanted redemption for my boxing loss, sure. I believed I had

---

2 A major misconception of MMA fighters is that they are crazy and like to hurt people. I've met thousands of fighters from all over the world and can't recall anybody who made it to any reasonable level in the sport whose intent was to fulfill their enjoyment of harming human beings. It's a sport like any other. It's about the learning, the art, the science, the networking, the money, the fame, the search for self, the practicing, the competing, the testing of abilities, being on a team, engaging in an act that dates back to some of the earliest Olympiads, the self-defense, the confidence it builds, the fitness, and more. MMA is often about everything except what people think it's about.

the drive to be an elite athlete and that MMA was my calling. Looking back, I wanted redemption because I was tired of blaming myself for my father's absence. Was it something I did as a son that drove him away? In pursuit of answers, I knew of no other place to go.

I'd hit the video store and rent three, four, five MMA videos, spending my senior year of high school alone, watching and rewinding, watching and rewinding. Studying the techniques. Thinking hard. As a result of my obsession to find answers in life, I sank into reclusiveness. I skipped the prom to watch fight videos, to bite my nails and think. The more I learned of life the more I feared life. My thinking led to the realization that life can't be controlled. Someone you cherish can kick you when you're down. Someone you love could be run over by a Mack truck.

Clueless about what I yearned for in life, I wanted to stay in the nest of mom and Altoona until I found a passion and myself. I applied to and was accepted by Penn State Altoona—only a few blocks down the road from home. I knew I wanted to enroll in a program there that would allow me to live at home all four years instead of transferring to State College for the final two. While Penn State Altoona didn't offer a bachelor's degree in fields relating to exercise, it did have a four-year B.A. Criminal Justice program. *Hell yeah. I'll take that then start locking up the world's assholes.*

Penn State Altoona allows (or forces depending on how one looks at it) students to take plenty of electives. I studied the class offerings carefully. Introduction to Business? *Hell no.* Family Relationships? *With the mess I'm in? Hell yes.* Introduction to Poetry? *Psshh, yeah right. A class with chicks talking about roses are red and shit. Wait.*

Voices came from my idols:

"Float like a butterfly, sting like a bee." – Muhammad Ali
"Using no way as way. Having no limitation as limitation." – Bruce Lee
"Flow with the go. This is the point beyond knowledge." – Rickson Gracie

That's poetry. That has to be poetry. Those are three of the most badass hand-to-hand fighters in the history of combat. Intro to Poetry? Sign me up.

***

Lee Peterson—a yoga-built, reddish-blonde thirty-something woman—taught Intro to Poetry. Her award-winning book of poetry, *Rooms and Fields: Dramatic Monologues from the War in Bosnia*, wasn't flowery and rhyming but it somehow still flowed in a way I could sense and feel but could not yet articulate. It spoke about the immediacy of struggle, death, war, of finding inspiration in life's crumbs and it did so through imagined voices. Holy shit. My preconceived notions of poetry were shattered. Notions that must have come from high school English teachers who didn't know or care about contemporary poetry.

On the first day of class I looked at the other students sitting around the circular table: *Girl, girl, gay guy, girl, definitely a gay guy, is that girl talking to herself? Yes, she's talking to herself. What the hell did I get myself into?*

"Go outside and look around," Professor Peterson directed during the first class. "Just look around. At people, at trees, at buildings. Don't talk. Just bring your notebook and write down observations. Write what you observe. Write what you hear. Write what you smell. Don't just see. Observe."

Some students laughed. One said, "Recess!"

But I wasn't laughing. There was something about the calmness with which she spoke. Something about the wrinkles around her eyes and the way those eyes settled on mine and seemed to know or share my struggle. I trusted her fully from the moment I met her. I would do whatever she told me to do.

So I went outside and stared at a tree. A few leaves fell. Death. Most stayed connected. Life. The tree gently rocked in the wind, gave in to the force but for its own sake—I researched: when trees sway in the wind it strengthens the woody material developing the stem and limbs and promotes the spreading of its roots. I moved closer. I couldn't see the full tree now but I could see veins on individual leaves. I could hear the wind rattle the leaves. I took a few more steps forward. Ants crawled through the bark. I reached my hand out and felt the bark's ridges. I saw the initials SAE + BMC carved into the tree. I looked up to the hilltop on my left and saw an entire forest. I realized I couldn't see any details of the forest—no veins on leaves or initials in bark—but I could see the vague outline of a forest. I felt myself really observe the way Professor Peterson intended. Then I felt angry with myself and angry at the city where I was born, the city I had yet to leave for more than a few days. Why hadn't I viewed anything in my life prior to this moment with such focused intensity, such openness? I flipped to the final page in my notebook and scrawled.

This is life.

I've been so sheltered in old, white, religious, racist, Republican Altoona my entire life that I'm without any perspective of thought, of people, of places, of myself. I judge people before I meet them and believe wholeheartedly in those judgments. I hear nigger and gay jokes every time I step off this campus. I think everybody who commits a crime is a bad person and should be locked up for life. I don't see their lives, I see moments of their lives. I don't see their story. I don't see stories in general. I judge people and books and ideas by their covers. Son-of-a-bitch. I'm lost. Dear Altoona, I've loved you and will always love you. You grew me. My roots are yours. But I am climbing English ivy. I need to spread. I need to see observe what else is out there.

***

The way I loved BJJ, I loved poetry. The goal of poetry seemed to be to show new ideas and perspectives that broadened and deepened human understanding of each other and the world. What greater inspiration could there be? I stumbled on Allen Ginsberg's quote about poetry. "The only thing that can save the world is the reclaiming of the awareness of the world. That's what poetry does."

Reclaiming awareness. Yes. Why is everything hidden? Is it hidden?

I wasn't aware of the Bosnian war, the Darfur crisis, or that my country possibly goes to war to feed its natural resource addiction. I wasn't aware of how ridiculous and dangerous it is that a humongous cheeseburger is cheaper than a few carrots, of how fast-food chains have turned farms into unsustainable corporations, how this causes lower-income people to eat their food (it's so cheap compared to fresh, locally-grown produce) and how those "less-fortunate" people, usually minorities, now have much higher rates of obesity, diabetes, mortality. I wasn't aware of how Native Americans and their estimated sixty-million buffalo were slaughtered and replaced with white "landowners" and nice, tame cows. I wasn't aware of how people on billboards and television commercials are enhanced to "perfection" with graphics editing programs so we feel bad about our own complexions, bodies, scent, teeth, hair and out of depression buy a company's product. I wasn't aware of the verbal tricks by which a news station can manipulate language to make a story fit their dogma. I wasn't aware of how difficult it is for homosexuals to enter the hospital room for their lifetime lover's last breath. I wasn't aware of how (for all its good qualities) religion is possibly the most separating, destructive, preposterous, and deadly idea in the history of humankind. I wasn't aware.

Poetry awakened me. There was more to life than Altoona. There was more to life than ESPN and Halo and even MMA. There was more to life. I wasn't aware until I embraced the constant questioning curiosity that is poetry. Poetry brings awareness not only through writing but also by encouraging thought, reflection, and research into ideas outside of what we're spoon-fed to believe. It's an art form where emotional intelligence and thought matter. Not regurgitated thought. Original thought.

Students with differences were respected rather than shunned in poetry class. The girl who sat in the corner and talked to herself wrote poems that opened our eyes to our interconnectedness as humans, to new images and to new ideas or simple metaphors to help us understand complex emotions. Being a bit bohemian was cool because it meant you weren't brainwashed by the almighty dollar or didn't fit the suit-and-tie-I'm-off-to-the-cubicle-from-nine-to-five-what's-for-dinner-tonight-honey?" mold that Americans are so easily baked into. It meant you might bring your unique thoughts to the table rather than lines spewed from a talking head on CNN or Fox News. For once in my life I felt okay that I didn't have answers to all of my problems. The poets in class thought I was cool just for being in pursuit of answers.

I took the same critical approach to fighting and poetry. I instantly saw both as arts. I learned about metaphor, iambic pentameter[3] and the subtle details of language within a poem. I started noticing the subtle details and dimensions of human emotion. I began independently studying exercise kinesiology, researching functional training strategies and experimenting with different nutritional intakes. I revisited a documentary called "Choke" that I had watched years earlier. "Choke" followed Rickson Gracie—the

---

3 The rhythm of iambic pentameter is created through the use of stress, alternating between unstressed and stressed syllables. An English unstressed syllable is equivalent to a classical (Ancient Greek and Latin) short syllable, while an English stressed syllable is equivalent to a classical long syllable. When a pair of syllables is arranged as a short followed by a long, or an unstressed followed by a stressed pattern, that foot is said to be "iambic." "Penta" means five. So there are ten total beats. Here's a classic line from William Shakespeare:
Is this / a dag- / -ger I / see be- / fore me?

fighter who everybody in the Gracie family, including Rickson's half-brother Royce—claimed was the family's best fighter. Rickson was as technical as Royce *and* well trained in all facets of human physical and mental conditioning.

What all viewers of "Choke" recall is the intense yogic pranayama breathing technique called Nauli Kriya. Rickson could focus so intently on his abdomen during breathing that he could vacuum it (suck all the air out) then separate each segment of his abdominal wall and move it at his discretion. I had never seen such absolute control of the human body. He would swim in freezing-cold streams for mental toughness. Fighters now do this, or sit in an extra large garbage can filled with water and ice, on a regular basis post-training because it's been shown to reduce inflammation and enhance recovery from strenuous workouts. I incorporated new exercise ideologies into my routine, experimented with ways to increase strength while allowing me to maintain the same body weight. I did naked yoga alone in the wilderness of Altoona. The poetry class and Rickson's influence somehow worked synergistically and made me feel comfortable enough to pursue my spirituality and individuality.

As a sophomore in college, I began picking up extra hours in the produce department at the grocery store, where I'd worked since the summer after I graduated from high school. I began making the four-and-a-half hour trip to the Renzo Gracie Academy when I had the finances, usually about once a month. The academy is in the basement of a business building; there are no signs posted to advertise.

Renzo (a cousin of Royce and Rickson) stands about 5'9" and weighs about 175lbs. "Hey, my brother! Welcome!" he says to students, hugging them as they walk onto the mat. He is the most naturally charismatic man I've ever met—the life of the party when there is no party. There's no plain-faced Renzo. When he is training hard his eyebrows furrow, his forehead wrinkles, and his eyes open unbelievably wide as though he's trying to also see what's behind him. But I'm convinced that Renzo spends the other twenty-two hours of his days either smiling or laughing.

Because I blended the BJJ techniques of the Gracie family with my background in wrestling and physical conditioning, I began winning no-gi jiu-jitsu tournaments (athletes compete wearing only shorts and not the traditional martial arts jiu-jitsu "gi," a white, two-piece uniform) throughout Pennsylvania and Maryland. Along with the name I had established for myself at the boxing club over the years, these victories gave me the cred-ibility to begin my own MMA Basics class at the Building II Athletic Club in Altoona on the weekends. Because I'd been a member there for years and because Carl Bennett, the owner of the Building II, liked me and had been hearing about my success, he approved my course curriculum without hesitation. The classes ran from nine to noon every Saturday. The cost was eight dollars per student per session. I gave the Building II three dollars and kept five. Each session was split between striking and grappling techniques. My goal was to focus on the fundamentals—how to generate power from the hips when throwing a punch, how to keep the eyes open when an op-ponent's punches are approaching, how and when to breathe and relax while grappling. It began as something selfish. The reason I taught was to learn and solidify my own knowledge. Relationships with friends and women were put on hold. I went to school, came home, did homework, trained four hours, and finished the day surrounded by fruits and vegetables at the grocery store.

Just days before my twenty-first birthday, while a junior in college, I made my MMA debut. Alongside the development of my mixed skill set, my body had developed physically—I was 5'7" and 155 pounds. Matched against my high levels of maximal strength and strength endurance from weight train-ing, low body fat from cardio exercise and a healthy diet, and knowledge of BJJ from world-famous instructors, was a residing, pounding insecurity about being small. And about being a quitter. And about that miserable box-ing match in Pittsburgh years ago. And about how and why my father left when I needed him most. To say I had hunger, I had fire, would be, to use a word I learned in poetry workshop, *litotes*: A dramatic understatement.

***

It was fire I'd seen in the eyes of my favorite boxer, Arturo Gatti. Two years before my MMA debut, fate made me drive the wrong way onto a one-way road and into a parking garage in Atlantic City directly beside his limousine. My sole purpose for the trip was to see him fight. I wouldn't have known it was Arturo if he hadn't rolled his window down so I could see his eyes. Shark eyes. I saw his fire. Here I was looking into Arturo's eyes just two hours before the eyes of pay-per-view viewers worldwide would be on him. He ended up winning the vacant WBC junior welterweight title that January evening in Boardwalk Hall against Gianluca Branco despite breaking his hand early in the bout. I screamed myself hoarse while cheering for him.

On the drive home I had plenty of time to think in between the gas station stops for transmission fluid (the transmission blew in my 1991 Plymouth Acclaim on the way home). Rather than dwell on how the $1600 dollars I'd busted my ass to save for a trip to train Muay Thai in Thailand would now be spent on this old beater, or even think about Arturo's miraculous victory, I thought only of the fire in his eyes. I knew I had this fire too. From that moment on, I knew when the time came to make my MMA debut that I would purposely wear a beanie at all times to distort my appearance, to cast a shadow over the fire in my eyes. I didn't want anybody seeing my fire until I burned them with it.

On the undercard of the Gatti bout, a professional boxer I thoroughly beat during a sparring session at the A.B.C. put up a solid fight in route to a unanimous decision loss against a top prospect boxer with a 24-4 record. For years I carried the confidence from knowing this top prospect couldn't finish a guy I knew I could have finished at any moment—I sprinkled this confidence on my morning oatmeal, into my bath water, and behind my eyes to help me see the world in brighter colors.

**

I'd sparred, grappled, sweat, and bled in Altoona, State College, Pittsburgh, Ebensburg, Hollidaysburg, Chambersburg, Huntingdon, Hagerstown, Richmond, Manhattan. Not yet in the state of Ohio.

My MMA debut would take place April 21, 2006 at the LC Pavilion in Columbus, Ohio. Professional MMA was illegal in Pennsylvania. As of this writing in 2010, professional MMA is banned or not regulated by an athletic commission in Alaska, Alabama, Connecticut, Delaware, Indiana, Maine, Massachusetts, New York, Rhode Island, South Carolina, South Dakota, Vermont, West Virginia, Wisconsin and Wyoming.

Steven A. Allred, Chairman of the Athletic Commission of West Virginia, (West Virginia is famous for its Toughman contests and the many deaths associated with this disgusting, unregulated spectacle of violence) wrote, "We think that MMA is Brutal and Dangerous and we will NEVER allow ANY such events in our State as long as I am in charge!" and "It is assault and battery." Allred has been accused of protecting his friends within the boxing and Toughman circles. If MMA is made legal, the boxing business will take a shot to the gut. Allred himself fought five professional boxing matches from 1982-1985. His record is 2-3. That Allred (and others like him) can hold positions of power is the reason for the bags under my eyes.

***

Date: April 19th.
Location: the bathtub at my home in Altoona.

To get clean, I shower. But the bathtub filled with the hottest water I can tolerate is for practice. I seek to find comfort in discomfort as I rest on my back and bring my legs over my head while trying to maintain calmness and a steady breath—fight simulation. For three years leading up to this fight I'd been practicing holding my breath under water to develop lung expansion and maximal capacity. Each exhalation is complete only when I make the desperate, dinosaur-like sounds of Jean Claude Van Damme when he's in pain in the movie *Bloodsport*. (As cheesy as it sounds, this is my gauge for knowing I can't possibly exhale any more air.)

Everything seemed to be a sign, and I began to notice things previously unnoticed, like the trail of hair running along the middle of my abdomen and into my belly button.[4] The majority of hairs slanted to the left. I wondered if this meant he'd have a hell of a left jab or left hook. I keep a glass of cold water beside the tub so I can maintain my levels of hydration while submersed in the hot water. This time though, a sip of the water traveled down the wrong pipe. Gasping for air as my eyes watered, I speculated that the fact I was choking in my tub might mean I would get choked in the cage. "Tap-Out or Pass Out," a poem I wrote in an undergraduate class, came back to me. The poem outlined a premonition about my first MMA bout, a vision that I'd be in full mount throwing rapid-fire punches, forcing my opponent to turn onto his stomach in order to protect his face and me capitalizing, applying the rear naked choke.[5] It ended with me crying and hearing the

---

4 Crazy word of the day. Omphaloskepsis: gaining wisdom from staring at your belly button.
5 The rear naked choke is considered the checkmate of BJJ. It means you've positioned your chest against your opponent's back – a dominant position worth four points in sport BJJ – and choked him. The rear naked choke is referred to as Mata leão in Portuguese. Mata leão means lion killer.

applause of a wild crowd. It would be a great possible outcome to a fight, but it was an amateur "tell-not-show" poem. Here's that poem, after many revisions:

Cage Fighter

Men dance like capoeira giraffes,
mercurial as mercury, unrelenting,
like the male praying mantis
who continues sex
for hours
after decapitation.
In this cage, there's no more wrapping
escarole, no more cleaning dog
shit from the yard. Knees,
thirty-five mile per hour head-on
car crashes. Elbows
slice brow flesh, a paring knife
through a ripe Anjou.
Chokes, like boas, the space
after exhalation.
In this cage, men dance, and when they look out,
their world is shaped
like diamonds. (2007)

Because this was my final bathtub routine before leaving for Columbus, I stepped out of the tub, threw on shorts and walked into the yard for yoga even though it was 2 A.M. I needed to cleanse all the toxins from food pesticides, air pollution, the trace amounts of prescription drugs that are found in tap water, all the negative thoughts of experiences with my father, all the brainwashing and manipulation by television and billboard advertisements, all doubts I had of what I could do or become in this world. Anything that corrupted any part of me—out. I tried to breathe it all out. Besides, I'd tossed and turned in bed for three hours a night the past three nights due to anxiety. Pharaoh, our Jack Russell terrier and Chloe, our Pomeranian mutt, deserved a night of rest and they would get this while I was out in the yard.

It was cold for mid-April, but my internal temperature was revving from the bathtub heat. On instinct, I dropped my shorts and continued my routine of yoga, downward dogs and all. I stretched hard until it hurt, until I could imagine the deepest fibers of muscle tissue breaking down to rebuild stronger. I exhaled until it hurt, until each rib was exposed, until I could imagine particles of impurities in all 100 trillion cells exiting my mouth. Pain meant purity. Pain brought pleasure.

The moon was blindingly bright. The cold dew on the crisp grass pricked my warm feet, sent an energy through my body and out my freshly shaven head. I looked up, followed the steam's trail as it rose off my body, and believed it was being sucked away by a vacuum, the moon ferrying my impurities. Merged with nature, I felt Lacan's jouissance[6] and finally understood what Penn State Altoona English professor Dr. Ian Marshall had been trying to tell me during a lecture he gave a few weeks prior on psychoanalytic literary criticism. With chills came normalcy, the cleansing process was complete.

***

The event in Columbus was called Extreme Fighting Challenge and the promoter was a man named Bo Kimley. Bo was a portly fellow in his fifties who hailed from Stockholm, Sweden, and sounded every bit of it. He paid for our hotel room on the night of the fight and I paid for it the night before so I didn't have to spend hours on the road the same day the fight took place. My two good friends, Tyler Rickards (a Clinical Neuropsychology student) and Mark Cooper (a graphic design artist) shared the room with me. While Mark was there for moral support, Tyler, though not competitive, was a martial artist in his own right. At 6'1" and a solid 220 pounds, he served as a tremendous sparring partner. During the months leading up to the fight we'd put on the gloves and spar wherever we could find space—mostly racquetball courts, though we frequented overgrown grasses of abandoned farms several times. The room was two single beds and a toilet. (Nerves forced me to spend more time on the latter.) Tyler and Mark packed into and shared a bed. I rolled restlessly in the other, agitated and anxious. I felt

---

6 Jacques Lacan (1901-1981) was a French psychoanalyst. His term "jouissance" meant an overwhelming feeling of pleasure and pain mixed together, a feeling of being at the edge, beyond the self, meditative feelings of being one with the universe.

like there was a warm itch on the inside of my body. The only way to nullify it was to move.

I turned on our radio to distract myself only to hear an announcer intone, "Come on out to the Extreme Fighting Challenge to see cage-fighting warriors punch, kick, and smash their way to glory...." I turned it off. Marched into the bathroom to shit again.

Mood-swings. Being less than five-percent body fat with a couple pounds of water weight to lose before I could make weight will do that. Even the precise process of weighing in is an art form. I counted the peaceful sleep-breaths of Tyler and Mark and mumbled to myself, "Do you have to breathe so fucking loud?" They were so attentive to me, helping in any way they could. But it didn't matter. In that moment of stress and dehydration I hated their peacefulness. I hated their closed eyes and their relaxation and their sleep. I turned on the TV to distract myself.

"The baddest no-holds barred extreme gladiators and the sexiest ring card girls, come on out to the Extreme Fighting Chal...."

***

The day of the fight. Tyler, Mark and I arrive early at the weigh-in and rules meeting to see the barbaric cage being built piece by piece. The cage looks unified on television, pristine. Perfectly cut into an eight-sided shape with a smooth, glossy, promotion-patched floor. I was aroused by this structure—even its name "The Octagon" had a euphonic ring. But seeing it built from the ground up scared what shit was left in me out.

Here were workers specifically hired to build a steel cage to enclose humans whose goal it was to kill each other while adhering to a few rules.[7] It

---

7 As of July 2010, there have been two deaths in fifteen or so years of professional MMA as a result of injuries sustained during sanctioned fights. Because gloves are smaller and fights are stopped in a larger variety of ways in MMA, the brain trauma suffered is so significantly less that it cannot even be compared to that found in boxing. The American Medical Association Council on Medical Affairs and Dr. Michael Schwartz, clinical instructor in the Yale University Department of Medicine, says that boxing is safer than football, auto racing, and horse racing. The same study calculated deaths per one thousand participants. The results show that the sport of boxing suffers 0.13 deaths per thousand competitors, compared with 0.3 in college football, 0.7 in Motorcycle Racing, 1.1 in SCUBA Diving, 5.1 in Mountaineering, 5.6 in Hang Gliding, 12.3 in Sport Parachuting, and 12.8 in Horse Racing. Horse racing is nearly one hundred times more deadly than boxing. This means that regularly eating fried food is more dangerous than MMA.

seemed absurd. The mad cacophony of hammers and drills wasn't what I expected. With each pound and crank my mind moved further and further away—so far away that the sport's brutality blurred its beauty. I felt ashamed of what I worked so hard to achieve. I felt proud of my body, the battle it went through, but the actual act of fighting filled me with disappointment.

The pounding continued. As the audience poured in, I heard snatches of conversation. "I'm ready to see some fuckers get fucked up," and "Front row seats baby! Close enough to get splattered with blood!"

Judging by the fans I'd seen and heard, I believed the majority of people weren't here for me to showcase my talent. They weren't paying the big bucks to watch my art. They were here for blood. They were here to see testosterone-fueled men pound on each other and out-of-work porn stars shake their asses as promised by the sport's promoters and the countless pay-per-view channel advertisements. They were piling into this arena to see how much punishment a human could take. They were here for the rarities: the broken bones, misshapen noses, and above-the-eye cuts that send blood coursing down the face to stain white shorts red. They were gathering, just as people have throughout history to see someone hanged, for the spectacle of watching human-on-human violence. Our ageless curiosity to cause and experience pain vicariously, in that moment, was what most ate at me. *I'm not here to hurt somebody or be hurt by somebody. It may happen, but it's not why I'm here. This is what they crave.* I thought *they* to myself as though referring to some sort of object. As though saying, "The crayons? *They* are over there." It didn't hit me until later that the audience also viewed me as an object. This primal thirst to see people not only psychologically vulnerable, as in a theatrical play, but physically vulnerable, was the main reason this arena would have a sell-out crowd. The first impression of my dream was one of disgust. I tried to play it smart, get there early, see my environment, adapt to it.

The way I adapted was by sitting on the toilet. From the stall I could still hear the pounding and clanking. It wouldn't stop. The fight would begin with a similar sound. I remembered that pounding *ch-ch-ch* ten-seconds-left-in-the-round sound followed by the metal bell I'd heard prior to quitting in Pittsburgh. Quitting.

I traced the slightly raised marking of the tattoo across my abdomen:

WARRIOR

So come on, I told myself. *Be one!* I left the stall and asked the workers if I could get in the cage. I wanted an intimate relationship with what scared me. I knew a warrior would live by this code. I felt the cold canvas give under my weight. I brushed the material with my fingers in the shape of the number 3. Three always reminds me I'm imperfect, I'm striving. It humbles me. It's not the continuous, flawless energy band of the number 8 but, with the way its arches curl, it's damn sure trying to get there.

I weighed in at 154.7 pounds, barely under the 155-pound limit for my weight class, and then I reached into my bookbag—which had been filled with poetry books during the semester—for olive oil, protein bars, fish oil pills, bananas, and the staple of any smart fighters post weigh-in meal, Pedialyte.[8] My weight was above 160 pounds before I stepped into the cage. This meant I'd have a bit of a size advantage on my opponent if he stepped into the cage at 155 pounds. Every little bit of an advantage matters—even if just psychologically. In this instance, it helped calm me because I felt the electrolytes coursing through my body. I felt confident that I'd have more functional muscle on my frame than the guy standing across from me when the cage door shut. Plus, I'd already confronted the cage by standing on its mat, touching its bars, and experiencing its enclosure. The dieting, the training and the restraining were over.

I could hear the promoter yelling in the hallway outside of the dressing room where we warmed up. "Cameron Conaway and Paul Compton is first fight. First fight is Cameron Conaway against Paul Compton." My psyche transformed. *This is my fucking time. These fans are going to see the best fucking fighter in the world.*

Fighters are notoriously egocentric and arrogant in thought and speech

---

8 Due to cutting water weight, the body loses electrolytes such as sodium, potassium, chloride, calcium, magnesium, bicarbonate, phosphate and sulfate. Electrolytes, among other roles, maintain the body's functions by regulating intra- and extra-cellular chemical balance. Without electrolytes the body can't send nerve signals or create muscular contractions. Pedialyte, which is designed for children with diarrhea, quickly replaces electrolytes while replenishing the body's water levels. Bananas are full of potassium as well as fructose – a quick energy sugar source. The protein bars provide recovery for muscles and most are filled with vitamins and minerals. The healthy fats found in olive oil and fish oil promote optimal brain and cardiovascular function and also have properties that reduce inflammation of the joints.

immediately prior to a fight. I never thought it would happen to me but it did. It's as though to stifle insecurity and doubt, the brain's instinct is to move entirely to the opposite end of the spectrum. Unlike most sports, an MMA fight truly engages the fight-or-flight response—it feels like a life-or-death situation. The human brain is built to survive by any means possible.

I thought of Ted Kooser's "and all the shuffling magazines grow still." I wanted to radiate that kind of valor. I wanted to bring the audience to that sort of absolute stunned awed silence. *Let's see how they react to greatness.* I heard a swarm outside the door of the dressing room. I opened the door and taped to it was the full fight card.

Fight 1: Cameron Conaway vs. Paul Compton

This was real. MMA wasn't just this thing I trained for and watched and talked about, it was something happening right now against a man, a man with a real name, a man who had also been training to fight. I paced. I wore the red Under Armour swim trunks that I cut with scissors at the sides so I'd have greater range of motion. They'd gone to hell and back with me and made it through. I wore a t-shirt that read "Fight Cystic Fibrosis" so I could give props to my friend in the crowd who has the disease. I wore a gray beanie from UFC fighter Tito Ortiz's clothing brand that read "Punishment" in bold letters across it. I wore it when training as much as possible. *The more I punish my own body through intense training, the better I'll be.* My goal would soon be fulfilled, or at least attempted. I pulled out the Theodore Roosevelt quote I carry in my bookbag:

> *The credit belongs to the man who is actually in the arena,*
> *whose face is marred by dust and sweat and blood; who strives*
> *valiantly; who errs and comes short again and again, who*
> *knows the great enthusiasms, the great devotions, and spends*
> *himself in a worthy cause; who at best, knows the triumph of*
> *high achievement; and who, at the worst, if he fails, at least fails*
> *while daring greatly, so that his place shall never be with those*
> *cold and timid souls who know neither victory nor defeat.*

> – Theodore Roosevelt, Citizen in a Republic. April 23, 1910.

The quote has been a guidestar since I read it in ninth grade. Until now, I never realized he said it on April 23, my birthday.

I sent Tyler and Mark out to scout Paul Compton. I wanted to know his build, his style, the way his breath smelled, anything. My strategy was stealth. I wanted to see him when he didn't see me. I wanted even that small advantage. I just wanted to know this body, this thing that stood in the way of where I was and what I worked so hard to achieve. Tyler and Mark were ten feet away. They nodded their heads as a way to say the man they stood beside was my opponent.

There he is. Taller than me but thin as a bird. Looks cat-like, probably great agility and cardio. I should own him in the clinch and on the mat. I'll neutralize his movement, close the distance, slam him to the mat and pressure him there. Blond hair. I can see the blood coming up through it now.

My friends and I talked strategy. The promoter posted a "revised" fight card over top of the original fight card on our dressing room door.

Fight 1: Clint McWorter vs. Cameron Conaway

I was still first but facing a different opponent. Now I was fucking pissed. *This fight organization is a goddamn mess.* I sent them out again. I wondered if the reason I was listed second was because I would be announced second. I wanted this because it would seem as though I'm the champion. It would ice the opponent. The stresses of iambic pentameter couldn't touch the stress I felt.

The event's disorganization continued. My fight was slated for 9 P.M. but at 9:20 the promoter told us the required ringside fight physician flying in from Las Vegas was running late. This meant even more trips to the toilet— for nervous shits and because it was a secure, private place. I was prepared to be enclosed and to fight. The openness of space, of people milling around and talking was breaking me down. I didn't know when to warm up because nobody had any idea when the first fight would go on. First fight nerves suck out enormous energy, so I didn't want to warm up for an hour only to be drained once I got to the cage. Being first is terrific when the show goes according to schedule. You know exactly when you'll fight, a luxury fighters elsewhere on the card do not have. When the company is in disarray though, fighting first is the worst.

During one trip to the bathroom I found a group of my friends in the crowd. "Man," I said, "The guy I'm fighting looks like he's going to ride a Harley into the cage. How the hell am I supposed to armbar or choke a Harley?"

They laughed but their laughter faded quickly because of their worry for me. Their grins, no matter how fleeting, relieved me. I went back to the locker room we shared with the other fighters and trainers to get ready and to see what the hell was going on.

At 10:10 P.M. the physician burst through our training room door and slapped a heavy black suitcase on the room's only counter. My shadowboxing stopped. She was a petite, fragile elderly woman whose frizzy gray hair reminded me of Johnny Robertson. She looked like she'd been shocked one too many times. She opened the suitcase. A defibrillator.

Time to go at last. A panic seemed to glue my feet (à la Pittsburgh) and I felt like I couldn't move. They called my opponent's name, and I heard the crowd roaring even louder than the heavy metal music. I watched him walk down the entrance and into the cage. This was a good sign, being introduced second, like a champion. I bounced lightly on my toes, completely covered in clothes, the beanie hiding my fire. *Fuck defibrillators.*

I heard the first few seconds of the music the promotion chose for my entrance. Then my introduction rolled out of the speakers.

In his first fight. A mixed martial artist. He specializes in boxing and Brazilian Jiu-Jitsu. Hailing from Altoona, Pennsylvania. Please welcome: Cam-er-on Con-a-way!

The crowd was louder than ever. I could feel it. Their ruckus sent tremors through my body but I didn't hear a lick of it. All was silent. As though the sound sense shut down in order to heighten those senses essential for a fight.

Something suddenly exploded in me. Something beyond arrogance. Indestructibility. There was nothing this other body could do to hurt me. I had done everything possible in training. All doubts evaporated about my cardio, my strength, my grappling, my striking or my state of mind. The nights spent fighting sleep's pull into darkness, standing up to my father, my mom front row like she had been at every basketball game, everything in my life came to fruition and wiped my slate clean of any insecurity. I didn't hear the music and I didn't hear the fans. I felt primal, pure, and ready.

I flung my shirt and beanie to the ground. The ringside attendants fastened five-ounce gloves on me and I climbed the stairs and entered the cage.

I stomped around feeling my feet on the canvas like an abstract artist preparing to paint a masterpiece. I was the panther I'd watched prowling in his cage the previous summer at the Pittsburgh Zoo.

Mark Matheny, a nationally recognized UFC referee, made me show the required mouthpiece and cup. I shuffled my weight from foot to foot but my eyes never moved. I stared straight into the eyes of my opponent. *I am the best fighter alive and there isn't a damn thing you can do about it. I'm going to run through you. I'm going to fucking run through you. Look me in the eyes. Stop looking away. Look me in the eyes, bitch. I'm going to smash you.*

Matheny settled into the center of the cage. "Are you ready?" (looking toward my opponent), "Are you ready?" (looking toward me), "Let's get it on!"

We touched gloves and sixty-five seconds later my opponent tapped-out to a rear naked choke. As I took his back and the choke deepened I saw his face go purple. He clenched his teeth to hold out for a few more seconds, so I held the choke with one hand and punched his face with the other. Then I repositioned my arms and my grip and sank the choke in deeper, tighter, and his face turned darker, faster.

He tapped-out. But it wasn't until he jerked the desperate shudder preceding unconsciousness that the ref threw me off and I let go. I wanted everyone in the cage and the arena and the city and the state and the country and the world to know who was the better fighter. I was not letting go of the choke just because he tapped-out—who knows if the ref would have seen it. I wasn't letting go until I received ultimate finality—the ref prying me off, or the feeling of my opponent's limp body. I wanted there to be no doubts. I had worked too damn hard for a fluke to happen. Either the ref was going to tear me off the back of my opponent or my opponent would be left unconscious. There were no alternatives.

The most passionate emotional response of my life ensued. I threw my mouthpiece to the mat and screamed to the fans, "I told you so, I told you motherfuckers!" At that instant the fans were the father who I believed had given up on me when I was thirteen. The man who didn't teach me to shave, see me in love, or see me graduate from college. The man who wasn't here now, for the greatest moment of my life—the culmination of not only the development of my body, but the development of my mind. The fans, my mom, my stepdad, my friends, everybody screamed my name.

The name I share with my father.

CHAPTER 12

Post-Debut Living

It's been three weeks to the day since my cage fight in Ohio, the fight for which I trained off and on for six years and won in sixty-five seconds. The whole event left me wondering, wandering, and wanting.

"I was wondering if you offer any student discounts or travel vouchers to study abroad?" I asked the Penn State Altoona Education Abroad Advisor.

Steve Sherrill, the author of a novel titled *The Minotaur Takes a Cigarette Break*, and I had become quite close over the years when I'd taken several of his and his wife Lee Peterson's writing workshops at Penn State Altoona. So when he came to me and said he was teaching a "Writing About Art" class and that the last two weeks of the class—for an additional one credit— would be a trip to London, I felt both excitement and disappointment. Excitement because I knew the class would be enlightening and count for one of my upper level credits. Disappointment because there was no way in hell I could afford to go.

The presented opportunity paired with the possibilities of receiving a $500 grant and taking out additional student loans. This forced me to think a little earlier than I probably would have about what I wanted to do with my degrees in English and Criminal Justice. The dream of being a professional fighter still itched me the same way a local band is always itching to find someone to sign them while they work part-time jobs washing dishes or bartending and dream of that lucky break.

I wanted to be a writer. I wanted to be a teacher who wrote. I wanted to be a writer who taught. I wanted an office like Todd Davis's, the man who became a mentor to me at the end of my sophomore year and still is to this day—an office on the second floor with wall-length windows overlooking the campus duck pond. I'd looked out those windows into the crystals of light the sun reflects off the water, watched the multi-colored autumn leaves sway and float care-free in the air and sat in awe as a dusting of snow created a surreal wonderland.

Todd sat in his office and read works by students or books off his shelf. Between the university setting, computer, phone, bookshelf, and the view outside, it seemed to me that Todd had the world at his fingertips. Students came to him for advice. The advice of his that most stuck with me was a quote he pulled from John Gardner's *The Art of Fiction*, "The qualities that make a true artist—nearly the same qualities that make a true athlete." He spoke of sharing quality time and of hikes into the woods with his teenaged boys Noah and Nathan. He spoke of the unconditional love he both gave and accepted from his wife Shelly. He spoke of his quiet time for writing and his active time playing pick-up basketball or lifting weights. He spoke of skiing at Breckenridge, Colorado, in March with three generations of powder hounds: his 80-year-old father, himself, and his sons. He spoke of the many people he'd met and studied. He spoke of Kurt Vonnegut, Jim Daniels, and Henry David Thoreau.

I knew if I persevered and became a professor, I still wouldn't make much money. Regardless of my financial situation, I took a quote by Thoreau to heart.

"How vain it is to sit down to write when you have not stood up to live."

Money was the reason I clocked in all those years using the same six-digit numerical code while at the grocery store. I began feeling more inhuman and more like 0-4-8-0-6-6 as I began my fourth year of employment there. I logged large chunks of my life surrounded by watermelon and cantaloupe bins. Sometimes I loved it, sometimes I hated it. But at all times I knew there was something else out there for me. I didn't know what. I began feeling that if I wanted to pursue happiness, especially as a writer, I'd have to stop living so conservatively. I'd have to take risks. I'd have to live. I'd have to adhere to the belief: "Fuck money, get loans and live."

Penn State Altoona did offer some discounts and vouchers and I was able to obtain a loan to help me afford the trip to London. I was confident and fearless after my fighting debut and ready to take on the world. That I avoided maps throughout my life because traveling was a pipe dream and wouldn't have been able to point to London if I had one in front of me didn't matter.

I'd never flown before. I clutched the back of Steve's seat as the plane's momentum forced me backwards and I said, "I can't breathe, I can't breathe." Steve turned, brushed strands of vibrant silver hair from his forehead and offered not a word, but an empathetic smile. Seconds later I settled in.

I'd studied photographs of artwork by everyone from Caravaggio and Cezanne to Velázquez and Vermeer during college and these studies had intensified during Steve's "Writing About Art" class. The deeper I got into studying visual artists, the more I realized that great artists are great artists no matter what their field. It doesn't matter if they are a slam poet, a painter, a chef, an actor, a businessman, a dancer, a teacher, or a kung-fu practitioner. Masters are masters, and the way I would become a master of my craft and of myself would be to study those I believed to be the best. The chief purpose of this trip was to travel to renowned art galleries in London and write about our experiential emotions as they related to the pieces we viewed. I visited photo after photo in my head during the ten-hour flight, but I also visited other thoughts. I wondered, at the age of twenty-one, exactly why I was still a virgin. I wondered what it must feel like to engage in the intimacy of sexual intercourse. I wondered, at the age of twenty-one, exactly why I seemed to be the only person I knew never to have had alcohol. I wondered what it must feel like to have a buzz, to get drunk and wake with a hangover.

I wasn't a churchgoer, but I believed physical purity led to successes here on earth and possibly in some afterlife. I tried to define what I meant by physical purity while I heard the hum of airplane dings and whistles, seatbelt signs here and passing pissers there. For me, it meant ingesting only the foods and drinks that kept my body clean. Drugs, of which I included alcohol, made the body filthy. When I had been in an environment where I had to inhale cigarette smoke, I felt I had to cleanse myself through a more difficult workout or through a bathtub routine where I sweat out the impurities. In the sexual sense, giving myself to someone I didn't intend to spend my life with felt like the ultimate impurity. It had nothing to do with adhering to biblical values (or maybe it did, subconsciously) and everything to do with the weakness and grime I felt when I gave in to pleasure for pleasure's sake. Pleasure, I believed, never led to successes or achieved goals the way pain did. Stretching beyond discomfort and feeling the burn of the hamstrings, working the heavybag and allowing the shoulders to sing their song of pain, getting up in the morning to study when I didn't want to—these were all forms of "pain" and it was only through pain that I could gain…something I couldn't yet put my finger on.

We met at an arts conference many years before in New York. I was attracted to her femininity yet physicality and also her life experiences (she was almost forty-years-old) and her world travels—she was a cinematic dance choreographer and this allowed her to travel wherever the movie was being shot. She was attracted to my drive and diversity—a fighter who took poetry seriously. We kept in touch but I wasn't interested in a relationship at this time, especially given the distance. But, she'd be in London for work when I arrived so I knew we'd meet up for coffee at some point.

The twelve of us students arrived at Lancaster Hotel in London. Steve gave me and my friend Cassie Ross (the other students mistakenly thought we were dating. More on Cassie in Chapter 15) our own rooms while the others had to double-up. I was upset that he treated me differently, but grateful—I didn't do well sharing a space with others. I'd tried it before and couldn't tolerate the laziness I encountered or the inequality of spending late nights taking care of drunks, drunks, so I thought, who gave in to pleasure's pull.

We all traveled the area, visiting art galleries throughout London and writing of our experiences and of how they fit into the history of art. This trip was far more "living" and far less "writing." Thoreau would have been mighty proud.

Night two. I decided to hang out in the bar of our hotel with the other students. Reruns of soccer games were on all the television sets and the locals were screaming for their team despite knowing the outcomes. Unadulterated passion. Many of the students offered to buy me a drink. At about my fifth denial, I told them all I hadn't tasted alcohol before, let alone been drunk, which sparked more pressure to drink. I looked around and saw the deep conversations, the smiles and the general warmth that filled this bar. That I was excluded from it in some way hurt me. I wanted to enjoy an experience. I worked my ass off, dominated my fight, and had been the one student chosen to represent the English department with a full-page interview in the *Altoona Mirror*. I felt on top of the world (or at the least, of a small town). What would Thoreau want me to do? Would he find it reasonable to have a drink even if he knew my father and grandfather both had problems with alcohol? What, exactly, did it mean to live? How much of living is trying and how much is being?

C'mon, Cam," my friend Chris invited. "Try anything on the menu. I'll buy."

"Honest to Christ, Chris," I said. "I don't know what any of this means."

"Well, I know you, man. Let's get you something healthy-like."

"Like what?"

"Excuse me," Chris said to the bartender. "You got a healthy drink with alcohol in it? My friend here is a fighter."

"We've got one with thirty-one different types of apples."

"I'll have that, Chris. If that's okay."

I sipped and talked, sipped and listened, sipped and became one with this scene just like everyone else. Chris ordered me another 32-ounce bottle and after my slow sips emptied this bottle over a few hours, I went to the bathroom to piss and to look into my own eyes. My pupils were dilated and I felt the warmth in my body that seemed to flow throughout the bar downstairs. I felt another surge of confidence and began shadowboxing in the mirror after I pissed. I felt unstoppable. I don't think I'd ever felt that unstoppable. I went back down to the bar, exchanged e-mail addresses with the new friends and said I was calling it a night. I ran the steps back up to my room, floating like a butterfly and fully expecting my head to be stinging like a bee in the morning.

I woke to a pounding not in my head, but outside of my door. Only half awake, I couldn't tell if it was my door or another one down the hall. "It's me," a voice murmured. "Can I come in?" It was my thirty-something friend. Prior to the trip I had told her the hotel name but nothing more. I glanced at the clock, 2:45 A.M. I got out of bed nervous and unsure what to do if I let her in and she tried to make a move on me. "I can't find the key to my room," she said. "Can I sleep with you, Cameron?"

My heart raced. I was wearing only my Altoona Wresting mesh shorts. I ran to the dresser and quickly grabbed the first shirt I felt in my hands, a white, wrinkled, long sleeved button-down dress shirt, so I didn't give her any signals. I opened the door a crack and she opened it the rest and flung her arms around my neck. She pressed her hips into mine and wrapped her left leg up around my lower back. I could smell the alcohol on her breath mixing with the sweetness of her perfume. "I'm sorry," she whispered softly into my ear. "I can't find my room key. I hope that's okay with you." I felt her tongue caress my ear and then my neck and then...

...blood surged. I knew she wanted me, sober or not. My body wanted hers right then and there. I fought the urge, lifted her up onto my shoulder like a fireman's carry, and she lightly ran her nails all over my back. I was crazed with lust. I delivered her gently to the bed and pulled myself out of her arms. I tenderly held her face in my hands.

"I don't want to do this," I said seriously. "I can't do this right now."

"Okay, I understand. I'm so sorry, Cameron."

I turned away from her and felt her do the same. We slept butt-to-butt. I woke again an hour later to her warm breath against my neck and ear. "Cameron," she whispered, her lips touching my ear. "You've told me you're a virgin and proud of it. But real men have had sex. You're not a real man until you have sex. I want to be the one to make a man of you."

Upset that I saw this coming and still allowed her to sleep beside me in a bed barely wide enough to fit one person, I replied quietly, "What the fuck do you know about real men? Who the fuck are you to tell me what a real man is?"

"Okay, okay, I'm sorry," she said. "You'll never know how good I can make you feel, the things I will do for you. Anything you want. You'll always wonder. You're right, though. And I'm sorry again. Goodnight, Cameron."

I woke again less than an hour later to the warmth of her breath next to the head of my penis. The tremendous sensation controlled me. I enjoyed it. So much so that I did my best not to stir, to pretend I was sleeping. I felt her soft hands on me and then warm moisture as her lips and tongue and mouth took me in.

"What the hell are you doing?" I yelled, as I sat up a few seconds later.

"You deserve it, Cameron. Just enjoy something in your life God damnit. What the fuck is so wrong with enjoying me sucking your cock and being a man?"

"Get the fuck out my room," I said. "I don't want to talk to you the rest of this trip. I'm sorry I lead you on. I'm sorry I let you in. I fucked up. But you know I didn't want this. I've told you how many fucking times I'm not ready. It's all about power to you, isn't it? Power and control and using your age to get what you want. Find your motherfucking room key and get the fuck out. Get out!"

She scrambled for her purse and dug through it. Her credit cards, nickels, dimes, and driver's license were scattered across the floor. "I can't find the key," she said with panic. I grabbed her purse and stuffed everything back into it. My breath quickened and my blood rushed, but this time it was out of absolute anger. I directed it at her even though it was mostly about myself.

"A real man never would have turned that down," she said. "Are you gay or something?"

"This is how a man acts," I said, shoving her purse at her. Her room key fell out of her purse and I picked it up and put it in her hand. "This is how the fuck a man would act. You're seeing it right now. You have no fucking idea what a man is." I grabbed her by the shoulders and pushed her carefully out of the room and slammed the door shut. "Fucking A," I whispered to myself. "Neither do I."

I spent the next hour or so in yoga poses while thinking how I was going to face her. If I was going to face her. If she would ridicule me. If she would remember. If she would tell our mutual friends and how I would face them. I closed my eyes and eased into deep stretches and wondered how I could have handled it differently. What if I'd had sex with her? I didn't even have a condom. What if I let her suck my cock? What would that have meant for us? For me? Why am I so different from everybody else? Will I always be? Why do I not allow myself to fulfill bodily desires of food and sex? Is it because they are ephemeral? Because they're not practical, with long-term benefits?

Yoga and thought took me into a profuse sweat, so I showered and at 6:00 A.M. went down to the hotel lobby for the buffet breakfast. Steve and Lee had a table and invited me to join them.

"How was your night?" Steve asked, as he stirred tea.

"I can't fucking stand how alcohol changes people, Steve. Why can't they just drink socially, why get tanked every time? I hate feeling self-righteous and all goody-good, but I just don't like it. What's so wrong with that? I tell people I don't drink. I don't go into why, I don't belittle them. But they make me feel it's because I'm all holier-than-thou. I'm not, man. I'm just a dude who doesn't want to drink. I think people who drink are more self-conscious and insecure about their drinking in front of those who don't than those who don't are when around those who do. But it always seems like it's the ones who don't drink that are the ones made to feel bad about themselves. Am I rambling here? I'm a freaking mess."

"So you had a great time, eh?" The way Steve stirred his tea calmed me. Zen.

"Sort of. She (speaking of they-knew-who) feels like she can control me because she has ten years on me. Well, that's a load of shit. Do you care if I train with the London Shootfighters today?" I had mentioned to Steve before the trip that I'd like to wander off and train at the London Shootfighter Academy one morning instead of attend an art gallery.

"Seems as good a day as ever for you to go," he said. "When you get in, give us a call so we know you're back."

I grabbed a blueberry muffin and a carton of milk and hit the streets of London. According to MapQuest, the academy was less than five miles away, so I decided to walk. Beginning in the hustle and bustle of downtown London, I soon found myself lost in the middle of a grass field surrounded by brick roads. A dark brown horse galloped toward me and stopped on a dime as though expecting me to pet its mane. I did. I petted that horse for over an hour, just an empty field, the horse and me as I delivered a long-winded soliloquy about what it is to be a man. This moment will forever feel like a dream to me. I can't imagine moving from the most people-filled area I've ever seen to one of absolute people-less peace and natural majesty.

Practice at the London Shootfighter Academy began at ten, so I parted ways with my friend, asked around a bit and found the academy with time to spare.

After introducing myself to the main instructors, Alexis Demetriades and Paul Ivens, I bowed and joined the circle of cross-legged sitting fighters. One of the other MMA trainers walked into the center of the circle, sat down, and closed his eyes. He reached out his hands palms-up in front of his chest.

"As fighters we must fight," he said with a Buddha-like peacefulness. "Patience, bad luck, life, death, caring for each other, making decisions: these are all fights and, in the long run, probably more worthy than stepping onto this mat or into a ring or into a cage. But, as fighters we must fight. Introduce yourself to the man to your left, whether you know him or not. Learning is a form of fighting. We are fighting ignorance. Meeting somebody new and feeling awkward is a form of fighting. We have a newcomer here from Pennsylvania joining us today. Let's welcome him the London Shootfighter way."

The members of the class turned to me and bowed their heads. If I never felt more disrespected the night before, I never felt more respected than I did here. I couldn't help but think the "fighter" of his speech was synonymous with "man." My mind rolled around ideas as my body rolled during grappling positions. I learned a new technique for controlling the hips of an opponent when trying to pass their butterfly guard position. I understood the definition of a man would never be a compact Thoreau-esque quote; its definition will continue to contract and expand with each contraction and expansion of my lungs. It has a breath of its own in the bodies of every person. I may still not know what it is to be a man, but I felt I knew more about myself than I did before I left for London. I could add that to my box of definition puzzle pieces.

Around 11:00 P.M. that same night, I took a short walk from my hotel and headed for Trafalgar Square. On the way I saw several openly gay and lesbian couples, smelled marijuana, and dodged people trying to sell me out-of-date theater tickets—all things I was rarely exposed to at home.

Trafalgar Square is the gray paved area in front of the world-renowned National Art Gallery. I'd visited the gallery the day before and listened to the story of a guitar-playing beatnik.

How the World Works
My dad was a bastard, but I moved
to Germany when I was 19
and I met a beautiful woman.
She asked if I've ever made love before,
I said no, no—I was nervous you see.
She played Beethoven that night
so of course we made love, and that morning
my feet were no longer splayed
and I no longer stuttered, I swear to you.
Then, about six months later
I got hit by a car
when I was riding my bike. (2006)

statement made by Brian Pope, 72-year-old aspiring artist, at Trafalgar Square, London

The Square contains striking outdoor fountains and monuments that create a people-packed social scene even late at night. I brought a pen, a notebook, and some red wine in a water bottle thinking that if I could control another fighter in a cage and my own bodily urges and do so while balancing two majors in college, surely I could control alcohol. This night, I felt an adrenaline rush very similar to what I felt inside the caged octagon. I wrote in my notebook.

Three couples are intertwined like swans, two of which are stroking each other's hair in perfectly synchronized movements. A group of five men are following—rather aggressively—two visibly younger women. The men are yelling profanities. My writing must be sloppy now because I am writing while I watch.

The men are becoming a little more aggressive and my writing is becoming a little more sloped. I'm looking down. The women are backing into the corner near the bottom of the stairs. My right hand is preoccupied writing, but my left is anxious. I picture my fighting stance, bringing my left fist right off my tucked chin, taking the step needed to close the distance, and landing the half-arched left-hook that has dropped heavybags and sparring partners. I place my left hand into my pocket to keep it from shaking. I'm going to go down there to help now.

I'm back. Two yellow-vested Trafalgar guards appeared and handled what could have made a classy scene a crime scene.

The majority of people and pigeons have now left Trafalgar Square so, like them, I too will retire soon.

Why is it that I want to be the fly on the wall and part of the scene? Why is it that part of me wants to watch as a writer and part of wants to act as a fighter? Is it possible to do both? I always want to do both. Tonight, wanting to do both pulled me apart. Luckily, I didn't have to fight. I enjoy the company of myself as much as the company of others. Maybe that is part of the definition of manhood. Either way, I'll never know and I'm fine with that. All I've wanted all these years is to accept myself. Today, I took a big step. I accepted that it's acceptable to not be sure about certain things in life. A period is sure. I'll commemorate my newfound respect and acceptance of uncertainty by withholding the period at the end of this sentence

11:47 P.M.

Log 7

Uncertainty. Have faith in the indirect, uncertain benefits of hard work.

Log 8

Withholding. Much of fighting is withholding. Energy, foods, friends.

CHAPTER 13

Support Your Locally Grown Professional Wrestlers

Premise Nineteen: The culture's problem lies
above all in the belief that controlling and abusing the natural
world is justifiable.

– Derrick Jensen, *Endgame*

A rhythmic pyrotechnics display interrupted my text message conversation with my stepbrother Bobby and signaled the beginning of the World Wrestling Entertainment's (WWE) Cyber Sunday pay-per-view event at the US Airways Center in Phoenix, Arizona. Bobby sat at home in Altoona and ordered the event. I sat in the sold-out arena and tried to regain whatever it was that drew me to this form of entertainment when I was a little boy. Plus, it was my final year in the MFA Creative Writing Program at the University of Arizona. I desperately needed writing material.

The smell of the fireworks' smoke and the feel of their heat reached my lower level balcony seat. Obese, middle-aged men on either side spilled their flesh over the armrest and invaded my space. I crossed my arms and leaned forward to avoid claustrophobia. *It brings me closer to the action*, I told myself in an attempt to remain positive. *It brings me further away from the scent coming from my left and right: dried armpit sweat splashed with nachos and cheese. This is professional wrestling? It's not like I remember it. I guess the passing of time can clothesline the bliss of ignorance.*

It pains me to call these entertainers "professional wrestlers," because it discredits the many athletes who train and compete in "real" wrestling yet are called "amateurs." By real wrestling I mean folkstyle, freestyle, Greco-Roman, and variants thereof—the kind of wrestling styles that are high school, college, and Olympic sports. In contrast to the real, this "professional" wrestling is the stuff that occurs in a ring similar to boxing rather than on a mat, that allows steel chairs, barbwire-lined baseball bats, aluminum garbage cans, and anything else for that matter to be used as weapons. From here on out, when I say "wrestling" or "wrestler," think entertainment, not sport.

From the age of six to fourteen, I followed wrestling. The walls in my bedroom were postered tributes to the superstars I watched weekly on TV and live once or twice a year at the Jaffa Mosque in Altoona or at the Bryce Jordan Center in State College. My pillow was a two-foot-tall plush "Ultimate Warrior" wrestling buddy. Action figures of "Rowdy" Roddy Piper, "Stone Cold" Steve Austin, "the Undertaker" and many others lined my dresser drawers. Especially after my folks' divorce, I half-believed that the toys would come to life and fight on my side if somebody tried to break in to the house and hurt my mom or sister.

More than anything, I realized it was my father's lack of communication skills and his code—that fighting can make up for it—that I lived by until college. It was our daily script for years:

"Now what do I want you to do, Cameron?"
"Not take shit from anyone."

My father and I never talked any deeper than a "How was your day?" level. I was too young to know how to go deeper, and I believe he was too incapable. Accordingly, other personal relationships remained on that surface level. I didn't probe deeper with questions to my friends nor they to me. The few times they did (often questions about girls I liked) I remember feeling uncomfortable and awkward and answering monosyllabically. Along with alcohol, it was this attribute of my father that most contributed to the divorce from my mom. But, the communication attribute only represented half of his code of beliefs. I graduated from Penn State University with a Bachelor of Arts degree in English.

My father's other half, the "Don't take shit from anyone" half, erupted during the divorce. To quote Tennyson, he fought "red in tooth and claw" not *for* my sister and me, but, I believe, *against* my mom. He didn't take shit. Apparently, I would often think, my mom must have been giving him some serious shit. So I came to hate people (including mom at times) who gave shit to others. I wanted to do something to stop those who gave it. I graduated from Penn State University with a Bachelor of Arts degree in Criminal Justice.

Wrestling served as bookends to the before and after of the divorce. Every Saturday night I'd watch good guys not take shit from bad guys. I'd yell at the television screen as bad guys dished out plenty of shit. Wrestling was the code of belief my father taught me encapsulated in a two-hour program. It was a continual fight against shit-taking. Of course, I was naïve and I didn't understand actual fighting or the continuum of physical pain that can come from it. I thought it was normal to be knocked unconscious several times during a wrestling match. Anytime in church, in school, or anywhere in the "real world" I saw a folded steel chair (the predominant weapon used during these events) I felt a sense of safety akin to when I slept under the "protection" of my wrestling figures. I thought taking a punch from a man who jumped off a turnbuckle must hurt infinitely more than one from a man standing a foot away. I finally arrived at a natural understanding of real fighting because of maturity, puberty, and a few rented movies of actual hand-to-hand combat produced by the UFC.

Around the age of fourteen, I lost interest in wrestling. The show and characters and drama and high-flying acrobatic maneuvers no longer controlled my emotional core. The days of hiding behind the couch when the Undertaker came out or when my favorite wrestler (always a good guy) took punishment (shit) from a bad guy (a heel) were long gone. A new era began, an era where I studied as many practical martial arts as I could, an era where I rented three or four UFC videos at a time and rewound and reviewed the many techniques used by the fighters to gain the upper-hand or bring the bouts to an end.

Once, I rewound and reviewed a UFC VHS tape so frequently I had to put a band-aid over my thumb because it was blistered from the remote control buttons. The Ultimate Warrior wrestling buddy who had protected me and kept me comfortable at night now became a dummy for me to practice armlocks, leglocks, and chokes. Of course, he couldn't verbalize whether the move worked or not, so I spoke under my breath for him.

On weekends, I didn't socialize with others. I studied these fight films, partly out of the fascinating switch from my days of watching the fantasy fighting of professional wrestling to the actual fighting of the UFC, and partly out of the remnants that remained buried inside of me from my father's code of beliefs. Theoretically, I believed that through studying these tapes and training my body to perform the moves, I wouldn't have to take shit from anyone.

Two organizations dominated national television when I watched wrestling:

the World Wrestling Federation and World Championship Wrestling (WCW). In 2001, the WWF bought the WCW. If having only two companies controlling the market for years was bad, now one held an absolute monopoly. Later that year, the World Wildlife Fund—the world's largest independent conservation organization—sued the WWF for breaking a business pact established in a 1994 agreement over the use of the initials. The World Wildlife Fund won, and the next year the WWF became World Wrestling Entertainment.

To watch a three-hour WWE pay-per-view event on an average-sized television set, we burn about one pound of coal. Coal has an old-school feel to it. We picture black-and-white photos of miners pushing wheelbarrows, but we seldom actually see coal. It works behind the scenes so we don't know about it, or we don't care. It's the same with smoking. If the damage done to a smoker's body occurred on the outside the way it does on the inside, most who smoke would quit immediately. By nature we respond to obvious, external stimuli. We buy gems that shine yet serve no purpose but to make us "look" better despite the killing and torturing of countless slaves around the world to procure them. We undertake surgeries that make our boobs and pectoral muscles larger but serve no additional function in feeding our children or lifting heavier objects, that make our asses fuller but serve no function in excrement removal, that smooth the lines on our forehead but serve no purpose in reducing the stress from which they grew.

If a naked human body broadcast on television 24/7 like a reality-show represented our environment, we would see the gross effects of our overabundance. We'd see tumors grow from the face and legs, skin discoloration, teeth become dark and brittle. Coal is still our most abundant energy source. According to the Department of Energy, burning coal generates half the electricity consumed by Americans. Half. The lights on right now in my house, the monitor allowing me to see what I type, my refrigerator purring in the background. I often think of the billboard sponsored by some coal association I see when driving through West Virginia, "Wind dies, sun sets. Think coal." Idiots spreading idiocy and infecting others. The ideology of the Holocaust.

Such was my eco-friendly train of thought as I filled my gas tank and made the two-hour drive from Tucson to Phoenix (a desert with an all-you-can-eat seafood buffet, a place so "economically developed" that at no point did I feel in the desert) to reflect upon how I view the wrestling scene differently now that I've been removed from it for so many years.

In the early days of the UFC, Ken Shamrock actually gave up his career as a professional fighter to become a professional wrestler with the WWF. The money was much better, he became a nationally recognizable name, and he never had to worry about state jurisdictions deeming his actions illegal. This is one of many reasons that fans of MMA call Ken a pioneer of the sport. When he entered the WWF and became famous, he helped bring thousands if not millions of fans to the UFC, and as the popularity of the UFC increased, so too did the pressure on state athletic commissions to begin implementing rules that would eventually sanction and legalize MMA.

An enormous, lit-up projector called the "Titantron" is a staple of any WWE event. On it fans can view the pre-recorded entrance highlight video of their favorite wrestlers as well as live footage when they emerge from behind the curtains to strut down the ramp to the ring. The matches are much larger than life on the huge screen. Close-ups of blood, pained facial expressions, and shredded abs. Because fans from around the world could vote on which matches took place by sending text messages, Cyber Sunday was touted as the "most interactive wrestling pay-per-view of all time." And to represent it, the Titantron was shaped into a cell-phone as tall as any house I've ever lived in and as wide as a two-car garage. Amid the shouting and cheering, the movement and action, and my own texting, I found myself thinking about how technological advancements have given us lives of such unbelievable comfort that we've let our lives and lands go to absolute hell. I thought about how far I was from home.

By many accounts, Altoona's population has dropped by half over the past fifty years. It's working class. It's get up early, clock in, get dirty, come home to eat and sleep and do it again. Pap worked eighteen-hour days at times as a truck driver, spending his life either on the road or loading and unloading butchered cows from the back of his truck. Gram raised four kids, mostly alone, while he was gone. I had tasted some of that drudgery, but not nearly to that extent, and just as I began to reflect on its bittersweet flavor, I was swept away into a new life.

It took me a week to rack up the hours at the grocery store that Pap or my mom clocked in one day. I cut cabbage, prepped parsley, hefted fifty-pound bags of potatoes on my back the way I imagined Pap did with cow carcasses. The mindlessness was a welcome change when I clocked into work, and I believe that time was a sort of mindless meditation that carried me through the intensity of my studies.

Now, at the US Airways Center in Phoenix, I was ashamed at myself for feeling different, feeling "better" than the majority of the Cyber Sunday fans. Mostly middle-aged men, many were emphatically overweight. Many were dirty. They spoke with the curse-crazy language that reminded me of the years I spent pounding the basketball into the pavement of all the local playgrounds—the language Pap admittedly used as a trucker. People complained about waiting in line, about how the nacho cheese wasn't warm enough, about how the cardboard plates were cheap and flimsy, and how the Pepsi was flat. They wiped their noses on their forearms, coughed without covering, screamed "suck my dick" and "fuck you" to wrestlers they disliked despite being in the presence of children.

The more matches I watched, the more I realized the WWE characters seemed to be devised solely on stereotypes embraced by the fans. Unwritten and unofficial requirements seemed to be:

For most African-American wrestlers: Dew-rag, low jeans so underwear hangs out, silver or gold chains, Timberland boots, cornrows. Must be proficient in rap, must dance. Silver or gold in mouth. Athletic abilities above and beyond the majority. I heard the following phrases from the fans: Kick his black ass. You rap like a white bitch.

For International wrestlers: If you are Russian, you must show no emotion. If you are Italian, you must be stupid and arrogant. If you are French, you must be overly dainty. French wrestler, you will be called: faggot, gay, homosexual.

Requirements for women wrestlers: Make men fantasize about sticking their penis in you. Two things will be said of you: (1) What a stupid bitch. (2) I'd fuck the shit out of that bitch.

Do certain careers keep intelligence and empathy from evolving? If I had worked only in the produce department, would I have absorbed the racism my co-workers harbored and occasionally released when customers upset them? Without academia, would my thoughts more accurately reflect the city in which I was born, a city where very few leave and ninety-six percent are white? If generation after generation inhabits the same environment without leaving, does it become a cesspool, with thoughts infinitely more outdated than Cyber Sunday Pepsi? Pennsylvania congressman John Murtha once said that small-town Pennsylvania is racist. Is this because no one leaves? Speaking specifically of Altoona, was it because the black population was so small yet so heavily represented in the area's crime? If people rarely see local African-Americans other than in mug-shot profiles on the nightly news, how much does this taint our view of the race as a whole?

I suddenly felt ashamed to be an American. I felt ashamed to be the grandson of a truck driver yet unable to relate to the working class around me even though I earned less than $14,000 a year as a graduate student. I wondered if the stereotypes propagated in wrestling during my youth influenced my current thoughts, and if so, how buried is my subconscious prejudice? I felt ashamed for thinking such thoughts while everyone around me cheered for chokeslams. I couldn't enjoy the event. Would they vote against Barack Obama because of his race? Would they even know they were doing this, or would their racism be so deep and hidden within even themselves that they'd mask their hatred of him with other reasons? How would their kids grow up? When I become a professor, could I make the positive difference in their lives the way my teachers did for me? A counter to a jab is a left hook. What's the counter to prejudice?

I wondered if my life was worse or better now that I'd become "learned." Over the announcers voice, the rock music and the raucous but happy fans, I recalled this passage from W.E.B. Dubois's "On the Coming of John," where his sister speaks to him:

"John," she said, "does it make every one - unhappy when they study and learn lots of things?"

He paused and smiled. "I am afraid it does," he said.

"And John, are you glad you studied?"

"Yes," came the answer, slowly but positively.

She watched the flickering lights upon the sea, and said thoughtfully, "I wish I was unhappy, - and - and -," putting both arms about his neck, "I think I am, a little, John."

WWE wrestlers average 300 days a year on the road. There is no off-season to train and perfect their skills. Their lives are literally spent on tour. While the WWE touts this schedule as brutally demanding and as a way to show the fans how hard these entertainers work, I once again think about sustainability—both for the body of our environment and for the bodies of our wrestlers.

The Environment's Body

The Amazon rain forest produces twenty percent of the oxygen we breathe, twenty-five percent of the medicines we take, and half of our animals, plants, and insects. Every second, every inhalation and exhalation, a football field's worth of rain forest is mowed down. But the environment is vast and we don't see these effects.

The pollution we cause effects the food we eat, the water we drink and the air we breathe. We know this. And we know of global climate change. But we often can't see the havoc we wreak. It occurs too slowly for us to notice in our fast-paced lives. The environmental body is disguised, but our own bodies do a hell of a job masking the garbage we eat, drink, and breathe to make our own degradation seem equally invisible.

The Wrestler's Body

Wrestling is labeled as "sports entertainment." Fans expect the drama of a soap opera costumed in chiseled chests and backs that ripple like the sharp ridges of Arizona's mountains. No question, the skill and dedication involved in wrestling is phenomenal. Not only do the wrestlers have to have a stage presence, charisma, and the skills of an actor, but the best also have the body of a superhero and the coordination of a gymnast and martial artist. But, again, our culture is all about the surface. We could not care less what's actually happening on the inside if it looks good on the outside. So how do many of the wrestlers maintain their physique and control the pain from the many bruised muscles and torn ligaments? Hint: not through grass-fed beef and organically grown vegetables at a farmer's market.

Steroids and painkillers kill wrestlers in the same way the use of DDT nearly wiped out many creatures including the world's fastest animal, the peregrine falcon, and our national bird, the bald eagle. Wrestlers use a move they call the "DDT," named after the chemical. One wrestler front headlocks another and falls backward so the opponent's head is "buried" into the mat the same way the insecticide is "buried" into the soil. It takes an animal eight years to metabolize half of the DDT it consumes and about eight seconds for a wrestler to act like he's hurt and rise to his feet after receiving one. The numbers of the peregrine falcon and the bald eagle are on the rise thanks to Rachel Carson's book titled *Silent Spring* and the subsequent 1972 ban of DDT, and it's the wrestlers now who are an endangered species.

Extinct Species
"The Canadian Crippler" Chris Benoit, 40—From an article by ESPN (June 27, 2007. Mike Fish).

"Pro wrestler Chris Benoit strangled his wife, suffocated his 7-year-old son, and placed a Bible next to their bodies before hanging himself with the pulley of a weight machine. Investigators found prescription anabolic steroids in the house and want to know whether the muscle man... was unhinged by the bodybuilding drugs, which can cause paranoia, depression, and explosive outbursts known as 'roid rage.'"

Researchers later found the human brain deteriorates over time from the same drugs Chris consistently ingested. It is widely thought this deterioration led to his rampage.

"Mr. Perfect" Curt Hennig, 44

Hennig's death is listed as acute cocaine intoxication. But his father believes a combination of steroids and painkillers led to his son's death.

"Ravishing" Rick Rude, 40

Rude's death was listed as a heart attack, but it's widely believed it was brought on by an overdose of steroids and GHB, a drug used for anything from helping athletes retain muscle while in a calorie-restricted state, to inducing a "rave party high," to combating depression.

"Flying" Brian Pillman, 35

A former NFL player, Pillman had a history of abusing steroids and painkillers before he too died from a heart attack.

These athletes had all been famous within the small circle of the wrestling industry. They were not people who never made it. They were former champions in the sport entertainment industry for which they gave their lives. Also, these deaths occurred within the past eleven years. What's sad is there were likely twenty or more deaths during the same time period.

For the sake of our wrestlers, we need to support the locally grown. "The 3,000-mile Caesar salad" has become a cliché in environmentalist circles, yet we are doing little to make it cease. The food we overconsume and the distance from which it comes prepackaged is causing the destruction of our environment. We disregard the local wrestlers who work part-time jobs or are part-time students at the local community college. Local wrestlers seem to use less sexist and racially motivated stereotypes and more creative characters. They work just as hard at their craft but they avoid steroids and painkillers more frequently than those who build a career around a culture where drug use is damn near a necessity in order to "make it big," both of body and career. Still, attendance at local wrestling shows is embarrassingly small. We can get the same thrill WWE wrestling provides us, and on a more frequent basis, if we pour our money into our local wrestlers. Let's donate the money we would normally spend on t-shirts supporting convicted wife-beater "Stone Cold" Steve Austin, or pay-per-view purchases of events run by a monopoly, and into the guy who splits his energy use between delivering pizzas and flying from the top turnbuckle. It'll give us a chance to meet the people who live near us, (which lengthens our lives and reduces crime) and it'll empower our youth to keep working hard towards their passions.

If we can tone down our excitement over real-life look-a-like superheroes we may save mainstream wrestlers from dropping dead of heart attacks or hanging themselves from the weight-lifting apparatus they may know more intimately than their wives. If we can take this same "go local" approach and implement it into the foods we eat, we may allow ourselves and all those who live around us to survive and thrive in cleaner air and soil and water and conscience.

The wrestlers I saw at Cyber Sunday were the same wrestlers I cheered as a little kid. "Stone Cold" Steve Austin, The Undertaker, Shawn Michaels, "Rowdy" Roddy Piper. There are very few newcomers in the business. Is this the result of so few people able to sustain such a demanding schedule? Probably. Is this to appeal to that audience base of middle-aged men who feel they are still young by watching those they cheered for as kids still compete? Probably. Is it indicative of our society's inability to make certain changes? Probably. Very little changed in twelve years. Wrestlers are either characterized stereotypes or stock character-remnants of when wrestling's popularity peaked in the 1990s.

Famed author and environmental activist Edward Abbey's quote often comes to my mind: "Society is like a stew. If you don't stir it up every now and then the layer of scum rises to the top." I believe I was born into an environment where the chances I would be stirred up were low. Where I could have easily become scum. Luckily, several mentors directed me to college which stirred me up, which led to Arizona which stirred me up, which leads to the year-long trip to Thailand I'll soon embark on that will stir me up. I avoided scum by moving throughout my environment, but I required a stroke of luck to get my own stew moving. There must be ways other than changing locations to stir the stew. I want this essay to be a spoon.

Log 9

"Essay" comes from the French word "essai" which means "to try." Say "essai" when exhaling during punch combinations. A reminder of life's meaning.

CHAPTER 14

Inexact Number of Ways of Looking at a Red-Tail

"Thirteen Ways of Looking at a Blackbird" by Wallace Stevens.

I

Among four-hundred-fifty students and over one-hundred faculty members, the only moving things: the Red-tailed Hawk and me.

Pile the height of ten basketball rim poles one atop the other. One hundred feet, give or take. That's how I judged the distance between me and the burgundy walkway rail that the Red-tailed Hawk's pencil-thick sun-reflecting black talons gripped.

It was a bright mid-June morning at Franklin & Marshall College in Lancaster, Pennsylvania. I was teaching "Crafting the Essay" for Johns Hopkins Center for Talented Youth (CTY). CTY is the premier organization for nurturing the academic talent of gifted youth. It was the first program of its kind to identify academically talented youths and then provide them with learning opportunities. Mark Zuckerberg (co-founder of Facebook), Blake Eskin (web editor of The New Yorker), Sergey Brin (co-founder of Google) and Lady Gaga (American recording artist) are a few who have taken classes with CTY.

I was on edge and intellectually intimidated during orientation. I wondered if I was in the right place. I never did well during high school. Some of my students are twelve-years-old and already have higher SAT scores than me. Two other teachers I met could rehearse Homer's epic poems the *Iliad* and the *Odyssey* in English *and* fluent Latin. Others enthusiastically spoke in mathematic formulas rather than sentences. I spoke of wanting to go to the bar down the road on Saturday night to see if it would air UFC 86.

I was making copies of famous essays for the late-afternoon class. Annie Dillard, David Sedaris, Raymond Carver, Scott Russell Sanders times twelve. The copier's sour smell of warm ink and warmer plastic mingled with cleaning-crew lemony-alcohol Pine-sol. Twelve copies weren't enough to park it, so I paced. Copier to window. Window to copier. Lunch at 11:30. Must get copies back to class by then. The warmth made me sweat. Paper clip, paper-cut, paper clip, paper-cut. I finished, pissed that, of course, the paper cut in my left index a day ago—the one no longer than a small staple, somehow became a target large enough to snag everything in the entire world. So it goes.

This was the end of week four out of six total weeks teaching. I was on auto-pilot. The erudites here called it "functional fixedness," but whatever the name, it helped the days smoothly tick down. I took on a machine state. And I liked it: the militaristic consistency. I was TV-less, so devoid of newscast's sticky little negative fingers from marking me. Emotional highs and lows? Nonexistent. A laugh here and there at the cafeteria didn't tip the scale. Steady-state all the way. Until the hawk.

I swung each step inadvertently scuffing forward—how I walked didn't matter, all that mattered here at F&M was the effectiveness of my teaching. I spotted the hawk. I wanted to get as close as I could to it without it being spooked. My inner Steve Irwin ran wild. I tried to get closer but realized the brightness of my orange University of Virginia shirt was probably a dead giveaway. Steve's voice came: *Crikey mate, anything's a dead giveaway, it's a Red-tailed Hawk!*

Fifty feet.

Modifying fear for practicality's sake and suppressing enthusiasm for focus' sake: these two abilities carried over from my competitive fighting career and exhibited themselves in this moment as my body approached the raptor's body. I scuffed steps no more. The talons were threatening, but I wanted to get closer. I wanted to see each feather. I glided closer, no sudden moves. *How close could I get to see this beautiful thing?*

Twenty-five feet.

What was that perfect distance—close enough to observe but far enough away to react and defend myself if he attacked? I sat the stack of Dillard, Sedaris, Carver and Sanders down on the grass. I squatted and duck-walked closer.

Closer.
Closer. I could almost touch him. Three feet away.

Stopped. Afraid it would move. What I learned: All-black eyes are frightening. There was no way to tell where the hawk was looking, he wouldn't face me. I'd been taught that animals who can't look you in the eyes are more passive. I decided he wasn't facing me because he was indifferent towards me. I meant nothing. No threat. The thought never crossed my mind that he might be ill or injured. He stood too strong—chest muscular and proud, the quick, short movements of his neck seemed to be his attempt to tease me with his speed.

A squirrel dashed under the walkway rail and the Red-tail squared up to it, lowered its head—a perfect straight line from the tip of its black beak to the meat of the oblivious squirrel's body. The hawk's tail was more a boiled caramel color, a lighter shade of brown than its body.

A few steps closer while his back was toward me.

Suddenly, the hawk forgot about the squirrel and about-faced me. Black eyes, black beak-tip, black talons. *Here are my weapons he seemed to say, black and glistening in the sun. Glistening like that essay titled "Buckeye" by Scott Russell Sanders in the grass to your left. It's a detailed account of what his father taught him when he was younger. Yes. The buckeye can be seen as a metaphor for how both he and his father believed life's simplest moments were also life's most profound. I know those essays. I know your every move and thought. Nothing you do will surprise me.*

II

We were of thirteen minds, like a tree, in which there is one
Red-tail and eleven squirrel parts.

Maggie was fresh off the plane from volunteering with Cross Cultural Solutions in Costa Rica (with a plethora of her own animal tales). "Do you think you'll ever see that hawk again?" she asked. I said, "I doubt it, once-in-a-lifetime deal right there."

[My ten-minute moment with the Red-tail sparked interest and some research. Did you know the great horned owl, the largest owl in North America, doesn't make its own nest? It steals the Red-tail's.]

My students, a dozen thirteen-year-olds, meet at 8:55 A.M. in front of a large, leafy maple tree. I'd named it "Samson" because its power of presence came from, as one student said, "its huge hair." We took the walkway as usual, only this time I tried to squeeze the passion I'd felt for this hawk into a five-minute conversation with them as we walked to class. "He just let me look at him," I said. "No qualms. He opened his wings for me, stared at me as if he knew every mistake I'd ever made. It was as if he knew more about me than-"

"My uncle is a falconer," a student interrupted. "He's rich, but I remember him telling us how he uses Red-tailed Hawks. They land on his arm like this," he said as he bent his arm and raised it chest level.

[The majority of falconers in the United States use Red-tailed Hawks.]

A group of kids were launching a frisbee around as we passed the burgundy walkway rail and began the slight ascent to our classroom. Launched one right up into the tree just as we approached. I waited for it to come down so I could tell the kids to be careful with the frisbee when people were walking by, that it was all fun and games until someone loses an eye. It rustled in the leaves then stopped.

The rustling continued. More rustling. Then the Red-tail emerged from the tree directly in front of us, with me just ahead of my students. Wings wide, he screamed…

[Because of its robust crispness, a certain recording of the cry of the Red-tailed Hawk is a cliché cinematic sound effect. This high, piercing scream is often featured in the background of adventure movies to give a sense of wilderness to the scene.]

… and dropped what looked to be the tail and back leg of a squirrel mere inches from where I stood. The scream continued as I shook and the Red-tail landed atop an adjacent building. He seemed to watch us walk to class. "Oh my god," I said to the class. "Did you guys see that?"

"Didn't you hear us yelling, Cameron?"

"That was sick," said the student who mentioned the falconer uncle.

I continued to have the jittery shakes as I got to class. I felt like this hawk was trying to tell me something, felt like I had to tell Maggie.

"Listen how ironic this is, Mags," I said when I told her the story later that evening. "Just last night you asked if I'd see it again…." Maggie and I are what you could call "in love." She's got an athletic spirit, she's empathetic, has practical smartness and emotional intelligence, values communication and conversation, is so damn beautiful, unrelentingly curious, can find humor in anything and is a lover of life's natural gifts—luck-willing I'll marry her someday. A man and a woman are one. A man and a woman and a Red-tailed Hawk are one.

[The Red-tailed Hawk reaches sexual maturity at two years of age. It is monogamous, mating with the same individual for many years. In general, the Red-tailed Hawk will only take a new mate if its original mate dies.]

Maggie lives in Charlottesville to my Tucson. Although we went to high school and lived in Altoona for the first eighteen years of our lives, we somehow didn't find each other (like this) until after college. Handwritten letters: Charlottesville to Tucson. Tucson to Charlottesville.

[The same pair may defend a nesting territory for years. During courtship, the male and female fly in wide circles while uttering shrill cries. The male performs aerial displays, diving steeply, then climbing again. After repeating this display several times, he sometimes grasps her talons in flight briefly with his own.]

I grappled with what this hawk was trying to "tell me." What could this whole experience mean? Typical me, couldn't just let it be. I had to dig deeper, turn over rocks that have been just fine where they were since the beginning of time.

[The Red-tailed Hawk is second only to the Peregrine Falcon in the use of diverse habitats in North America.]

III

The kids were moving. The Red-tail must be swooping.

It was the last night of the CTY summer course. Evening session ended at eight instead of nine so the kids could have more time for their final dance. At 8:05 P.M. the quad was empty, the campus quiet. Strengthened through research, the sinews of my brain surely sharper-edged now after grappling nights away, I felt I knew this hawk. If I ever saw him again, I knew I could look at him the way he looked at me. I was satisfied. I could never see him again and I'd still be happy for the moments we shared.

On the way back from checking my faculty mailbox—in which I received a handwritten letter from Maggie—I was walking back to my dorm room to rest and reflect on this entire teaching experience. I was ready to contemplate my search for meaning. Should I question a raptor specialist when I headed back to the University of Arizona? What about a shaman's take on the situation?

Suddenly I saw a flash of motion. The Red-tail flew, no, streaked from atop my building right at me. I nearly hit the ground when I ducked. Had I not moved I'm sure he'd have struck me. It screamed again and again, so loud it rang in my ears and I couldn't tell if he was actually screaming again or if I was just hearing the echoes. He then settled on the lowest branch in the tree directly outside my dorm.

Here are my weapons it seemed to say again, they are black and glistening in the sun. I read your every move and thought. Nothing you do will surprise me. Did I just surprise you?

I watched the hawk for minutes in absolute silence. I couldn't look at him as he looked at me. He seemed nonchalant. But I was filled with awe, with unadulterated envy of his confidence, his life.

"Here is my body," I said to the Red-tail. "I've sharpened it over the years. This is my weapon." I sat, then sprawled flat on my back against the grass directly underneath him. With my arms spread open, back and neck relaxed, my thoughts stopped. I continued to watch amazed that he would let me get so close. That he would get so close. He opened his mouth once, twice, as though trying to say something to me other than a scream. As though he wanted to communicate in a different way than we had been. I lifted my head slowly off the ground to hear what wisdom he had to say and then the fur and bone of regurgitated pellets came my way.

It was evening and would be when I woke. No matter. From the maple tree the Red-tail spoke.

Bracketed information from http://en.wikipedia.org/wiki/Red-tailed_Hawk

Log 10

Sleep. From The Harvard Women's Health Watch.

1. Learning and memory: Sleep helps the brain commit new information to memory through a process called memory consolidation. In studies, people who'd slept after learning a task did better on tests later.
2. Metabolism and weight: Chronic sleep deprivation may cause weight gain by affecting the way our bodies process and store carbohydrates, and by altering levels of hormones that affect our appetite.
3. Safety: Sleep debt contributes to a greater tendency to fall asleep during the daytime. These lapses may cause falls and mistakes such as medical errors, air traffic mishaps, and road accidents.
4. Mood: Sleep loss may result in irritability, impatience, inability to concentrate, and moodiness. Too little sleep can also leave you too tired to do the things you like to do.
5. Cardiovascular health: Serious sleep disorders have been linked to hypertension, increased stress hormone levels, and irregular heartbeat.
6. Disease: Sleep deprivation alters immune function, including the activity of the body's killer cells. Keeping up with sleep may also help fight cancer.

Source: https://www.health.harvard.edu/press_releases/importance_of_sleep_and_health

CHAPTER 15

Caged—Part Two

August 19, 2006. Or August 19, 200 B.C. It didn't much matter. Before the audience was allowed to enter the LC Pavilion in Columbus, Ohio, I stood alone in the cage before my second fight. The same venue. The same cage. The same buzz in the air. But four months had passed. I felt the emotions my centuries-ago predecessors must have felt. I could see myself along a continuum of fighters. Closing my eyes, I pictured two gladiators standing in the center of the Roman Coliseum, their loincloths slit along the side for ease of movement just like my Under Armour shorts. I imagined their minds reflectively racing through memories with family or of the grueling training they'd overcome or about strategies for the biggest battle of their life—the one in front of their face. The storm before the calm.

I sat cross-legged in the center of the cage, closed my eyes and imagined closed-door fights in the gyms of Rio de Janeiro in the sixties, seventies, eighties, nineties, now. I saw the gradations in picture quality—from black and white to sepia tones to brilliant full colors. I pictured a Gracie family member entering a windowless room along with a fighter from another academy. One member representing each school was allowed in to serve as referee. The men battled hard to find out if what they've been studying actually works. Their fathers and grandfathers did the same. They were progressing the art of the fight, improving the most practical art in human history. For the Gracie family, there was no nobler act. There is no more gratifying, more glorifying way to ensure the practicality of true in-the-body learning than to demonstrate skills against an opponent. The outcomes of those fights were rarely leaked to the public. Each fighter held the result in his heart and passed the information on to his team so they could also reap the benefits of his win or loss.

I opened my eyes and stood up. I knew the history of what I was engaging in, knew it more intimately than I'd known it during my first fight. In many ways, I'd become a fight historian. And I took pride in being part of this history.

The cage, this time, did not conjure up thoughts of violent and shameful human spectacles. Instead, it was lifeless compared to the warriors who entered it. I saw its soft corners and compared it to the sharp muscular cuts of a fighter's forearms. The real cage was the one I lived in daily; this physical cage stood only as metaphor.

The walls of the cage were glazed to a silky finish. A few short months ago I only noticed its barbarous appearance, not its visual appeal. The overhead lights reflected off the dark, diamond-printed steel the way the sun reflects on wave crests at dusk—leaping to new views in unison with each step taken. My hands were calloused and rough from heavy deadlift training over the past four months, but when I smoothed my fingers over the cold cage it felt good. It no longer intimidated me. Instead, it acclimated me as I'd hoped it would. The first time, the cage had looked like some medieval torture device. Now, on this humid August night, I felt another side to its personality—the coating of paint along its bars had tamed it.

As a small boy learning to breed rabbits from my father in the backyard, I remember taming them. I slowly counted to one hundred every morning as I petted their thick, shedding winter fur one hundred times to make them calmer. My father said the more I petted the rabbits the better their temperament would be. Even when I was seven, I sought to bring order to something as abstract as temperament, to make the unquantifiable quantifiable. To me, one hundred was a magical number. Count to a lower number and the rabbits wouldn't turn out as nice. Count higher and they'd take it for granted. In my mind, one hundred was the concrete number that would give me control.

The idea that numbers were the only paths to improvement, to control, continued on even through college, when I logged every single repetition and the exact amount of weight used on every exercise. I felt as though I only improved in life when I could either perform a higher number of repetitions or could lift a heavier weight. Through poetry, I came to see there were values to life outside of those that could be counted. Emotional intelligence was more important than Pi = 3.14.

I'd roll the thick clumps of the rabbits' shedding fur between my fingers and throw it into the yard for the robins to make nests. I never felt more productive than when I'd see robin nests made of rabbit fur around our house. I even named the mother rabbit "Robin" because the act moved me so much. I pet her day in and day out. The muscles in my frail forearms would burn with the repetitions, but I persevered. "Tame rabbits would have nice babies," I told my father, as though the idea had been mine all along. And they did. In the early evenings, when the mother would struggle and writhe and yelp during the birthing process, we would put the male into another cage. Then, miraculously, one by one, tiny, wet, furry babies no larger than my thumb would appear. The mother would nudge them with her nose into the nest she made by chewing alfalfa, spitting it out and mixing it with her own fur.

The octagonal cage though, the one trained adult MMA fighters compete in, would always be too indifferent to contain and care for babies. It had been coated to prevent lawsuits, so if a fighter's face was split-jagged and bleeding, it wasn't the cage's fault. And by association, it wasn't the promoter's fault. Nothing was.

After my debut fight, I established the identity I knew I lacked. The absence of my father for nearly the past decade no longer subconsciously drove me to impress him. I realized that trying to fill the void he left with accomplishments was like putting sand in a strainer. The process of training was undoubtedly fueled, in part, by my past experiences with him.

I'd wanted my father to see what he lost. I'd wanted to rub it in, no, to splash the alcohol not in his mouth but over his open wounds, from a distance. I'd wanted him to read the *Altoona Mirror* newspaper and see my writing and fighting accomplishments, see the full-length article about me as the representative of Penn State Altoona's English Department. I'd wanted all of this so he would question himself, admit and then reflect on the way he treated me. I wanted to impose my will on him in this mental way, the same way I physically did to my opponent in the cage. I wanted to force learning and self-improvement down his throat so he would vomit up acknowledgement and apology.

After that debut fight, when the fans screamed my name, for the first time in my life I didn't feel the dead weight of my father hanging from each letter. Our name, in that moment, for a moment, became only my name. His fingers slipped off the curl of the capitalized C of Cameron. His part in "our" name disappeared—not the way a teacher removes a student's correct answer from the chalkboard, one swipe, but the way the waves erase a loved one's name written in the sand, slowly eroding it until it is going, going, gone.

From the time I can remember until my junior year in college, speaking in front of a crowd brought bouts of a mechanically stiff tension through my in-need-of-WD-40-jaw and down into my trapezius, before finally kicking its shoes off and calling my heart its home. Preparing days ahead of time, I carried water with me at all times the way toddlers carry their favorite blankets. I wanted to make sure I was properly hydrated so my mouth wouldn't be dry come speech time. It never helped. From the time the first person presented their speech until it was my turn, my mouth filled with phlegm so thick I couldn't spit or swallow. This, of course, was a precursor to stuttering words I'd read aloud hundreds of times. I could hear myself stutter but absolutely couldn't stop it. I can fight in cages with thousands watching, I thought, but speaking in front of people makes my nuts recede.

Junior year in college, I had copped out by presenting a "how to" speech that was more of a demonstration with a partner about BJJ moves—the triangle choke, the omoplata and the gogoplata—instead of presenting an informative speech about the history of MMA (what I really wanted to do). During senior year, my friend Cassie invited me to watch her audition for the role of Medea, in Penn State Altoona's production of Euripides's play of the same name. I was the top dog of a small campus. "So audition," I asked Cassie, "is basically a cool word for try-out?" Being a guy surrounded by sports my entire life, I knew all about try-outs. "Just come watch," she said, "you'll see." Cassie was truly audacious, letting herself become completely vulnerable in front of people she was either competing against for the role or didn't know at all. And she reveled in it. During the audition, she laughed—the uncontrollable type when you know you shouldn't and need to hide it or excuse yourself from the room. She became a serial killer—brooding, pacing, shoulders hunched, hair wild, eyes blank. She bawled—the type where you can't breathe, the type that becomes more a fight to inhale oxygen than about the cause itself. She trembled afterwards from what seemed like a coming back to reality, a shock from residing within herself again rather than in a fabricated character.

I congratulated her with the slap on the back my junior high basketball coach used to give after I took a charge on the opposing team's biggest player. Later, in a bathroom stall, I too shook. The beauty of what she did amazed me and also upset me because I knew acting would be a tremendous way to expand myself but I also knew it scared me too damn much to try. I gritted my teeth. I was being split in half by a desire to do something and a desire not to do something. With me, the desire to do something to better myself always wins. I hate that it always wins because sometimes I don't want to pursue personal growth. Sometimes I want to sit back and relax and watch a Steelers game. I didn't know what the hell to do. Fear and insecurity bubbled to the surface like boiling garden-variety spaghetti sauce, thick clumps thrown, sticking and burning. I shut myself in a bathroom stall. I put my face in my hands and cried.

Through Cassie's performance I learned that the more I cared what people thought of my appearance, from clothing to the facial mannerisms I couldn't control, the more I became their prisoner. The reason I'd always been shy was because I was not confident in what I said (my ideas), how I said it (my voice), and the package with which I presented it (my body).

My debut fight had been more a battle with fear than with my opponent. This time, the cage wasn't what scared me. What scared me was that once again I couldn't control my incessant pre-fight bowel movements, that all the eyes in a sold-out arena would be on me, that I might lose in front of those I loved. Though it rarely happens, I was afraid I'd get seriously hurt, that I'd sprawl to defend against a takedown attempt and blow my ACL or be too stubborn to tap-out soon enough and have my shoulder dislocated or be knocked unconscious or break my neck. I was afraid my family and friends might see me in such a battered, weak state.

What must a mother go through when she watches her son's neck jerk to one side and his body go limp from a left hook? When the audience is silent as a fighter is unable to move on the canvas, what must the silent voice of a mother be saying? I imagined her fighting the instinct to rush from her seat when she sees blood on his face. I wrestled against these fears, trying to trump them by thinking the outcome would be self-elation and an unharmed body as the referee raised my hand. This could be a jumpstart to a possible career.

Confronting these fears led to me finding my own place as a man, out of the shadows of my father. A certain peace overcame me each time I subdued the negative thoughts that infiltrated my mind—a peace that came from pulling my knowledge of the history of what I was about to engage in to the forefront. I'd developed a more tangible appreciation for the clichés "hard work pays off" and "the lesson is in the journey." This fight—the maximum length it could last was fifteen minutes—wasn't what mattered. What mattered was that through all my training, the mental meditations as well as the physical exertions, I found that my path to spiritual happiness was a result of a balance between the two. I found—through my post-fight, instinctual, primal screams—that as sophisticated as I try to be (attending art galleries wearing a collared shirt and nibbling on exotic cheeses) that I am still very much a wild animal, evolved to a far lesser extent than I previously imagined. And it was through this that my respect and connection with nature began. I realized I'd learned little in my barely-over-one-minute first fight. But I had learned a tremendous amount through the years of preparation and self-reflection.

I entered the realm of fear when I stepped into the cage for that first fight. Win or lose, I knew I had won a battle with myself. Now, I did not stand alone in the cage. I stood with the unconditional friendship of experience. The best way to confront fear is to knock on its door and once in, to head straight for the kitchen, robbing it of sustenance. I learned this lesson because I had broadened my personal definition of what it means to be a fighter. And because I partook in the act, I fought.

I applied this lesson to my other fear, the fear of being in front of people. I auditioned after all and I won the lead male role, Jason of the Argonauts, Cassie's co-lead, Medea's husband. I researched Jason the way I researched anaerobic energy systems for fight training. Obsessively. It helped that he was a warrior. I hung Post-It notes in my room: WWJD? What Would Jason Do?

Jason would strap Glossophobia[1] to a wooden raft, rest coins on both its beady eyes for admittance into a kingdom, set it aflame, and send it afloat. Through him I found a new side of warrior.

It was the summer prior to senior year and rehearsals weren't until the start of the fall semester. I was taking fifteen credits so I could graduate with

---

1 Word of the day part two: Fear of public speaking.

two Bachelor degrees in four years. Twelve credits were part of an Intensive Spanish class in State College, Pennsylvania, a fifty-minute drive from Altoona. The other three came from an internship (a necessary final step in attaining the Criminal Justice degree) I had with the Blair County Coroner. The hectic schedule provided ample time to develop stress, bags under my eyes, and a recurring nightmare that still wakes me sick from time to time. It's the day before opening night of *Medea*, I don't have a clue what my lines are and I'm too afraid to admit it to Robin Reese, the woman who, come fall semester, would split almost every waking moment between being my acting coach and the director of the play.

As for now, the Spanish class taught me much about a new language and culture and more about my own culture. Four Penn State football players were in the class of twelve. They, and I use "they" to signify how close-knit of a group they were, were assholes. I'd had to take out a high-interest private loan for $7,000 for these fifteen summer credits and I was driven to do the best I could. Studying a language in academia is half outside-of-class personal preparation and half in-class partner practice. I did my fifty-percent, but the football players sure didn't. I was pissed that I cheered for their team on national television. I was pissed that they were even on national television.

The players consistently made sexual remarks to the female instructors when they turned their back to write on the board. They joked around and watched pornographic videos on their iPods. When the teachers left the room during intermission they'd turn the volume up so everybody could hear the moaning. I always found myself partnered up with one of them (often the one who now plays in the NFL). I'd spend my nights listening to audiotapes, working hard to earn an A. Then I'd enter the class and waste time with lazy jocks who earned a scholarship simply because genetics gave them the gift of athleticism.

Okay, I admit, I can be a bit of a tight-ass. I work hard, play by the rules and love doing my best. I also love to have a good time when it's the right time. When I became a teacher, I made my classes as fun and engaging as possible, but as a student trying to get his money's worth and being distracted by porn-watching "athletes," I had little tolerance. I felt bitter that I followed a warrior-code of discipline, yet wasn't given nearly the same attention or respect as the players. They were nationally televised, had die-hard fans from every walk of life, and were going to school for free. I was $50,000 in debt and my sport was illegal. They received A's for the class just as I did.

On the other hand, the internship with the Coroner forced me to confront and think about death. When I'd walk in and see a man who had blown half of his head off with a shotgun, while the television flickered in the background and the flies flickered around his still-moist brain, I couldn't help but come to terms with what it means to die. Even in the cruelest deaths, poetry blossoms.

Suicide Sighting

"Sometimes you just get so tired of being tired you just need to sleep. I'm sorry."
– Message on the man's suicide note.

newspapers, tv dinners
burnt spoons, chandelier

cobwebs
decorate the trailer's
entrails
collect
smells of dog shit

    of burnt beef

embalm.

there he is.

    slouched
on the couch watching seinfeld
without eyes.

single-shot shotgun
    in his hands

a remote control.

maggots and blood

the rice pilaf he'd make

filling the bone bowls
of his split skull. (2007)

I learned to dislike how depression medications are handed out like candy despite their dangers. More importantly, I came to view death as a part of life rather than something separate. As I was a fighter on some sort of historical continuum, so too, I thought, was life. I believed that when a person dies here on earth they are born elsewhere—as a particle of dust on another planet, as a squirrel in their backyard, or as someone or something in another world. I refused to believe that things just ended, especially when nothing in my life ever just ended. When the face-to-face relationship with my father stopped, it continued in my mind. The first fight came to a close but never will. Everything ends and never ends. We humans are so interconnected in this world that when we die we still live on. Death is but a masked transition. So I believed.

In the scraps of spare time between the Spanish class, the internship, memorizing lines for *Medea* and working part-time at the grocery store, I was preparing for my second fight. Because I was no longer drawing motivation from my father's absence, I imagined the beliefs of everyone close to me. I believed they all felt my MMA debut victory was a fluke, that because he had slipped and I capitalized with the rear naked choke, I hadn't won legitimately. They couldn't see the preparation and didn't understand the sport's complexity enough to know how much work went into creating those sixty-some seconds.

My only consistent outlet to combat nerves and problems in life was through physicality. I signed on the dotted line for my second fight. With that signature came an *I'll show them* attitude mixed with an *It's the world against me* mentality. I brought this fire into every training moment so I could lift heavier, punch harder, stretch deeper. There was only one problem. Because the first fight stripped the vines of my father that had wrapped themselves around me and forced me to untangle them, I'd lost the ability to find reasons to go that extra round, extra set, or extra repetition that make all the difference. However, in believing that my friends and family thought I had it easy and that their congratulations were lies, I forced my back against the proverbial wall. As a cornered dog, I found the intensity necessary to train for a fight—the intensity that had left with my father's shadow. I'd be back in the cage on August 19th, one week before rehearsals for Medea.

I prepared my body as Cameron, the MMA warrior, and my mind as Jason, son of Aeson. I would prepare to slay the dragon of insecurities, and slay the dragon guarding the Golden Fleece.

My fight training couldn't be as intense because of my schedule, so I took more to the weights, wanting to become the iron I grunted to lift, and to online MMA instructional videos, hoping to at least retain what I knew. The farms surrounding State College became my training partners. I woke at five each morning, trudged along sleepily to an abandoned farm, shadowboxed for fifteen minutes then did sprints through grass rivaling deep snow in difficulty, making sure to bring my knees as high as the seedpods on the weeds. The round pods represented my opponent's face. Wet bales of hay challenged me for explosive overhead throws, which I hoped would improve my ratio of fast twitch fibers. I hoped the increase in strength I picked up from these workouts would cancel out the lack of technicality I'd bring to the cage due to lack of sparring and rolling. Through my morning screams of bodily pain and incoherent trash talking to family, friends, ex-girlfriends, and myself—the farm was a hell of a listener.

They called my name first this time, and rightfully so. Out of respect for my elders—my opponent was thirty-two, ten years older—I was fine with him entering the cage second, like the champion, with the chip of ten years on his shoulders. My friends and I had a theory (half serious, half joking) that if a man worked physically as he aged, he'd acquire a functional, practical strength when he woke up on the day of his thirtieth birthday. "Man strength," we called it.

Pound for pound, I believed my opponent couldn't match my prowess in the weight-room. For the two years leading up to this fight, I no longer performed the bodybuilder-style endless repetitions. This style causes microscopic muscle tears so the body adapts to the stress by rebuilding muscles larger than before. It also expands the muscle's volume by filling it to the max with blood in order to stretch the muscle tissue. This makes it easy to add muscle, but adding muscle isn't necessarily the best way to add strength. So feeling the "pump" didn't matter to me. Instead, what mattered was getting stronger while maintaining the same bodyweight. This was achieved through a mix of heavy and explosive lifting which enhances the motor unit recruitment ratio at the cellular level. It's often more exhausting neurally than muscularly. At one point I deadlifted three times my bodyweight. The deadlift is considered one of the best lifts for measuring overall strength. In drug-free powerlifting competitions, my lift would have broken several states' records. I prided myself on this, and knew if I needed to pick my opponent up off the ground and slam him that I'd have no problems. Because the deadlift strengthens the muscles surrounding and supporting the entire spinal column, I knew through developing this lift that I had also developed the most important muscles for reducing risk of serious injury.

As in the first fight, I again met my friends in the crowd on the way to the stall. My concern about my opponent's man strength was also the concern of one of my friends as well, the one who was a medical student studying the molecular underpinnings of Neuropsychiatric disease.

"Fuck man strength, man," he urged me. "Cardio counters that. Take him into the deep rounds. Take him into the deep waters then drown him."

In other words, he wanted me to make the fight a battle of cardiovascular conditioning and sheer will rather than one of brute strength and the exhaustion that accompanies such short bouts of action.

I met my opponent (though I didn't know for sure he'd be the one) the night before the fight. I arrived at Bo Kimly's Martial Arts Alliance, where the fighters fill out paperwork, then headed to the hotel where we would all stay overnight. Again, I was hiding my fire under my beanie. I overheard my future opponent talking about his weight. "About a buck fifty-four," he said with a twinge of southern accent, a bit of an overconfident raspy bar voice. "Won't know the dude I'm fightin' til tomorrow night." I sensed this was the man with whom I'd struggle in hand-to-hand combat. My right knuckles itched, as though they wanted this bout to come as soon as possible so they could cascade into his jaw and save me from the stress of a sleepless night. I heard someone call him Hockenberry. He looked soft. His eyes relaxed droopily, which I reframed to mean laziness.

But I'll be damned.

The fight began and after my initial off-the-mark jab he stormed out with a burst of man strength. He aggressively marched me close to the back of the cage with a flurry of wild, bad-intentioned left and right hooks that fell just short of my nose. With nowhere to go but into him, I sprang forward, initiated a clinch and wrapped my interlocked hands across the back of his head. My head rocked back from a crisp inside uppercut. Man, this guy was not soft. I tried to stay tight to avoid damage. The closer I remained, the less momentum he'd have to land one of those haymakers. He remained reckless—which made me juiced to the gills with the adrenaline only desperation can bring—rather than him vulnerable to an attack. A reckless fighter with wild punches is only dangerous if his opponent responds with panic. Well, I did, even though I taught my students not to, even though I knew better. A calm fighter would find the openings and counter hard. Seconds later, both my feet left the ground for a split second as I launched all of the force of my right knee directly into his right inner thigh. No momentum shift. Adrenaline counters pain. The knee landed clean but didn't seem to phase him. Shit.

They had announced him as a wrestler and BJJ fighter, which meant he probably felt more comfortable on the mat rather than standing and exchanging blows. I continued an out-of-control strength struggle with someone I couldn't win it with. I threw another knee-strike and purposefully left it hanging in mid-air—baiting him to latch on. The guard position—where a fighter on his back wraps both legs around his opponent's waist—is the foundation of BJJ. I feel more comfortable there than any place in the world. If he took me down, I could pull guard—wrapping my legs around his waist while my back was pressed into the mat and therefore staying close so I could ride his wave of energy and remain unharmed.

He took the bait, grabbing my leg and diving in with a single-leg takedown that put me on my back. I could feel diamonds from the cage imprint themselves on my shaved head as I withstood his man-grip. I tried to keep him at bay with submission attempts so he knew I was dangerous enough to catch him if he overexposed himself in an attempt to hurt me. I did this so he wouldn't attack more. I did this so I could catch my breath—I must have held it for the duration of the bout. I was spent and we were only thirty seconds in. Hanging on until round two was my only hope, literally and metaphorically. I wasn't trying to finish the fight. Taking him to the "deep rounds" to "drown him" was the last thing on my mind. Actually, nothing was on my mind. I forgot to breathe, my vision blurred, and all I could see was his sweaty chest in my face. But survival coursed through my blood.

We were in the area of the cage where his cornermen were. Their faces were separated from ours only be the fencing. "Grind his face into the cage," they shouted. "He doesn't like that! Elbows, elbows, elbow his nose god damnit!" Because I heard them and knew what was coming, and because I'd watched thousands of MMA fights over the years and imagined myself in the position of all the fighters, even the ones taking a beating, I began to feel calm. I began to feel like I'd been here before. I began to find rhythm to my breath. The white bubbles of his cornermen's spit flew into the cage each time they yelled. My opponent continued to use his man strength to drag my body closer and closer to where they were. "Hock-en-berry, Hock-en-berry." The crowd chanted his name. The fans always cheer for the most aggressive fighter, but passivity can be more lethal than aggression.

The blue mat had become his swamp, and he was taking me to the deep-end. He was like an anaconda trying to drown me.

I shifted my hips, grabbed his right forearm with both of my hands and pressed it hard against my sternum while I clamped the pit behind my right knee across the back of his neck and my left calf against his forehead. I extended my body by thrusting my hips forward and his arm became straighter and straighter and, I hoped, hyperextended. This is the armbar from guard. I was going to snap his arm if he didn't tap-out. I've practiced this move under the guidance of some of the world's best. My intent was to break his limb in half. It's BJJ's maxim—to use the entire body to prey on a single joint of your opponent. I wanted to break him so he couldn't break me. I continued to forcefully extend my body and came close to breaking his arm when I was lifted into the air.

Man strength.

He shook me off and followed the escape by smashing his fist just below my nose. I heard the *Oooh's* of the crowd. We were still in his corner and I heard his cornermen scream, "Yes! Pressure him! Finish him!" I scrambled and regained the guard position. Had his punch landed on my nose, a mere half-an-inch higher, the fight would have been dramatically different. My nose would have been broken and sent blood everywhere, including in my eyes. Or my eyes would have filled with tears so I couldn't see enough to defend myself. Hockenberry would have proceeded with repeated punches until the referee stopped the fight. Instead, the punch landed on and just above my upper lip. Protected by my mouthpiece, I felt the pressure of the punch but no pain.

Tyler, who had again come with me from Altoona to serve as my cornerman, yelled, "You're in control, Cameron!" "Control" reminded me to breathe, the breath being one of the few things we can usually control in this world. Fatigue's slow, grinding numbness overwelmed me. *Breathe god damnit,* I thought to myself. *Hang on and breathe.*

"Hockenberry softening up the ribcage," the announcer yelled as my opponent landed three lefts to my body from on top. I saw the punches in slow motion, again felt nothing but their pressure, wondered if I was having an out-of-body experience. *Were the punches seriously damaging me?*

True desperation, I found out, comes when the body discovers it's in a life-or-death situation. True desperation can give birth to cleverness if cleverness means survival. Again, we were chest-to-chest and I was on the bottom. I trapped his arms above the elbow between my armpits. This trapping is called "overhooks." They allow the fighter in guard to stall by taking away the top fighter's ability to throw punches, but they also take away much of the offense from the fighter on bottom. I stalled because I wasn't sure if I was hurt or not. I heard the crowd's reaction and needed time to compose myself and check in with my breath and body. He forced the point of his chin into my lips, driving through the powerful base of his legs in an attempt to inflict pain on the soft tissue of my face. This is one aspect of fighting boiled down—how to best use the hardest parts of your body against the softest parts of your opponents' body. I let it happen. As long as it meant he struggled. As long as it meant he burnt energy. *That bell is going to ring soon,* I told myself. *Go for it. Burn him up so he's exhausted for the next round.*

I let go of one of my overhooks and used my free hand to grab the top of his head and pull it tight to my chest when he wanted to rise up to rain down punches. I pushed his head up when he wanted to grind his chin into me. I pushed his head to the side when all he wanted to do was press his head into my chest to center his own base. The top fighter must have a centered base or else the bottom fighter in guard will be able to "sweep" the top fighter so that the bottom fighter would then attain a dominant top position. This fight was a game of counterbalances. If I was cut, if I bled, so be it. If I died, so be it. It was my time to go; I died learning something new and testing myself.

I slowly sapped the energy from him, made him overwork to perform un-important tasks. I used a variation of the guard called the "Rubber-Guard." It's part of a BJJ system reliant on flexibility that was developed by grappler Eddie Bravo. I'd spent thirty minutes each day in the fields of State College flipping though the pages of his book *Mastering the Rubber Guard*. I also had a chance to grapple with Bravo during a seminar he gave. It paid off. Hockenberry constantly had to reach back behind his head to try to stop my legs from clamping down on the back of his neck. The Rubber Guard allowed me to threaten him with potential submissions like armbars and chokes but I wasn't intending to finish the fight. I wanted him to expend energy and he did so by my being seriously annoying, irritating, and just plain pesky.

"Stop it or I'm gonna tell Mom."
"Stop it or I'm gonna tell Mom."
"I'm stupid."
"I'm stupid...."
"Hey!"

Finally, finally the ten-second sticks announcing the close of round one, and I pressed my game for those last seconds. I focused on taking three or four deep breaths. I stood up nauseated as the round ended. I questioned whether I had enough left in the tank to take another intense round. I was frustrated for being controlled physically and for not controlling what I could control: my breath. I felt absolutely spent, heavy, and sluggish. The sixty seconds between rounds passed and my body—acclimated to sprint-ing through weeds and resting for sixty seconds, sprinting through weeds and resting for sixty seconds—began to remember the purposeful rhythm with which I trained for moments like this. I settled down. I focused on what I was going to do. My right hand itched again. I felt light and agile and powerful. *As soon as the round begins I'm putting him down and out with a straight right hand flush into his jaw. As soon as the bell rings I am marching across this fucking cage and ending the fight.* That's all I wanted. Nothing else mattered. I felt murderous. I could see his crumpled, misaligned body after I landed this one shot. *Kill him before he kills me.*

Seconds before the round two bell rang, I watched him take three deep breaths into his upper chest rather than into his abdomen like a calmer fighter would. He was bent over and his hands were on his knees. The disadvantage of man strength is that it's short-lived. Ding-Ding-Ding—Round two.

Instinct made me abort the straight right hand. Instead, I feinted a push kick, which brought his hands down to defend his abdomen, then I came back upstairs and landed a leaping right hook to his temple that rattled him. He wiped his cheek immediately afterwards and smiled. A stunned smile. I've watched enough fights to know that when a fighter smiles after a blow, it means they're hurt. I saw weakness and pounced. I launched a crushing Thai leg-kick, whipping my hips and unleashing the density of my tibia into his left quadriceps. In all of my life, nothing felt more natural than this battle for survival. It was primal. I was surviving and it felt fucking incredible. After he received my strikes, he didn't want to stand. He urgently took me back to the ground with a single-leg takedown. We were back into his waters, where he had found control in round one. I achieved the guard position and he buried his face into my chest to establish a secure base. *Here we go again. Be more patient this time. Lull him to sleep then explode for the finish.*

This time I heard his gasping, throaty inhalations and felt his chest fill with air as it pressed into mine. I could feel him gathering for one last go-for-broke maneuver to knock me unconscious. He exploded upwards, and I abruptly released my tight hold around his head. This is the beauty of fighting, to control while letting go. He rose onto his knees and away from me, came down with a clenched, arced right hand. I blocked it with my elbow and then trapped it with an overhook. I worked for an omoplata, a move where I take one of my legs that was wrapped around his waist and hold it against his neck while forcing his head away from that leg and onto the mat. This puts me in a position where I can use the entire strength of my body to crank on his shoulder joint. It's a move rarely seen in MMA, requiring excellent timing and flexibility. I nailed it. The announcer and fans went wild. I felt the bones in his right elbow shift and pop and grind like gears.

Something broke.

But he escaped again and somehow mustered enough energy to swing that same right-handed swiping hammer fist I'd tasted in round one. I dodged to the left and his fist landed flush into the mat, crunching his knuckles and rolling his wrist forward into a position unable to support his weight. He didn't howl in pain and he didn't panic. But when I hopped out the side, stood up, and got behind him, he tucked his arms in and curled into a ball while on his knees. He was a tired man with a possible broken arm and a broken will.

This is the position to secure the rear-naked choke. Instead of going immediately for the choke though, I went for the open, unprotected flesh of his body. I wasn't tired at all and if I could land brutal body shots it could suck what little life there was right out of him. Clean headshot knockouts make the highlight reel, but the knocked-out fighter always wakes up wondering what happened. A body shot's beauty can shut down all movement while the opponent helplessly watches his body crumple. They never have to ask what happened.

I unleashed a left-right-left hook combination to his kidneys as he crouched on all fours with his head tucked in and I stood above him and looked down like God. No longer did I want to annoy. I wanted to prove that I was the better mixed martial artist. No longer was this fight about anger or revenge or insecurities. I wanted to paint my skills with large brushstrokes for all to see. His body stayed like a turtle. I felt my fists pound his flesh and I heard the pained whimpers that nobody in the audience could hear. He gasped from my third body blow, sucked air that wasn't there, tried to swivel around to grab me for a sloppy single-leg takedown.

But I held my position behind him, sprawled my weight on top of him by planting my stomach and chest to his back, and threaded my legs through the space between where his elbows and knees pressed into the mat. (This is called getting "the hooks in" and is another step to maintain control of your opponent.) I rolled him on top of me and now my back was on the mat. My left arm was wrapped around his neck, my right was under his armpit to maintain control so he couldn't roll out of the position. My legs clamped down over top of his legs so he couldn't kick or squirm and free himself. When he used his left arm to try to pry one of my legs off his, I quickly threw my leg higher and trapped that arm as well. Systematic. He now had no leverage and only one arm to defend me from choking him. I've been in his position thousands of times. I've scrambled and panicked. I've relaxed and tried to be technical. It doesn't matter. When all the steps of BJJ come together like this, it's checkmate. I sank in the rear naked choke, deep, as in my debut. Each time he exhaled my position got a little looser and I'd tighten it to fill the minute spaces his body created. This meant each time he exhaled, the position and the choke became tighter and tighter. This is how anacondas kill. He took a deep breath to expand his ribcage and create some room, he raged and raged to escape.

I waited. A huge inhalation means a huge exhalation. When the exhale came, I followed it by squeezing as hard as I could. I squeezed the lies out of this world. He tapped-out. The ref jumped in and pulled me off. I could barely breathe—fatigue mixed with exultation. I brought my hands over my head in an ostentatious, Tony Montana*ish* "look at me now" gesture to shut up the naysayers. *Is there no one else? Stay down, bitch. Whimper. Stay down and show the crowd how bad you've been beat. Stay down.*

Then I came back to reality.

Get up. Please get up. God damnit, I hope you're okay.

With the help of the ref, Hockenberry stood up. He was groggy and disoriented, but he was up. "Are you okay?" I said. He nodded yes. "Thank you for meeting me here, for fighting me," I told him. "You're a warrior, man." He smiled and we hugged. The referee grabbed our hands and led us to the center of the cage. The announcer said, "Winner. Round 2. Via rear naked choke. Cam-er-on Con-a-way!" The referee raised my arm and Hockenberry and I again hugged. I raised his arm to the crowd and they cheered us both.

Ring card girls came into the cage and posed with me for a few pictures. I no longer wanted eyes on me. *I'm just standing here. I'm not performing,* I thought. As I left the cage, I kissed the fencing. I felt a connection I didn't understand until a few years later. I admired the fencing. It was strong yet compassionate, able to withstand but also able to give in. It was hard to break, but soft. *Perform,* I thought again.

After the fight, I sat in the passenger side as Tyler drove me to the Taco Bell drive-thru—a celebratory splurge meal for us. When the woman at the drive-thru window asked "Can I help you," I thought, *You sure can. I just*

performed in front of a live audience and didn't even know they were there be-
cause I was in the moment of the fight. Will acting be similar? Will something
about fighting temper Jason of the Argonauts?

"You sure can," I said. "I'd like six soft chicken tacos."

Log 11

Temper my temper.

- heat of mind or passion, shown in outbursts of anger, resentment, etc.
- to bring to a proper, suitable, or desirable state by blending.

CHAPTER 16

On Acting

Constantin Stanislavsky (1863-1938) was a Russian actor and theater director. He devised a method to train groups of actors to invoke personal memories as a way to spark the natural emotions needed to play a believable role. He noticed that because of the intense nature of reliving their pasts, especially the times they were most emotionally vulnerable, many actors using this method were overcome by bouts of hysteria. Though he still believed in the process, which he called "Emotion Memory," and continued to implement it into his method, he began to embrace and incorporate other ideas already present at the time, such as using imagination as a means to find and unlock the realism in the given play.

His search for realism grew from this very basic idea: He did not want his actors to fake emotion on the stage. He believed the best acting came from rigorous training and a continuous, critical self-analysis. The more actors knew themselves by exploring both their immediate and buried pasts, by studying their mistakes and even by understanding their strengths, the more credible they would be when performing. Through training, he wanted actors to develop sensitivity and awareness of externalities such as voice, diction and physical movement.

My acting teacher Robin Reese once told me, "I'm heavily indebted to Stanislavsky." Robin is a Jewish Buddhist. Though she stands a little over five feet, her thick, frizzy brown hair bounces when she moves and her charisma fills rooms like water fills cups. She believes (and those who meet her will come to believe) that she shares a kinship soul connection with cats. She may meet you for the first time and say "Meow" or she may simply ask you a question you haven't asked yourself before. Conversation with her is never dry, never predictable. Her creative spirituality exudes from the edges. She's either focused and as intense as any fighter I've ever met or she's laughing. But she's always observing.

As Ken Shamrock made me believe I could be a professional fighter, as Todd Davis made me believe I could be a university professor, so Robin Reese made me believe I could be an award-winning actor. The "method" with which she used to train us, capped off by a week of two-a-day performances, proved to be every bit as demanding and fascinating and frightening as my experience preparing for and eventually competing in a steel cage. Stanislavsky's name stuck with me and I researched him extensively. One thing he said has stayed in my mind ever since.

"In the creative process there is the father, the author of the play; the mom, the actor pregnant with the part; and the child, the role to be born."

Though I felt the importance of this quote while I was an actor, recently I've begun to feel it resonating a different sort of energy, one that can be applied not only to acting, but to life as well. After all, is life not the ultimate creative process? I've reworked Stanislavsky's quote to better reflect the feeling it provides me. "In life there is the past, the author of action; the present, the actor pregnant with the role; and the future, the role to be acted."

In life there is the past, the author of action;

I cried in front of absolute strangers during the first week of rehearsals for *Medea.* The training took place at Penn State Altoona. We worked on kinesthetic awareness—moving our bodies however they wanted to move, forgetting about the way we are used to moving, the way society orders us to move. As we floated around the black stage floor, we let whatever inhabited our mind at the time exhibit itself through physical actions. Some people hopped around, dragging their knuckles like apes, scratching their armpits and inspecting the hair of others. Other people slithered on the floor like snakes while mumbling something their mother used to say to them as a child. Some became curious about the space between objects on the stage, like the varying views between each rung on a ladder, looking through the keyhole of a door or through the triangular space made by a person standing still with feet shoulder-width apart.

Here I was, one of twelve cast members of *Medea*, a stranger to all except Cassie. I was surrounded by actors ranging in age from just under twenty to close to seventy. I was scared in a way I never felt before. In fighting, there's the fear that you'll lose. But it's decisive and action-oriented. How do you lose when you have a lead role in a play? It's more a fear of failing others, failing the team, a team, in this case, of experienced veterans who viewed acting as their life's mission.

We hailed from Arizona to New Jersey, from Illinois to California. The only shared similarity was that we were students (in the broadest sense of the word) of the world, and that we were here now, in this same space. There were no preconceived notions about who moved around us, except for the unconscious stereotypes that arise from the way another human being dresses or looks. We were willingly vulnerable enough to stumble around a small stage as babies, monkeys, and white-space enthusiasts. The exercise stripped down the barriers we all put up during typical self-introductions: the prejudicing, the suspicion, and distrust. The more inhuman we became the more we understood each other as humans.

Robin always placed a thick blue rectangular padded crash mat in the corner of the stage for actors who relived an emotion too tough to handle. We were encouraged to act as our bodies wanted. More often than I could have imagined, my body wanted to punch and smash, literally, when the rough moments of my buried past broke through and sprouted up quicker than bamboo. I wasn't the only one who retreated to the blue mat to pound away or yell incoherent words. On more than one occasion, tears dropped atop the mat to form puddles wide enough for us to see our own reflections. We were encouraged to continue moving about the stage as a fellow actor let loose on the mat. But I watched a few times, and the scenes I saw reminded me of the humor and humanness of Ralphie, the Red Ryder BB gun-toting young boy in the 1983 movie *The Christmas Story*—when he finally snaps, mounts the bully and begins to throw punches with reckless abandon.

At one point, Robin asked that I explore using the "method" as a way to act as angry and tormented as Jason of the Argonauts would be upon finding that his wife, Medea, had slaughtered their two children with a knife out of absolute jealousy. I recited my lines with a forced, fake anger knowing it wasn't believable. I felt embarrassed. I was a first-time actor with a lead role and surrounded by actors for the most part who have spent years perfecting their craft. As in my fights, eyes were on me, only this time I had no idea what the hell I was doing and lacked the confidence concealed preparation can bring.

I put my head down in disgust at myself. Suddenly an image formed in my mind: the image of my father putting his head down in disgust at me because he believed I didn't say thank you to his new wife for the birthday gift she gave me. Robin said my eyes fixated on the floor of the stage. She said I went somewhere else. I saw my sister saying *he did say thank you*, then saw my father hurling her into the garage door. I heard the sound her body made upon impact. I heard her pleas for life. I was sprinting towards him to kill him and I was on the blue mat screaming and screaming and dropping elbows into what I imagined was his face. My vocal chords hurt (Robin would later teach me how to scream properly), my elbows were brush-burned and bleeding and I saw my tears blend with the tears from others.

The eleven other actors surrounded me and Cassie knelt down and hugged me. I felt enveloped in warmth and caring. They knew a bad-memory bamboo-shoot sprouted, but they didn't question it. They saw me as human, as fallible, as brave enough to be all that I know of myself in front of them.

For the first time in my life, despite the years of basketball practices, I felt the inner strength a team can provide. It carried me through the consistent invoking of memories to improve my role. We were all there to simultaneously sharpen ourselves through sharpening our roles, not the other way around. During rehearsals the following day, I was able to recall that brutal moment and transmute the energy from it into the play. The practice of transmuting emotions comes from the Tibetan Buddhist tradition and it is mixed with Hinduism. Transmuting means that it is possible to move emotions from lower energy centers to higher energy centers and actually benefit from cultivating the energy of negative emotions. It's a practice I've been trying to incorporate into my life ever since.

the present, the actor pregnant with the role;

Stanislavsky also wrote, "When we are on stage, we are in the here and now." When fighting in front of an audience, when that little bit of tunnel-vision kicks in just enough to turn off everything but instinct, just enough to let the body act without acting, I was in the here and now. I didn't feel as though I was in the here and now because emotions are fleeting and are constantly, with each fragment of a millisecond, becoming the past. But upon reflection, I realized that because I was so unaware of my actions over the course of the seven or eight minutes I spent in the cage during two fights, for that time, I *was* in the here and now.

As I write this, I'm thinking of what I wrote *before* before. I'm constantly combing and re-combing so the words and sentences are shaped on the page just right, like I imagine a TV news anchor's hair must be before going on the air. I'm thinking, at unpredictable moments, about the passion-filled way my fiancée Maggie, when she came in the door from work last night, kissed me while both of her hands cradled my face. I'm thinking, from time to time, how I need to get to the gym, no, how I need to first flip through previous workouts in my journal, then formulate a workout for today, and then get to the gym. I'm thinking about how I need to adjust the way I'm sitting because my lower back is uncomfortable and tight from deadlifts a few days ago. I'm thinking about the e-mails to friends I need to send and the phone calls from family I need to return. Of course, the majority of the time I write, I'm in the here and now. It's one of the beautiful qualities of being a writer. I get to surf on words. But surfing on words means the occasional crashing wave (memory = past, which can = negativity, which can = not-in-the here-and-now when I snap out of it) that dislodges me.

Just as fighting gave me that blissful here and now for sixty-five seconds in my first fight and for 310 seconds in my second, performing *Medea* in front of a live audience gave me that feeling for more than an hour each time we performed. Because we were actors, we were the authors in creative control of our past. And as we became more talented as creative controllers, we were able to bring the past into our lives *only* when we wanted it. We could remember and summon up anger, fear, or grief and use them on the stage.

During rehearsals I had called up anger at my father to portray my anger at Medea for stabbing our children. After months of line study and rehearsal, when I was in that moment, I truly felt the memory become reality. I felt the anger and torment generated by my father years ago transform into genuine anger and torment in the present about Medea, my wife.

Medea, the woman I fell in love with and married, the woman I'd created children with, now was bludgeoning my babies with a knife. *That fucking bitch.* Over sixty minutes of this, twice a week. My real-life problems didn't matter. The theater was packed with the steady buzzing sound of a large audience when we stood behind the curtains. But when the show began, it was as though the audience and their buzz had disappeared. If the drive-thru Taco Bell lady could have answered my thoughts she would have said:

"Yes, everything will be just like your fights when the action is underway. You'll be okay."

The audience's energy was there, but the eccentricities that make them human and their judgments were not. It was me, basically playing a video game, where my practiced actions didn't matter when I turned the game off. That my children were slaughtered and I was drooling and panting and sitting curled in a ball rocking back and forth and pulling my hair on a stage in front of an audience that included my professors didn't change that I had a test in British literature the following day. It was pure here and now. Nothing else mattered. There was nothing short of the stage collapsing that could penetrate our here and now, not even the fact that as we were in the here and now, we were, unbeknownst to us, paving the way, pregnant with our future actions for our future roles in life.

CHAPTER 17

Lucky

When the mind is inside an octagonal cage during an MMA bout, it dissolves into the realm of physical action. Moves practiced thousands of times become automatic. Here's the Zen philosophy paradigm: All the practice is doing, but when doing comes without thought, what once was doing becomes *non-doing*. Action without thought is where a fighter reaches rapture. Thoughts can flood the mind: turn hips over with each punch, proper foot balance and movement, heart rate elevation, sweat stinging the eyes, pain and fatigue, what to eat before and after to properly recover, body weight and body fat. But in battle, the fighter is often free from thoughts. They are shed with the sponsor's t-shirt just prior to entering the cage. Win or lose, when the cage door opens again and the fighter exits, the thoughts flood back into his mind.

From there, some say it's back to the drawing board, but that cliché doesn't account for training sessions like the shark drill that are purposefully intense enough to mimic the fight mindset. The shark drill has many variations but the premise is this: One fighter stays in the ring while fresh fighters cycle in every few minutes. The fatigue becomes so intense that proper technique eventually gives way to instinctual survival. There are many times when my uncontrollable mind—feeling the body's exertion and burn in the hip flexors due to throwing knee-strikes and Thai push kicks, or the numb, spasmodic deltoids due to rounds of jabs and crosses—tells my body to stop. Then, the fire and determination of my controllable mind tells me not to stop—but to improve my technique and my mental strength and to prove to others that I am someone. Everybody has his or her reasons. The warrior spirit is *modus vivendi*—a way of living. Competition but one of many ways to express or refine it.

In the cage, the twenty-first century human becomes the basic *Homo sapien* of Paleolithic times. Instinct supersedes calculation. I don't have to clean up dog shit in the backyard, worry about the bill collector, or study for an upcoming test when engaged in hand-to-hand combat in front of an audience of close to a thousand. Being in the cage is the closest I get to the mindless primality from which I evolved.

All that matters—and this not with conscious awareness but with euphoric cloudiness—is survival.

All the knee-strikes I throw, the arms I hyperextend and the punches I land are not to do damage, but to survive. If I hurt my opponent, he will be less capable of hurting me. When I choke, I choke to finish the fight and better protect myself, since an incapacitated opponent can't hurt me. Political opponents to MMA focus on this violence when they argue for the sport to remain illegal in many states. These people are the types that see the world in black and white, but the world and the realities it contains—like violence—are mostly shades of gray, the spaces between. In choking to finish my opponent (which is altogether different than the demented or rage-infused violence of choking to kill a human being), I am saving myself.

Despite having roamed the earth for more than ninety years, Helio Gracie still calmly whispers into the ears of world champion fighters before they roll with him on the mat for practice, "You can't beat me." He never says he *will* beat an opponent, rather, he says they can't beat him. Meaning, of course, that he can survive.

In BJJ sparring, the manners and methods by which humans can die or become hurt is respected, studied, and used to improve the art. When a partner locks on a choke and you feel like it has the potential to make you pass-out (and eventually die if they wouldn't let go), you tap-out. You can fight against a technique or against an opponent, but you can't fight death. And this acknowledgement is why BJJ is so safe, why it has students in their nineties who have remained injury-free throughout their lifetime. There's a mutual gentleness in this process because it's an assumed learning experience and not an actual fight. Tapping out is a language the blind can see and the deaf can hear. It's universal. I've sparred with men I was completely unable to communicate with because of language barriers. Through our bodies and through tapping out, we established a system of communication that could set sparring intensities and take us to the limits of the art. There's nothing more beautiful than stepping onto the mat with an absolute stranger and trusting him with your life. The historic beauty of BJJ rests not with its ability to allow a smaller man to maim a larger man, but with its ability to allow any man of any size to survive.

When a football strong safety eyes a spry receiver about to catch a pass across the middle of the field, he does not think, "I will tackle him only as hard as I need to in order to bring him down." He thinks, "I'm going to knock this receiver unconscious so he drops the pass and thinks twice about coming here again." It is the same with a baseball player rounding third and about to plow into the catcher. Hell, it's the same with the baseball player swinging a bat, the soccer goalie clearing a ball, the hockey defenseman checking then clearing a puck, the shot-putter launching cast iron, the sprinter exploding off blocks, the ballerina leaping three feet into the air.

These moments of absolute explosiveness are merely parts of the whole in sports. Yes, many maneuvers are inherently violent, or are performed with violent intensity in order to tap into the deepest reserves of strength. My intent is never to actually take human life when fighting for sport. Of course, this intent would change if someone attacked my family or me. It perturbs me when ignorant talking heads claim MMA is nothing but "cockfighting" and interrupt any guest who might offer a different perspective. I would never partake in a "sport" where a referee did not look out for the welfare of the contestants and could not immediately stop the contest. It would not be a sport, nor I a gentle soul.

Honestly and with humility, I can say I've been greatly challenged mentally, emotionally and physically in my lifetime. As a result, I find sports without all three challenges to be unbearably boring. If MMA did not require years and years of practicing and refining techniques, if I did not see the way it can develop positive lifestyle qualities, if it was not as artistic as any art, as scientific as any science, as historic as anything man has ever done, I would not find it important enough to occupy a reader's precious time. I would not find it interesting enough to make of it a lifetime practice.

I love to fight. And I love to continually learn how to fight. The way an extra inch of flexibility can make a miserable situation tolerable, a tolerable situation neutral, a neutral situation advantageous, and an advantageous situation into victory both excites and torments me.

Excites because minutiae matters. The critical thinking skills I developed as an English major (Scrooge was the perfect name for a famously mean and stingy character because of the hard "sc" followed by the gross "eww" and ending in the "idge" sound, almost a grunt, recalling words like garbage and sabotage) are instantly applicable to analyzing the way my workouts and diet influence—positively or negatively—my overall health and athletic performance.

Torments because minutiae matters. The sun sets and I'm comfortable with the improvements I made for the day—learning a new sweep from half guard or hitting a new deadlift personal record. I'm comfortable for a second, until I feel the need to get a bath before bed to practice underwater breath holds and sweat impurities out. Later in bed, I feel the need to focus on my breath—inhaling and exhaling to the count of twenty—before visualizing and hopefully cementing the day's lessons in my head. It's an obsession. If it weren't an obsession I'd be increasing my risk of getting injured. It's a torrent of torment and it all has to do with calculating risk. On the surface, I've reaped the positives of obsession, but these torrents also bring in obsession's jagged shells and they've often torn apart my insides.

That's enough philosophical meandering to serve as prelude to the situations before and after having to mop up my own sweat and the blood that crept out from under my left eyebrow—from which gash a scar remains.

Interstate 80 East. 197.7 miles. December, 2006. 1991 Toyota Corolla Hatchback named Victor. 3:00 A.M. Unexpected blizzard. Destination: The Renzo Gracie Academy in Manhattan.

I'd made it to Renzo's in four hours and four minutes three weeks ago. This time it was over twelve hours and I damn sure wasn't proud enough to count the minutes. The trip to Renzo's is the *congratulations* I give myself for working hard through another semester of college and another semester in the produce department chopping celery and cabbage over a Rubbermaid garbage can in rhythm to elevator music.

Produce

As a capital E,
his knees against cold linoleum,
spinal erectors erect, right hand reaching,

gripping her left hip,
his left hand slipping…

Cara cara oranges color
a colorless room, stain the brain
with scents of citrus, scream,
as a six year old boy
scraping his knees on concrete,
like potato skins on a peeler.

…the peach-fuzz soft ear muff
over her right ear.
As a lower case e,
her varicose vein calves rest
on open leg pads, her back
curves as a quartered cantaloupe,
her hands…

Clanking, crashing shopping carts
smash into each other
as pots and pans and cutting boards,
when the baking sheet
is buried on the bottom.

…tremor against her wheelchair,
as on movie theatre arm rests
during their first kiss. His fingers move
at the speed of gray, as comforting as blue
cloudless skies. He covers her ear, soft
as kiwi, with the hand-warmed white ear
muff.

Wind rattles the jackets, stings
as habanero, the hands,
ears and eyes of the young couple
on the other side
of the window. (2007)

Every Friday, Saturday, and Sunday night in the darkness of the produce department cooler, throw jabs and elbows at boxes of Foxy or Dole-brand head lettuce (because they are soft), grab the top wooden pallet on a doubled-up skid (because it's shoulder height and therefore perfect for clinch work) then throw knee-strikes toward the bins of watermelon or cantaloupe below (careful not to hit the boxes of blueberries, never harm blueberries), expel breath (and hear its hiss and see its steam) in consonance with the sound my shoes make in the shallow water puddles on the floor (from the ice that melts inside certain boxes) while mimicking Floyd Mayweather's shoulder-rolls. Pretend potato bags are human bodies and lift them the same way I would perform actual takedowns: from the ground and up onto my shoulder. Carry them across the cooler like I am Matt Hughes and they are Frank Trigg. Always keep an eye on either door and stay in the middle of the cooler where it's darker so if a customer or manager peeks in I'll have time to pretend I'm working. Do not slip and fall in the puddles of water more than once on any given shift (seriously, you could hurt yourself). And balance is important for fighting.

Why I do it: because work means I get paid and getting paid reminds me of going to Renzo's and thinking of going to Renzo's while working a mindless job makes me anxious and the way I relieve anxiety is through physicality.

Hefting and chopping and fighting with all that produce paid next to nothing, so I headed for the cheapest place I could find: the Starlite Motel in Jersey City, New Jersey. Manhattan hotels were well out my budget, and rather than driving straight home after training at Renzo's, I got a hotel room for the night thinking it might make life a little easier.

At Renzo's I did two two-hour classes of BJJ and two, two-hour classes of Muay Thai. All classes begin with a fifteen minute warm-up of body-weight squats, pushups, and yoga exercises, followed by forty-five minutes of technique demonstration that we drill with a partner, followed by forty-five minutes of "open mat" sparring with a new partner every five minutes, followed by a fifteen minute cool down of yoga, stretching, and breathing exercises. The training was typical. What happened before and after was not.

Before

The drive to Renzo's was 197.7 miles of whiteout. Road signs and lines and cars flickered in and out of sight like a bad TV. Did I mention Victor is white? I felt invisible. I pulled over once at the eight-hour mark, unsure of where I was and desperately needing to take a leak, and I cried. Hard. I cursed and I cried and Victor retaliated by shutting off his heat. Fuck. I had an unknown time to go (four hours as it turned out) and now no heat. After the cold dried my tears, I stepped out into the blizzard wearing my Ringside boxing gloves and threw left-right combinations against the passenger-side door of Victor. Now that I look back, I wonder if the passenger-side door was my target so that I seemed to be in a ditch rather than in danger on the road—in no way can I validate this—or maybe because I felt so lonely in this pursuit and the emptiness of the passenger-side was a metaphor for my feelings. I felt lonely and in dire need of some sort of luck. A break. I followed the punches with a kick and felt the sharp pain of my thrice-broken ankle (all breaks caused by years of basketball, not MMA) and looked above and around into never-ending pockets of ground clouds, of absolute whiteness. I extended my arms, looked toward the sky and screamed *Fuck you!* as loud as I could. The you wasn't Victor. The you, I suppose, were the gods, or whoever rewarded my hard work during the semester with this punishment. I felt as though my enemy was the world, and I felt an inability to communicate my emotions because I've always resorted to speaking the language of boxing gloves.

In that moment, in the clouds of whiteness, of perfect-chaos, of opacity, I felt something that resembled the freedom I feel in the octagonal cage. It warmed me the way Victor couldn't. I had a backseat of poetry books in case free time arose. When my rage and conditioning finally wore down, I took my gloves off and got back in the car and dug through my book-bag for a poet's poem that could give me I know not what. I opened to and read aloud this previously highlighted passage from Tony Hoagland's "Lucky":

> If you are lucky in this life,
> you will get to raise the spoon
> of pristine, frosty ice cream
> to the trusting creature mouth
> of your old enemy
>
> because the tastebuds at least are not broken
> because there is a bond between you
> and sweet is sweet in any language.

After

Body beaten and blending with the stench of the twenty men with whom I grappled, *I arrived to you, Starlite, my precious Starlite,* the place where I'd get a warm shower, pull the covers over my head and forget all about the twelve-hour drive in the frigid blizzard and the fact that there was no place to park. I remember the poem I wrote while sore and bruised and looking out the window into an Altoona snowstorm:

A Fighter's Thoughts

2:36 A.M. I sit
while others sleep
watch the tips
of my cornerman's
cottonswabs
fall from the sky
a backdrop darker
than the warm black
pekoe in my cup
in this railtown
there's nothing
more to do
but sit and watch
sit and breathe
fog-breath
on a windowpane
smoothing the swelling
above my eye
picking scabs
from my knees
my elbows
wondering why
I'm tempted
to shadowbox
with the snow (2006)

Outside the hotel, an elderly woman offered me her shovel to make a space for Victor, but this came with a stipulation. She demanded I finish her home's driveway. "To finish would mean it would first have to have been started," I thought, but I didn't say it. She was wrapped in a thick black shin-length trench coat, and wore bright red sweatpants and a pair of fluffy white slippers. All I remember of her face was her nose. It hid her other features. Though maybe her nose is all I remember because her voice made me look at her less frequently than I would if the sound or subject were remotely pleasant.

I shoveled for forty-five minutes while she watched from her porch and complained if I missed a spot or didn't break up the ice well enough. The snow was heavy and I was exhausted, but I hate disappointing anyone, especially the elderly, so despite a searing headache I chipped and dug and heaved. I felt the sweat of the men I trained with dry on my BJJ rash guard (a spandex type of shirt worn when grappling. It's similar to what surfers wear) and become a sort of crust. I just wanted a shower and a bed and some rest, but the self-professed Greek woman began barking about how her country is disrespected. About how I "deserved" to be shoveling for her because, as she inferred from my last name, Conaway is Irish and Irish people are a "bunch of pale-ass drunks" while her people "invented philosophy and shit." Philosophy *and* shit. I felt knee deep in one of her people's inventions.

I finished her driveway, maneuvered Victor into a spot, walked across the street and opened the door to the motel where I would eat the trail-mix I'd been pining over all day. *Ahh, after all the foreplay of standing across the street and admiring you. Come to me, my beloved Starlite.*

As I opened the door, four gum-chewing hookers walked out. Red heels and all. *All* meaning scarred faces, running mascara, eye-watering perfume, and neck tattoos. The blondest of the bunch—the one with a prominent pink scar from the middle of her left eyebrow, through her eye, and down to the tip of her chin—whispered to me, "Do you want to get lucky?" and Iris (Jodie Foster's character from *Taxi Driver*) flashed in my mind. Travis Bickle (Robert De Niro's character) would have said,

> *Lucky? What are you talking about? You walk out with those fuckin'*
> *creeps and low-lifes and degenerates out on the streets and you sell*
> *your little pussy for peanuts? And I'd be lucky to get some?*

I said nothing. Only put my head down and walked in.

Many of Travis's intense lines, like the famous "You talkin' to me?" were said to the mirror. I wish I could have been some type of perspective-changing mirror for the prostitute in that moment, a mirror different than the cum-and-blood-stained mirror above the sink in the bathroom I would share with an entire floor at the Starlite Motel.

Park Avenue

> Three prostitutes walked out
> when I walked in.
> He paid for her
> time as I was handed
> the key to room ninety-five.
> Ninety-four's mattress springs
> chirped like mid-April robins.
> I left, got the trail mix
> from my Corolla hatchback -
> raisins, pistachios, walnuts,
> sunflower seeds and currants -
> held the door as she walked out,
> saw her sharp, creased face,
> the deep scar that runs
> through her left eye, a tear
> tired of falling, blending
> into a rain-stained
> concrete curb.
> Like her, it will lie
> unnoticed, lacking
> the individuality
> of a dry bag of raw trail mix. (2007)

The man in front of me at the motel counter was arguing with the night manager, safe behind scratched bullet-proof glass, as to why he had to pay for a full two hours instead of one. I waited. I fumed, in every definition of the word. Eventually, the manager handed me my key. It was a breath of fresh air to turn the lock and finally step in, a breath of the same, strong, eye-watering perfume from the hookers outside. The wooden headboard on the bed was stained with greasy hair product. Even my frustration was too frustrated to kick in. *My darling Starlite, you gave me a room of my own. A room with a view through an iron-gated window.*

The bed was all I needed. I bit down hard into almonds to block the sex sounds coming from room ninety-four. I walked out to the shared bathroom, passing a qualmless, middle-aged naked man with a Geraldo Rivera mustache. Shards of glass filled the shower floor and the splintered window above looked like the rest of it would crash in at any moment. My hand stuck to the left sink nozzle. Blood and snot or semen or a concoction of them covered the right nozzle. I filled my water bottle from the bathtub sink (while kneeling atop the shirt and shorts I wore at training because I believed they were cleaner than the linoleum floor) and dumped the cold water over my naked body. Again and again. I dried off with my Pittsburgh Steelers hooded sweatshirt in order to save my towel to spread across the bed. The chirping continued sporadically from all three sides throughout the night (*thank you for sparing me, iron-gated window*). Solace came from opening the window to the max—maybe an inch. The winter wind's howl replaced sex sounds and its cold periodically overrode my auditory awareness with a bodily shiver. A welcome change. A change that allowed for sleep.

I woke around five in the morning and while I was packing up Victor I realized the whiteout remained. I read Tony Hoagland's poem again, realized the "trusting creature mouth" of my "old enemy" was not the weather or the struggle or even myself. I have no enemies. The natural world is my ultimate teacher. It speaks the truth no matter how bad it stings, it shows me and allows me to unravel valuable lessons rather than lecturing to me on them. And although it teaches every second of the day, it puts the learning in my hands for when I want or need it. It *was* and *is* and *will*. It's the only constant. Energy.

Less than a year later, I enrolled at the University of Arizona, where Tony Hoagland received his MFA in Creative Writing.

Log 12

Great energy wrongly applied is negative energy. Negative energy is worse than wasted energy.

CHAPTER 18

The Difference Between Rice and Wheat is like Night and Dad

It's likely I'll never have a relationship with my father.

Sometimes I wish the decision of whether to see him again could have been cut and dry. Could have had even just a smidgeon of *easy* to it. Could have vanished the day I tearfully sprinted to the golf course pro shop. Yes, lessons were learned because it was difficult. But now and again, when I feel like bitching, I turn to Willa Cather's quote:

> *Artistic growth is, more than it is anything else, a refining of the sense of truthfulness. The stupid believe that to be truthful is easy; only the artist, the great artist, knows how difficult it is.*

I realize now that most of my life's struggle was the struggle for self-understanding and expression. Artistic growth. Artistic with a capital A. Uh-huh.

When I can say, "I will not fight again," I imagine the decision will be much easier to reach than the decision concerning a future relationship with my father. I've been out of the sport for three years. MMA has evolved human combat more so than anything has in human history. The evolution of technique that has happened within those three years—such a small period of time along the grand continuum of martial arts—is enough to scare the shit out of me. Is enough to make me realize my absence training in the sport might make a return to the cage too dangerous.

I suppose the reason the easy did not happen is because human relationships—those emotional connections between people—are complex and difficult and meant to be learned from. I still have quite a deep relationship with my father—or at least with my feelings about him. I'm writing—and therefore thinking—about him, while he, as reported by my sister Courtney (who still maintains a semblance of a face-to-face relationship with him), cries from time to time about me. That definitely fits the parameters of relationship. Chance encounters still happen when I spend time with my family back in Altoona.

Several years ago, for example, I held the door for him while he exited a gas station. I was just acting out of respect and recognized him at first glance, but it wasn't until our eyes met that I saw an indescribable blankness. No words were exchanged. "He may not have recognized you," people said when I told them about it. Well, maybe. But I'm certain *he did* recognize me. I think when you raise a son for the first thirteen years of his life you must develop a bond strong enough to persist through whatever physical changes puberty may cause. I will always remember his face in that moment. The blankness, the lifelessness, the just-going-through-the-motions. And I believe, in that moment, he remembered mine. I wonder what he saw in my face. Fear? I missed the keyhole three times before getting into my car because of an old familiar feeling of fear. Maybe I was afraid of an awkward or other sort of confrontation. Maybe it was fear that he could hurt me again.

When will I lose that fear? Will there ever be a "right" time to reconcile with my father? In the minds of fight enthusiasts and even doctors around the world, we all have an athletic, physical prime. For some, that prime may be as early as nineteen or twenty, for others, their mid-thirties. Even if my health and his health hold and we're given ample time and flexibility of schedule to meet, I believe we will never have a relationship. A deep one.

In fighting, it's impossible, even in our age of human genetics research, to quantify the given prime for each athlete. There will always be exceptions to any rule—Randy Couture headlined UFC 105 at the age of forty-six, and won. But considering how fast the sport of MMA is evolving, taking a few years off is crippling to a fighter's career. I'll soon reach the age at which I would be in my prime if I had continued training. But the breakneck evolution in terms of training and technical skill-set means I probably won't be stepping into a cage again.

It's easier to say that than to make a similar statement about seeing my father because as a fighter with a "body as temple" mentality, I would find the risk of being unprepared and possibly incapable too great. I want to control as many variables as possible—it's been my strength as an athlete. But now, I find myself thinking of being a father and husband and with these thoughts come too many variables to juggle. I'm more and more ready to say that I'll never fight again.

There are variables concerning reconciliation with my father that are beyond my control, but I can accept them because they lack the desperate decision-making of the fight game. I could pick up the telephone or pay him a visit, but I don't want to do either. While he is still fully alive to me in memory, in many ways he's dead to me as a person.

People probe about why I'm not interested in seeing him and I feel an underlying insinuation. Maybe the insinuation isn't from them, maybe it grows from my own guilt as an abandoned son who feels he coulda-shoulda-woulda and now doesn't wanta. Not including this one, so far in this chapter I've said the word maybe five times. There will be more.

I think people watch too many emotional reunions on Oprah and believe all reunions between parents and children end in tears of joy and happiness. Of course, this does happen occasionally, but TV has a way of making us believe things that just aren't true. Look at the rise in college criminal justice programs because of the TV show CSI.

Dear Oprah,

I'm not saying you can't invite me to your show to discuss Caged, because that would be a once-in-a-lifetime opportunity for a small-town guy like myself. I'm saying if you did invite me, I hope you wouldn't surprise me by having my father waiting backstage. I'd much rather be surrounded by those who supported me with unconditional love. Maybe, although I'm a horrible dancer and would just flail my limbs as though independent from my body during the entrance music she plays for her guests, I'm more of an Ellen kind of guy. I won't know until I get a chance.

Sincerely,
Cameron Conaway

Why don't I want to see him? I've reflected and brooded for years about my parents' ugly divorce. It's taken me a long time to articulate my feelings so when someone asks why I don't want to see him, I can calmly explain.

In short, I don't care to see him. We are so distanced at this point that when I heard he told my sister he was going to drive his car into a tree to try to kill himself, then, I guess, did so and was in a coma for a few days, I felt nothing. I'm perplexed that I didn't feel anything, but as the famous saying goes, "Feelings aren't right and they aren't wrong. They just are."

I'd see him only to please those people close to me, but that's because I'm a people-pleaser. It wouldn't be for myself. From what I know of him, even knowing that people can change, he's not somebody I want to know better. I don't have the time or dedication to develop a deeply enriching relationship, nor do I want to be an acquaintance with my father. I think an acquaintanceship would get under my skin, because I would not want more than that and I'd feel guilty for not wanting to maintain even that small bond.

I surround myself with people I care about, and I'm very grateful for them. If I felt the slightest "need" to have my father be part of my life I would act on it because it would make me a stronger person. The warrior code demands bettering the self by any means necessary. It's not telling me to meet him right now.

It took years for me to listen to the voices in my mind, to accept being asked questions by Maggie, and find my own answer. I feel confident with my decision. Experiencing painful moments is easy, they just enter our lives and usually we are helpless to do anything to stop them. But purposefully reentering the memory of those painful moments for the sake of learning is one quality in people that I greatly admire.

> It is easy to go down into Hell; night and day, the gates of dark
> Death stand wide; but to climb back again, to retrace one's steps
> to the upper air—there's the rub, the task.

~ Virgil (70 BC to 19 BC)

However, I feel there's an intangible quality as to why I could go the rest of my life without seeing him. I believe the answer remains scattered throughout this memoir in a way that isn't meant for the crispness of a few simple sentences. There's an abstract quality to the answer that paints the pages of *Caged* the very same color of the pages *Caged* is printed on, but, when under the right light of the mind, the abstract can become visible. When I've thought as deeply as I have for years and years, I trust in the power of mystery. The answer will always remain barely beneath the surface—like some large shark whose presence I can feel from glimpses here and there, but whose true identity I may never discover.

At this point, you are completely justified to think, "What in the high holy hell does any of this have to do with rice or wheat or any other cereal grain?" The word identity from the end of the previous paragraph leads me, as you shouldn't be able to guess, to rice. Yes, rice. In Malcolm Gladwell's book *Outliers: The Story of Success*, he addresses the issue of how where we come from, even if we are generations removed, can and still does influence our everyday lives. Particularly enlightening was the discussion of how the rice fields in Asia and the wheat fields in the United States of America have (and still do) continue to impact the choices many of us make. Gladwell states, "Working in a rice field is ten to twenty times more labor-intensive than working on an equivalent-size corn or wheat field. Some estimates put the annual workload of a wet-rice farmer in Asia at three thousand hours a year."

Due to the fragility of the rice crop, impractical dreaming on the part of the rice farmers was unable to grow. The day in and day out monitoring and the bent backs burning from muscular pain and unrelenting sun led these farmers to create motivational quotes to help themselves and those around them persevere through the times. "Don't depend on heaven for food, but on your own two hands carrying the load."

It's obvious to see how, as the men shaped the fields to grow the rice, the rice, in turn, shaped them. And Gladwell's argument continues on even further, as he links the mindset of Asia's rice farmers to the unbreakable work ethic many people feel is a stereotype of their progeny in colleges throughout the United States. He links the rice farmers' mindset in the fields to their mindset about learning, that with consistent hard work the mind will continue to grow better and stronger. He compares it to the soil of the rice farmers:

"In fact, one of the singular features of rice cultivation is that because of the nutrients carried by the water used in irrigation, the more a plot of land is cultivated, the more fertile it gets.

"But in Western agriculture, the opposite is true. Unless a wheat - or corn-field is left fallow every few years, the soil becomes exhausted."

To summarize, this accounts for why Asian students attend school many more days throughout the year than American students. We have a three-month summer break because we felt our mind, like our soil, would become exhausted otherwise.

You may be wondering how rice, or wheat for that matter, has shaped me. Truth be told, I've never been a rice farmer and I've only been in wheat fields to run sprints as I trained for fights. But just as the lessons of the rice farmer infiltrated their children and exhibited themselves in a new environment, so too did the lessons learned through my relationship with my mom and stepdad.

My mom still works in the Supportive Service department at the Altoona Hospital. It's an unpredictable job and she never knows when she will feel the workload begin to deplete her body or when she will feel an overwhelming sense of reward. As complex as it can be from day to day, she can never quite predict what will happen, as the farmer can't quite predict the weather or how the amount of rice they gather one year will differ from the next. All she knows, and this especially when she was raising my sister and me, is that the more she worked, the better her family would be. She never talked to us about it, except to say, "I want you both to have better."

The unspoken lessons she instilled into my sister and me have become so deeply a part of who I am that I do not know how to not work hard. My hard work though, like the progeny of those rice farmers only a generation ago, is being applied in a radically different environment than the one in which my mom works.

I remember the moments of being scared and crawling into mom's bed, but also the mornings after. If my father left me afraid and needing, my mother made me strong and free. From the first night my father no longer slept in our house, to today, I have had dreams of someone breaking into my house. The insecurity that arose because my father no longer protected us forced me to become the "man of the house." The tangles of nightmares are all similar.

It was always dark, but just light enough. I could make out the intruder's movements. I would see the flash of a face peering in through the blinds of my bedroom window, my mom's window, and then my sister's. I'd hear the soft touch of his black leather gloves against the metal doorknob and the ever-so-gentle rattle of the locked door as he attacked the keyhole, finally getting it to open. I'd hear our door slowly creak open. I'd see him creep closer and closer to my mom's bedroom. He was always dressed in black.

I'd be strapped down on my bed and unable to move or scream to alert her.

I fought and kicked to break free as he inched closer, fought so hard, that right as he reached out to grab her, I'd spring awake out of breath and in a sweat that made the pajamas stick to my body. Terrified and exhausted, I'd crawl into my mom's bed without waking her. Then I'd lie there, matching the rhythm of her breathing with my own.

The next time I woke up was as influential in shaping me as the nightmares that simultaneously increased the bond between my mom and me and made me tougher. It was the sound of her alarm clock at 4:30 A.M. Today we have cell phones that make all sorts of pleasant noises to wake us, but my mom had the most annoying clock in the world. And she slept so deeply that it would go and go for what seemed like hours before it woke her. When she got up I'd pretend to sleep and she would brush her hand through my hair and kiss my forehead.

Those moments, my struggles at night and the way mom always rose from that alarm clock are like the ever-fertile soil the rice farmers cultivated. Those nights were so different from the practical aspirations of the farmers. They were imagined and unrealistic, they were something that more than likely would never come to fruition. But that alarm clock was practical, it was the evidence of hard work and the fertilizer that helped me to grow into what I've become. The consistency of that alarm clock's annoying loudness, even if I was sleeping in my own bedroom and not cuddled into mom, was the year-around, never-taking-a-break mindset of the rice farmer. Pennsylvania surrounded me with opportunities to see field after field of wheat, but I never knew the way it depleted the soil after a period of time, and if I had known, I'd still have been without foresight and immune to its lesson.

It's 6:00 A.M. as I write this, but I woke minutes ago to a downloaded cell phone ringtone of Tom Petty's "I Won't Back Down."

A year or so after the divorce, my mother fell in love with Bob, a man of quiet strength who would serve as the scaffolding in my quest for becoming a good man. Bob and my mom eventually purchased a house and his three kids and my sister and I all lived together. We aren't sure how I came to call him Nab, but mom suggests it was a slip of some sort, an odd fusion combining the words Bob and dad. It still leaves the "N" unaccounted for, but I'll take it.

Nab and my mom recently married, but he had become my true father back when I was fifteen. For about ten years now, Nab and I have had a wonderful relationship. I watched first-hand the way he looked lovingly at my mom. I watched the same pattern of him getting up at the sound of the alarm clock. When I first met Nab, I watched him to make sure he was good to my mom. As time went on and I found that answer, I watched him because I wanted to be like him. For nearly thirty years, Nab has worked for a local envelope-machine making factory while volunteering his time to help with the machinist union.

He pounded away long hours on their concrete floors, which damaged his knees enough that he could no longer play softball with the guys for fear he was holding the team back with his lack of speed. But, because of that work ethic, he was able to raise his three kids as a single parent for a while as well.

The times I most remember and cherish with Nab were those quiet times, when we both—without speaking—made the pact to watch TV together, often watching our Pittsburgh Steelers in the living room. Here's what goes unsaid:

Nab: Hey Bub, (what he calls me) let's watch the Steelers game in the living room together even though I was watching it comfortably in the bedroom and you were watching it comfortably down in your room.

Me: Okay, Nab. How come? Is it that you enjoy my company even if we are not speaking? Is it that, through our non-speech, we are developing our bond?

Nab: That sounds about right, Bub. I enjoy and appreciate the little time we do have, what with you being in school and always reading. I feel our bond developing, us becoming closer and learning about each other even though we are just watching the Steelers against the Ravens.

Me: I do too Nab, but I could never explain it. I like when I'm on this chair and you are on the couch over there. It feels warm.

Nab: Yeah, I know. I feel the same, it's really amazing.

Me: You know what else Nab?

Nab: What's that Bub?

Me: I like when after the game, or if it's a blowout, when you fall asleep on the couch. It usually makes me fall asleep and I feel so safe and secure and loved even though we rarely say to each other "I love you" like mom and I always do.

Nab: That's true, Bub. It's like we are sleeping pills for each other. The sound of your breath when you sleep usually makes me sleep easier I think.

Me: Hey Nab?

Nab: Yeah Bub.

Me: I love you, Nab.

Nab: I love you too, Bub.

Quiet, unassuming moments like the ones mentioned here have been the imperceptible kernels of rice that have shaped me into the person I've become. Long after the moments pass they always remain stored in the well of my mind and so are always there for reflective learning. If you boil a grain of rice until it swells it will split, but in the form of a slit, like a mouth, like the rice is willing to talk to you if you are willing to listen.

Log 13

Listen hard to the body. Do not be rigid about your exercise regimen. Allow leeway. If your hamstrings are still sore and tight from sprints but it's sprint day, don't suck it up and "just do it." Just adapt. Listen as though trying to hear things like in Michael Herr's *Dispatch*:

"...damp roots breathing, fruit sweating."

Listen to others this way as well.

CHAPTER 19

Caged—Part Three

"Two shining arrogant eyes had established dominance over his face and gave him the appearance of always leaning aggressively forward."

– The Great Gatsby

Crippled, war-battered men with missing fingers lean back in their chair on the porch to relax. Half of a rocking chair's life is leaning back. People with dentophobia lean back in the dentists chair and await orifice-seeking, or producing, syringes. Children, legs asleep from leaning over their video game controllers for hours on end, lean back in beanbags to extend playing time. We've all heard common phrases like, "Lean back and relax" or "Lean back and take it easy." Rapper Fat Joe topped the charts in 2004 with his song "Lean Back." People around the world watched and mimicked his dance on TV, leaning back to the rhythm of his beats while standing.

On 3:00 A.M. trips from Altoona to train Gracie Jiu-Jitsu in Manhattan, my only companion a mug of green tea, I leaned back any time the song called for it. Not just to stay awake, but for fun.

But I didn't lean back when it meant laziness, when it meant rocking and not going anywhere. I trained myself not to lean back, but to apply pressure, to press my opponent back after a left-hook kissed his temple. I trained to *lift-up* a 450-pound barbell, *to press* 70-pound dumbbells, *to explode* in sprints through rundown farms in State College—lifting my knees to meet the tips of overgrown grasses. I learned to twist, to jump, to throw, to sweep, to force, to trap, to punish, but never did I learn to lean back. What's to learn about it? Loafers lean back. Even sex usually involves someone leaning back.

I revere fighters like Mike Tyson and Wanderlei Silva. They always come forward with their shoulders hunched and their trapezius muscle bulging just under their ears like the rolling hills of Pennsylvania. It's like a "my-hands-are-on-my-ears-because-I-don't-give-a-shit-what-you-have-to-say-I'm-coming-to-kill-you," style. Fighters with this style often win rounds even if they didn't land the cleanest shots. Appearance matters.

Top position always seems dominant in the fight game, but although I'd won my first two fights, I hadn't been on top. I never felt totally dominant. Did I feel I had a level of control? Yes. I'd won both fights by latching on to my opponent's back and not letting go of the choke until the referee pried me off. I finished fights with my back pressing into the mat, my opponents' backs pressing into my chest, my legs wrapped around their torsos. This position is called the back mount and it actually is the most dominant position a fighter can achieve. But, as with everything in this sport, there is a counter. If the opponent is able to spin one-hundred eighty degrees to face the fighter holding the back mount he can escape not only the vulnerable position, but the submission that comes as a result of the position, the rear naked choke.

The notion that the fight could change drastically from an opponent simply turning to face me simmered constantly in the back of my mind. Paranoia, maybe, but maybe not.

I was staying in a cheap-ass promoter-paid-for hotel in Sandusky, Ohio, for my third MMA fight. June 2007. Again, I had with me, not experienced fighters and fight trainers like most of the other combatants had, but friends, and we discussed a strategy for what I called my third and final MMA bout. It would be my first fight at the possibly too-lean weight of 145-pounds. We finally had a plan. First, my feeling-out process: landing several Muay Thai kicks to my opponent's thighs, moving around, seeing how he reacts. Then whoosh! Shoot in for a lightning-fast takedown—never attempted in my fight career—and initiate the top game. I felt that nobody could be as strong as I was at this weight, and I wanted to combine that strength with the gravity and smothering advantage that comes from being on top. I wanted to play the top game badly. I wanted the pseudo-dominance of being on top. A position I hoped would grant me the position to elbow-slice open my opponent's forehead with the ease of a knife through a ripe Anjou pear. I wanted to press the back of his head against the cage, make him feel my pressure before unloading with a furious sequence of punches that would force the ref to jump in to save him.

The weight class listed on the official Ohio State Athletic Commission website was between 136 and 145 pounds. I'd followed the most critical nutrition program I'd ever had in my life, backed by years of personal research, and I weighed in at exactly 145.0 pounds.

But shortly after weigh-ins, the promoter approached me. He was a shady businessman type. I knew he hadn't studied any of the arts that have proved to be most dominant in the sport of MMA for any reasonable amount of time, nor had he competed in any serious form of competition in the sport. Nevertheless, he was a teacher of MMA and a fight promoter. In my mind, he was doing what many other people were doing: cashing in on the popularity of the sport despite the fact that he had few, if any, MMA credentials.

He'd pay for one night at the cheapest hotel he could find for the fighters even if they'd have a long drive or needed to fly across the country to compete. If you win your fight, he offers you not congratulations or a smile, but tickets to the strip club where he found the ring girls. After the fights, he stands alone in the middle of the cage rolling stacks of twenty-dollar bills between his fingers, while the majority of fighters, after a great performance win or lose, are often forced to scrounge up what money they have for a celebratory meal at Taco Bell. He drives a flashy red sports car. He's a walking cliché. He's the white, poor man's version of boxing promoter Don King.

"I only listed those weight classes on my website so the athletic commission would get off my back about it. I never follow them," he told me just an hour before my third fight. I put my head down and looked at my shoes, unsure of whether to hold back my feelings or let loose.

"That's not right," I said. "Not right at all, man."

"Well, when you're running a business, not everything can be right," he said. "The state athletic commission has too many rules. I cut corners wherever I can."

I felt my temples pulsate.

"That's fucking bullshit. Our health is at stake here," I said. "As much as this is a business it's also a fucking sport." He waved his hands as though to interrupt me. "No, put your fucking hands down," I said. "Fuck you." I walked away.

About an hour later he had a messenger tell me I'd be fighting a man in the weight class above me, (155-pounds, my old weight) who had eight fights to my two fights. Despite the fact that other fighters had weighed in at my class, he paired me against an undefeated fighter who had fought for him for years, a fighter who got to choose his own entrance music, a fighter who obviously outweighed me by an amount over the five-pound legal allowance.

I had lost the mental edge of being the biggest and strongest fighter I could be at my weight class. I had lost the edge given to me by countless hours of research and dietetic discipline. All because I bitched at what I felt were the promoters' wrongdoings, all because I didn't lean back and let this shady promoter continue making a mockery of the sport. Whether he knew it or not, "his" ring girls were in the audience selling their hardcore porn videos to the spectators. Because I put the sport in front of myself and opened my mouth when I was heated, I was treated differently.

The more I understand what happened in my own situation at a "small" show the more I see it throughout the mainstream world of MMA. Some of the largest, most successful and most popular MMA organizations in the world, despite the millions and millions of dollars they are rolling in, somehow find a way to only pay former champion fighters who headline an event on pay-per-view, fifty-thousand dollars. It may seem like a lot, but compare it to other sports, such as boxing, whose popularity continues to dwindle. Headline boxers continue to make millions of dollars each fight.

The MMA fight promoters are cashing in big-time, but when outspoken fighters attempt to air their concerns, they are instantly placed on the undercard, given less exposure, dropped from the roster, and talked about less frequently by the announcers. That fighter's clothing brand is blurred-out when the camera pans across the arena. Politics and corruption are nothing new to combat sports—the mafia and other gangs have controlled boxing for years. Boxing may now be playing second-string to MMA. People just don't know about the corruption because the sports-news organizations are not covering it as prominently as they once did for boxing.

As the announcer screamed my name, I stood outside of the large aluminum storage shed—where the cage was—and said to Tyler and Mark: "Win or lose, I want to represent the Gracie family. Let's come out in a straight line, holding each others' shoulders and bouncing just as they do." We did.

Shortly after the fight started I was on the bottom, taking it. Taking glancing blows, remembering to find my breath as I learned in fight two and being the annoying son-of-a-bitch I'd come to be known as. I saw his mouthpieced grimace that resembled a smile, watched him struggle to pin my arms to the mat and to break the grip my legs formed around his waist. It was déjà vu. Acting as Jason of the Argonauts months prior to this fight taught me to be comfortable in front of crowds, ultra-aware of my surroundings. I heard the crowds' baritone Sandusky, Ohio, Bike-Week voices, my stepdad yelling from the back row, my opponent grunting like creatures I watched on Animal Planet. I even heard my breath.

After I landed two solid Thai kicks to gauge distance and begin finding my rhythm, I shot in for a takedown so I could get on top. He sprawled back and stuffed my takedown beautifully, pulling his legs just out of my reach, but I rushed in so I wouldn't be left vulnerable on all fours. I rushed and I rushed and I eventually football-tackled him around the waist but I quickly ran out of room to finish the takedown because his back was now pressed against the cage. *Deadlifts were for this*, I thought. It was time to lift him high and drop him hard and fold his head back down through his neck and into his chest and put an end to this fight.

But he grabbed onto the cage to prevent being slammed, which is illegal, then countered with a gorgeous, textbook knee-strike that shot up through my belly button and into the deepest gorges of my abdomen and took my breath away. I jumped into the air to wrap my legs around his waist and attain the familiar guard position. This would allow me to bide my time so I could catch my breath. Instead, he caught me in mid-air and slammed me to the mat with a thud that had the biker-fans revving like the motorcycles they rode in on. So it goes.

Now this was a fight. But I felt in the zone. Time slowed down. In seconds he would blow it and I'd capitalize, choking him until either he tapped-out or passed-out. Tap-out or pass-out, the phrase taped to the ceiling above my bed. I ended the day and started the new with it. The formula—finding the back and cinching the choke—had worked twice. 2-0.

His shoulders relaxed, his intertwined back muscles, the ones I'd seen glistening under the lights as he rhythmically bounced in the cage before the fight began, went slack.

Exhaustion, I thought. He gassed already. The fact that I consistently swam until my goggles filled with tears, not chlorine, ran hills until my thighs wanted to vomit lactic acid, and was the better-conditioned athlete had prevailed for the third time. His dead weight felt easily maneuverable. I remembered corpses from my internship with the Coroner. *No, they had rigor*, I thought. *They wouldn't feel like this.* My mind could drift outside of the fight, as though it wasn't so much a fight as it was a game that could be played at my discretion. Paused at will. I felt no desperation to do anything.

We were face-to-face and his right forearm was on my chest so I grasped it, forced it down my abdomen and brought my legs up high on the back of his shoulders. This is the high-guard position and allows for armbars and triangle chokes. He pressed forward into me and I locked up the triangle. The fans were screaming because they knew once the triangular was set and tight like I had it that it's usually game over. Rather than going for broke and clamping down as hard as possible, I decided to save some energy for the later rounds. Still, the more he struggled, the more the choke tightened and the more his face turned a deeper red. Those early mornings I got up to work on my flexibility and breathing so I could be relaxed while in awkward positions paid off. He was going to be put to sleep soon, not by the rear naked choke, but by the triangle choke. I'd show my versatility once and for all, then retire after this fight.

At that moment, he got off his knees and powerfully pushed through his feet so I was forced to support our combined weight on only the back of my neck. This is called "stacking" and is a last-ditch maneuver to defend and escape the triangle choke. He pulled out of my triangle, broke free from the web I'd tangled him in, and moved authoritatively to the dominant side mount position. From side mount he could have his pick of elbow strikes, chokes, and armlocks. I had never been so vulnerable but I was still composed. I scrambled and forced my left knee inside against his waist and eventually wrapped both legs around his waist to regain the guard position. I heard the ten-second sticks and knew if I didn't go balls-to-the-wall that I'd certainly lose this round in the judges' eyes. I exploded forward to sweep him and get on top and dominant him. He leaned back. At the same damn time I forged forward he leaned aggressively backwards. And I found myself in a position I've never been in. On top. *Time to unload*, I thought. *Time to finish him.*

But he had leaned back to secure a heel-hook—so named because its lever is the heel. It shatters knee ligaments. A cast iron wok through a window.

He leaned back, purposely, like a La-Z-Boy, but with the goal of inflicting great bodily damage. I tried dropping a right fist into his orbital bone but hesitated because it might have meant sacrificing the health of my knee. I wanted to land that shot badly.

Five seconds left in the round.

Four seconds.

Three.

Here comes the University of Arizona's Poet-in-Residence strutting down the hall… on crutches? How would I get to a class that was well over a mile away in a city I'd not yet lived in? Would I be one of those fathers who desperately want to play basketball with their child but can't because of injuries I suffered? He tucked my ankle under his armpit and began cranking. I broke this same ankle three times during my basketball career. I felt no pain, but the scary part about leglocks is that there's often no pain until a tear or break occurs.

Two.

It's not worth it, I thought. Checkmate.

One.

I tapped-out.

I learned my lesson. Acknowledged it by tapping the mat three times. I brought my hands in a prayer pose, bent down, and kissed the mat. Then my opponent and I shook hands, hugged, and smiled. "You were the toughest dude I've ever fought," he said to me.

"You've got a hell of a future in front of you," I said to him. This inanimate canvas was more real to me than so many people I've met. I exited the cage with a smile, excited to sit in the audience and enjoy the rest of the fights with my friends and family.

I learned a lesson I never could have learned by winning. I learned humility. I learned the yin-yang relationship of BJJ—that yielding can be as controlling as resisting. I learned that waiting can be as decisive and aggressive as attacking. I learned that my friends didn't really think about me the way I'd imagined they did. I could see in their eyes how much they cared for me. I learned that the reasons I fought this third fight were not the reasons I should have fought for. I loved the sport, but I was not fighting because I loved the sport. I wondered if I'd ever be able to fight for that reason alone. The training was for the love of the sport, but the reasons for fighting felt altogether different sometimes. I fought this fight for the love of those I wanted to love me. And I learned that they already did. Losing is awesome.

Log 14

Get used to being second at most. In MMA, there are so many martial arts to study, so many physical attributes to have. Even if I am the best at BJJ, I won't be the best in another discipline. Even if I'm the strongest, someone will be more flexible. If my hands are the fastest, someone out there will hit harder. If I beat someone in wrestling, they might dominate me in boxing. Don't settle, but settle.

CHAPTER 20

1631 South 10th Avenue
Tucson, Arizona

*I know and have explored the many reasons why I've been
drawn to the sport of MMA—from its history, to my own insecurities, to the challenges of it—but it is right now that I want to
admit and explore why I feel that love slipping away.*

On the way to 1631 South 10th Avenue in my green Hyundai Accent, I
passed thirty or so Mexican men on the sidewalk flailing orange flags and
Worker Pick Up posterboards. I wondered if their deltoids and trapezius
muscles succumbed to the sear of lactic acid from holding those signs with
outstretched arms all day or if they were numb to it. I wondered about their
success in slowing down cars, let alone stopping them. A nervous, desperate
wildness inhabited their movement. The quick, six-second glimpse of these
men while I sped past at forty miles per hour was deeply unsettling. How
must they feel when they open the passenger door or jump into the back of
a stranger's pick-up truck? How do the others, the unselected, feel? Do they
swarm a stopped vehicle with the same feverish intensity as kindergarteners
when getting to the recess room means first dibs on the new Nerf football?
How do those looking for workers determine which of these men to choose?
The one who approaches the car first? A quick head-to-toe physicality as-
sessment? Something here reeks of slavery. Or fighting. I hoped the history of these men would not hold them down. I hoped the factors out of
their control would not adversely effect them. I hoped their personal "tale
of the tape"—usually attributes like arm-length, height, and weight, but in
their case things like place of birth and the circumstances they were born
into—wouldn't hold them back in life. But I knew better. Still, in a burst of

positivity, I wrote a poem a few hours after this encounter. Poetry allows me to understand the roots of my emotions. This allows me to empathize with others. If we can understand ourselves, we can better understand others. When be better understand others, our world becomes more peaceful.

The tale of the tape

doesn't mean shit. Some stories
are in the 4 oz gloves, ask them about the glory,

the gory BJ Penn blood licks, the smell -
desperate sweat seeping through tape's glue -

they will stay quiet as breathlessness: an uppercut
under the ribcage. Hip control can't be quantified,

nor can instinct be liquefied, fit into a shiny can
advertised by a slow-motion-for-me ass with a tan

and what about the transition from position
to submission? The butterfly sweep to half guard

(pass that guard!) to full mount to triangle
from the top angle to an omoplata -

almost countered - to a gogoplata to fuck
he slipped out, back to the feet, duck

the left hook, (watch the right knee)
sink the single leg, against the cage,

breath-control controls rage,
sweep that foot, the soot of your life

under the rug for these three
carefree, fight-or-flight five-minute rounds. (2008)

A sign on the stuccoed front of 1631 announces Centro Del Sur, Pima

County. A brightly painted sun with orange rays and a yellow face bridges the gap from the O of Centro to the D of Del. A mosaic of a seated, cross-legged Native American man is pressed into the building, his flesh pieced together by russet potato color plastic chunks no larger than a stamp. An exaggerated red, yellow, and blue headdress radiates above him. At the far corner is a white sign: Pima County WIC and Food Plus. WIC stands for Women, Infants, and Children. This USDA program provides supplemental foods, health care referrals, and nutrition education for low-income pregnant women, new mothers and infants, and children up to age five who are found to be at nutritional risk.

I turn from facing the WIC building to look across the street where a painted ten-foot-tall cement wall extends down to the end of the block. It's broken into four segments by the rusted metal door that is large enough for vehicles to enter. As though gatekeepers, two tribal concrete totems of equal height border this wall. They are decorated with charcoal-color drawings of primitive humans. A banner streams from totem to totem and reads: Tucson Electric Power. 27th Street Substation. Danger High Voltage. Peligro Alto Voltaje.

I notice at the top of the cement wall is a painted merman—legs cut off where shins would begin. He swims downward, reaching for I know not what with something in his hands, an eraser maybe. A foot and a half past his fingertips, another painting, this of a crouched, well-muscled man sporting a deer-head headdress. The deer head looks to be either scalped and bleeding or wearing a red kerchief across its antlers.

At this point in my life, I was teaching creative writing in the Pima County Juvenile Detention Center. A teenaged student I connected well with was a Tohono O'odham Native American tribe member from Arizona, so I decided to ask her about what I saw. She told me that the mosaic is of the "Yaqui Deer Dancer," an iconic symbol of the Pascua Yaqui Native American tribe from along the Rio Yaqui in the Sonoran Desert of southwest Arizona.

A weathered white banner wavers behind him with a small black cross, the word BARRIO (Spanish for "district" or "neighborhood") stenciled and what looks to be scratched out letters painted on it. Directly below those muted letters is an ominous phrase that seems to encapsulate this area in Tucson and the continuous degradation of Native Americans and their lifestyles: The Violence!

My time teaching in the detention center served as inspiration and led to the creation of *Until You Make the Shore,* my first book of collected poems, to be published by Salmon Poetry. The poems blend reality with fiction and inhabit the voices of four imagined young girls at various institutional levels within the detention center. The Tohono O'odham student and the class on MMA I taught to the incarcerated girls served as inspiration for the following poem from the collection.

Eva

One

those two moves you showed   triangle choke   right?
        and gogo   gogoplata   they look cool and all
but i ain't never gonna pull that off on the streets

because streets have uncountable gravel
you have a mat

streets have knives
you have two gloves

        streets have eyes from all sides
you have one pair

and besides if i tried it
        that gravel'd stick in my back
make me bleed

        and it'd burn like busted heat
in the shower   it'd probably leave scars
        or something   and people'd ask

how it happen   or if i was born that way
        or if i was whipped at home

i mean   i wouldn't   feel sexy

scars are cool on the front you know

      but back scars mean you done
had it handed to you
      front scars mean you done took it lookin. (2010)

WIC centers and free public boxing clubs are often located in the poorest areas of a city. I am searching for the club because I miss the Altoona Boxing Club, because I can't live without the energy of fighting and writing and I've been without the former and knee-deep in the latter for the first three months of graduate school. I need my fix. Now.

Horns blare as a milk-chocolate, collarless lab-mix bobs and weaves through traffic with a poise that labels him a seasoned vet. He leaps onto the sidewalk, looks at me and nods in the nonchalant "what's up" way of men. There's a sunless silence. Rain trickles onto my notebook, leeching the ink from my notes about the mural into its little cilia fingers. From behind me, inside 1631, I hear the familiar sound of the three-minute training bell that signals the beginning and end of a round of jumping rope or shadowboxing or sit-ups or neck exercises or footwork drills or bagwork or of sparring: Ding-Ding-Ding! The sound I associate with my own maturation into a man. The reason I brought myself here.

I took a few deep breaths before I reached to open the door to the boxing club. *I hope I'll feel uncomfortable here,* I thought. *Being too comfortable kills the bodies and minds and spirits of humans. It destroys our desire to learn and reflect and see other perspectives, makes it easier for us to let our bodies go and to not care when our environment is being butchered beyond belief for the sake of making us a smidge more comfortable. Too much comfort kills. It makes tolerable situations miserable and makes miserable situations seem like the end of the world.*

I open the door and was startled to find seven or eight pregnant women waiting their turn to be called to the front desk. The automatic doorbell rings when I enter and they all shift to face me. In my quick glance I notice one woman has half of her face tattooed and that most of them are pregnant and have a child already on their laps. I close the door and the dog gives me another what's-up nod as he moseys on by. I walk around back to find another door ajar. The bell signaling the start and end of each round became louder. The mixed smell of worn leather, cotton, and sweat that I abhor when standing over the washing machine and that arouses me when in its midst, pulled me closer to its source.

I've never seen a WIC center and a boxing club housed in the same building. I wonder about how many pedestrians and cars pass the artwork on the outside of the shared boxing club/WIC center on a regular basis. Thousands? And how few are aware of or experience what's on the other side of those walls—the grit and fear of a man crippled by body blows who fights physical fatigue and the thoughts of ceasing that tease comfort? Of a pregnant single mom who struggled for bus fare to come here, who fights her fears that her poverty will inhibit the health and possibly the life of her unborn child?

Emanuel Steward, a highly successful coach and the famed trainer of former three-time world heavyweight champion Lennox Lewis and former six-time world welterweight champion Thomas "Hit Man" Hearns, opened this gym in Tucson after much success with coaching in and owning Detroit-based Kronk gym (so I was told by the trainers). Ralph Wiley, a writer at *Sports Illustrated* between 1982-1992, said of Kronk during HBO's *Legendary Fights* documentary, "You go down one flight of stairs, you feel the heat rising as you go down. In some ways I would imagine it's like Dante's Inferno. In the middle of all of this, is this little Merlin, this little man, Emanuel Steward." Steward can now be found behind the commentator's desk during HBO Boxing broadcasts.

Walking into this new gym, I gathered a new perspective—because of emotional and physical distance—of an act with which I've only viewed while being heavily engaged. For the first time in my life, while in an environment where fighters were training, I noticed myself standing back and observing with the mind of a writer rather than with the mind of a fighter. I felt scared. I felt like I lost part of myself and gained access to another.

A blue canvassed ring, identical to the ones I've stained red in other times and places, fits perfectly, Tetris-like, into one corner of the Tucson Boxing Club. Two speedbags hang like uvulas against the wall behind a long wooden desk with chairs on either side. A man wearing gray sweatpants and a gray hooded sweatshirt darkened by sweat begins striking the speedbag. It sounds like an intensified version of the dried leaves that used to antagonize me by skipping along the street faster than I could run. Pitter-patter-pitter-patter. With the bells and the bags and the heavy music I recognize how fighters always look like they are smiling when they try to talk while wearing their mouthpiece—though a smile is likely the last thing to appear when rigorous training is underway.

On the wall adjacent to the speedbags, I see an oil painting of "The War," the fight between the razor-thin and equally deadly Thomas "Hit Man" Hearns and the compact southpaw terror of "Marvelous" Marvin Hagler. HBO Boxing broadcaster Jim Lampley said the fight was "possibly the most memorable fight in thirty years of boxing on HBO. It's the most hellacious eight minutes of combat in modern boxing history."

The fight occurred April 15, 1985 in Caesars Palace, Las Vegas—eight days before I was cut out of my mom's womb and brought into the world at the Altoona Hospital. Reruns of the fight were one of my first tastes of passion's intensity—passion I wanted for happiness, for future love, marriage, children, for my career. A passion which, if extinguished, would make life meaningless. The painting captures absolute passion, with oil as the perfect medium, as though the fighters' bodies could blend fully into one by tilting the painting and allowing the captured colors of their battle to become something greater than either man could achieve alone.

A man noticed me after the thirty-second break bell rang, nodded his head in that familiar way as he fumbled to hold a water bottle with gloved hands. I was reminded of the way my Jack Russell holds his chew-rope upright without the dexterity of fingers. My writer mind was making associative leaps with everything I saw. This was my first visit to the Tucson Boxing Club. I could feel it would be the place for me, whatever that may mean. I was content to be a fly on the wall, to come in and watch and only watch.

One of the hopeful laborers leapt out onto the road with his orange sign as I was heading home. I braked and shook my head no and he let me proceed, but his disappointment crept into my day. In my mind I repeatedly saw his instantaneous postural slump at my refusal. I felt directly responsible. When I returned home, I cleaned my floors and shower and toilet and the entire time I kept envisioning that slump. His slump wasn't an act, it was automatic. It was real. I wondered whom he felt disappointed for—maybe his wife back home with a kid on the way. Maybe he was writing letters to a loved one in Mexico, bragging about his scant success in America. Maybe it was general disappointment in himself sprung from his past mistakes or maybe it was from the situation in which he was born into and had absolutely no control over.

Whatever the reason, a Marvin Hagler quote came to me:

"I worked construction for eight years and while I was diggin I was thinkin, there's gotta be a better way."

Combative sports like boxing and MMA make me push myself more than any other sport. In football, a weak-ass practice might be the difference between a missed tackle or a great one during a game, a win or a loss. In combat sports, a practice could be the reason for getting cut open, knocked out, or choked unconscious. There is a difference between defending the goalline and defending life.

Life. The Tucson Boxing Club, in my opinion, was opened in this particular area because Mexican men crossing the border (less than an hour away) hungered for a better life. Why else would the gym be here and not Pittsburgh, not NYC, not a wildly populated California town? Sure, maybe it was put here to help people in ways similar to the Altoona Boxing Club, but I'm feeling something else. Boxing to Mexico is like football and baseball combined in the United States. It's a sport less reliant on natural ability and genetics than on sheer determination, on hunger.

I do not know Emanuel's precise history or connection with this gym. I only know what I've heard from some respected martial arts instructors and police officers in Tucson. The two trainers who sit at the wooden desk and stare at you when you sign in also happen to be two of Tucson's largest and most renowned drug lords. By "largest" I mean not only that these two men control a sizable area and are more than stable financially, but that they are so morbidly obese that it takes a full sixty-seconds for them to open the door and remove themselves from a parked vehicle. Their necks disappear, turtle-like, inside their bodies when they reach along their waist to unhook the seatbelt. They have some sort of aura (and smell) that surrounds them that brings Martin Scorsese's *Goodfellas* to mind. Yet, despite being utterly out of shape, they are fabulous trainers. They taught me balance, how best to transfer power, how to make each step I took in the ring setup an attack or a defense against an attack. As I continued working out there, I received far more attention from them than the other athletes. Part of me feels it's because they may have seen dollar signs as they watched me shadowbox in the mirror.

The majority of boxing clubs throughout the United States are non-profit. They seek to take in "at-risk" youth and teach them through physical training the values of hard work, determination, focus, and goal-setting. And it works. Here in Tucson, I imagine a Mexican man crossing the border to start a new life, a man whose pockets are weighted with more lint than money, but who still *can* afford to go to a boxing club. Only the more affluent can attend "mixed martial arts" classes, though I believe boxing to be a martial art. Only the well-off can afford BJJ lessons at $150 to $200 a month. That's rent for the working poor. That's food.

So they turn to boxing and not MMA, with hunger in their stomachs and hearts. And they learn those lessons of boxing and then some.

I realized I'd become complacent during my time in Tucson. I'd reached a plateau with how far I could go and how good I could become in MMA without having a team. Having a team means shelling out hundreds of dollars each month. I've become bitter towards the sport that, in its infancy, was for everybody, but that now, thanks to its rise in popularity and resulting expense, has excluded an enormous part of the general population. This means those in lower-income brackets. This often means minorities.

Right now this means me.

I've become bitter that I can't push past nausea or those thoughts of quitting when I train and can't summon the desperate intensity that the teenaged son worried about his baby brother while his mom is in line waiting for a check at the WIC center can. Each time I drive to the gym, the sign in bold letters across the street from 1631 reminds me of the spirit I once thrived on and now lack. *Tucson Electric Power: Danger High Voltage.*

It's when I feel a lack of personal power that I somehow create the voltage to make my life work. Created voltage needs somewhere to go to make something work. I'm one of the youngest MFA students in this graduate school and I'm the Poet-in-Residence of the renowned Poetry Center—one of the most coveted positions for a poet in graduate school in the country. Of my friends in the MFA program, I received my acceptance letter the latest. It makes me believe I was at the bottom of the selection committee's list. As a writer and graduate student, I'm stressed and insecure and lacking personal power in unbelievable ways. But this means I have voltage. So much voltage I can feel it coming out of my ears. It's mental voltage, and I have no idea how the hell to release it other than to be dogged in my pursuit of studying and learning. It's Saturday and I've read four books this week.

Humor arises from pain as beauty arises from violence. I look back now and laugh at the half-a-spatula we have back home. Half-a-spatula because it broke over my butt when mom cracked me with it seventeen years ago during a fight I had over a toy with my younger sister. It depends, I suppose, on how much time has passed between the pain and the present. Here is a prose-poem musing I look back on now with laughter—finding humor in struggle's weathered, wrinkled face—though at the time it was devastatingly painful.

Brief History of My Life

I unfold my chair into the warmth of March, take off my
socks, feel the grass on my feet for the first time in months,
and begin to read poet Jeff Gundy. I turn the page to the
poem "Brief History of Life" only to hear the discharge of a
truck's airbrakes. A paint-chipped truck turns the corner and
stops in front of my house. The man walks toward me. I put
my finger between the pages and stand up. He hands me the
bill for five hundred and two dollars and asks for the head
of household. I tell him that she's working a double today.
He heads back to his truck. I return to my chair. Flip back to
page 19. Before I read a word, I notice the man is climbing the
telephone pole. When he reaches the top, he fiddles with his
shiny tool belt. He's cutting our power. I imagine his left boot
stepping on a rotted bracket, leg swinging away from the pole,
the rest of him falling, only air and concrete, and me giving
him the finger all the way down. (2006)

In the martial arts, beauty surely arises from violence. The martial arts began as a way to inflict and defend against violence. This does not preclude their movements from being beautiful. Striking or grappling combinations strung together like pearls are gracefully lethal. The exhibited, practiced reservoir of human fight movement is just as beautiful (and natural) as what we consider "the natural world" or "nature."

In Peter Paul Rubens's oil painting "The Lion Hunt," completed between 1617 and 1618, seven men pierce two lions with spears; two lions pierce seven men with claws, teeth, and fear. The title is beautifully ambiguous—who is hunting whom? And the oil paint seems to purposefully muddle colors and shapes as a way to show the scene's chaotic blur. The painting is about three feet wide and two feet tall. In the center, a horse falls, head flung back as though trying to see where pain's unreachable sting is coming from. One man is falling head-first towards the ground while a lion sinks its teeth into his abdomen. Two other men are already on the ground, one is unconscious or dead. The painting is still, but somehow moves with mayhem.

There I was in London's National Gallery, unable to stop looking. My fixation wasn't like morbidly staring at a car accident, where human nature for curiosity to see other humans vulnerable is strangely reassuring. It was more of a "how did Rubens create this wonderfully disturbing image?" type fixation.

From the reds and whites, blacks and tans, where did the scene come from? Did he actually see such a scene? If so, did he get it just right? How did he come to terms with angles of paws and heads? How and why did he give it a certain abstractness so the viewer can't tell exactly what is going on? Is that how the scene was in his mind? A way to capture the action component?

At London's Tate museum I saw Jackson Pollock's "Naked Man with a Knife" painting (1938-1940). It's an unidentifiable sprinkling of unattached limbs. Again, shapes and figures are distorted in what might be a way to capture the blind rage and fury of violence. In the upper left hand corner is a knife—is it plunging downwards? I don't know. I only know that the painting is beautifully violent or violently beautiful.

I remember the time when my mom was curled in a ball on the bed in her room and crying on the phone, begging with the bill collector to turn our heat back on in the dead of winter, telling him over and over that a check was on its way. I remember her mascara running down her face—the left-side teardrop racing with the right—as she mouthed to me, "This is why you need an education." My sister, only her head exposed from under the green sleeping bag on her bed, was flu-ridden and vomiting into a garbage can.

The heating company places a large metal lock over the outdoor heating unit when they turn the power off. It's similar to "the boot" for a car with excess violations. But what was a young man of eighteen to do when he's the man of the house? When his mom is crying, at her weakest, and his sister seems on the verge of death from cold? I grabbed a hammer from the basement, screamed to my mom, "I'm pounding that fuckin lock off!" She covered the phone with one hand and yelled, "It's a felony to take that off!" I brandished my hammer. "Cameron, please no, you'll go to jail!"

It took four full-body whacks to bust off the lock. Luckily, the bill was paid and I didn't have to go to jail.

Each winter one of us tells this story and we laugh uncontrollably. Or, at family gatherings, if the cliché "when it rains it pours" is thrown into the air by somebody (which has happened more than once) the three of us smile with our eyes at each other from across the room. From the depths of our cores, we've shared in what that cliché can really mean.

If pain is a pot of boiling water, humor can be the rising steam.

Where does passion come from when I'm comfortable, that is, when I'm not in pain? Humor can come from pain, beauty from violence, but what is the source of deep passion? I mean that hungry, til-I-die type passion as displayed in "The War" painting at the Tucson Boxing Club. How do I compete in a sport when, on all sides of me, men are training and fighting to win a few bucks to put meat on the ribs of their children?

I worked hardest physically when my family and I struggled. And I'd be a liar if I told you I have the same hunger today. I want it, but I can't summon it. My mom made less than $23,000 while supporting my sister and me—not including the chunk taken out for the ugly-divorce lawyer fees. As a graduate student, I made $14,000 per year - plenty to support just myself. I could buy ground beef, fruit, and vegetables at Trader Joe's. I was living the good life.

Ron Borges of the *Boston Globe* said on HBO's *Legendary Fights*, "When Marvin Hagler came out of his corner, he was carrying with him all the frustrations and broken dreams of his whole life…." What people don't see is that those things also carried him—through a brutal training camp filled with pain, sweat, blood, and vomit. I wasn't willing to last the extra two seconds for the bell to ring while my opponent had me in a heel-hook like a man needing the winning bonus so his wife can eat. I tapped-out. I cowered. I didn't want to be a "teacher hobbling around the hallways on crutches."

And even today, I train to stay in shape, to move well for longevity's sake. I call my training style "Sustainable Functional Fitness." Occasionally a fire burns and I train harder so I'm ready to fight if fighting means protecting those I love. Whether right or wrong, I feel pathetic next to a man with the fire I once had. I feel out of place. Wait a second. Yes. I feel uncomfortable.

Log 15

Uncomfortable.
While driving:

On a hot, humid day: Turn off the air conditioner. Roll down the windows. Breathe. Feel the heat on your seat. Feel yourself become a little sticky, a little uncomfortable.

On a freezing cold day: shut the heat off and roll down the windows. Let the skin on your face burn just a little, let your teeth chatter just a little. Bite down and smile through it.

When driving past a McDonald's, drive slowly. Savor the smells. Taste the fries through scent but deny. Be strong, go home, eat salmon and broccoli.

These build the mental toughness, the fighter spirit needed to maintain dedication to the health of the only bodies we'll ever have. These are reminders of how good we have it. Reminders that, over time, will make us complain less (because we are affected less) when we run out of maple syrup for our breakfast pancakes or when we cut soda from our diet. Such seemingly disparate (yet purposeful) discomforts are, in fact, related. There are parallels everywhere if we look hard enough. After a period of weeks of cutting soda and other sweets, we'll realize how desensitized we've become to sweetness. Eventually, we'll be able to taste the sweetness in vegetables. Even water will have a certain sweetness. And pineapple will be powerful enough to pucker our faces so hard that we may look, for a second, like MMA fighter Wanderlei Silva.

CHAPTER 21

Fights Begin and End with Handshakes

"There comes a time in every man's education when he arrives at the conviction that envy is ignorance."

– Ralph Waldo Emerson

Envy pumped through the vein that runs down my forehead. Envy behind my eyes. Envy in the bridge of my nose. Envy in my fingertips. Envy in the sound of my voice. Envy has burned me since I found out the news on February 8, 2010: Altoona fighter Charlie "The Spaniard" Brenneman signed a contract with the UFC.

Born in 1981, Charlie graduated from Hollidaysburg Area Senior High School, a mere ten-minute drive from my home in Altoona. He then went to Lock Haven University where he majored in Spanish and finished his collegiate wrestling career with a top-twelve finish at Nationals. Brenneman also holds a Master's degree in Sports Management from East Stroudsburg University. He returned to Hollidaysburg Area Senior High and taught for several years as a Spanish teacher.

Charlie and I first met at the Altoona Boxing Club some years earlier when he was twenty-five and I was twenty-one. It was the place in town where I had some clout and could usually pick apart most boxers regardless of weight class. I'd heard of Charlie through some friends, who said he was pursuing MMA seriously. When I saw a new guy at the boxing club with thick, curly brown hair I had a gut feeling it was Charlie. It was and I've liked the guy ever since.

Between the buzzers and grunts I introduced myself. He had heard of me because I was the first local known for competing in MMA. He was interested in training with me, and I with him—I could definitely absorb much considering his wrestling pedigree. I sparred a few fighters while Charlie watched and I had one of my best sessions in years, dropping two different opponents with the counter-left hook I'd been polishing. Johnny Robertson motioned for Charlie to put on the headgear. I took some deep breaths and thought I'd be going another round, but Johnny had another idea.

"Conaway, get out. Good work. Dan, you're up."

Dan and I had sparred a few rounds earlier. He only had about a month of training in at the boxing club, so he was still in the awkward, lumbering phase. About 5'8" and 165 pounds, Dan had a solid, proportionate build. Like Charlie, he'd been wrestling his whole life so his legs and neck were thick and sinewy. He had green eyes and a large "Italian nose" that he was "damn proud of" which stood out all the more because of his shaved head. I usually focused on movement when I sparred him, letting him land his looping punches on me just so he could get used to the distance it takes to actually land a punch. This is one of fighting's first and most difficult lessons: to hit somebody cleanly you have to be close enough for him to hit you. This is a major barrier to get past, and Dan was still learning the ropes.

"Dan, focus on movement and breathing. Charlie's new," Johnny said as he finished strapping on Charlie's headgear and gloves.

I skipped rope lightly and watched how Dan and Charlie matched up. They appeared equal in weight, though Charlie was a few inches taller. I was particularly interested in how Charlie moved. From all accounts he was a great guy, educated and respectful, good-looking and articulate. The same can't be said for most who entered the boxing club. He seemed someone I'd instantly befriend what with our MMA aspirations and academia backgrounds. But I was the town's MMA phenomenon. Animal instincts came. I must protect my brand, my niche. I watched him like I've watched few others.

Dan and Charlie circled left as Johnny instructed them to do—this is the typical movement for all orthodox boxers. Orthodox meaning left foot and left hand in front and the dominant right hand and right foot in the back. When the bell rang, Charlie came out of the corner wildly moving every body part except for his hands, which stayed glued to the side of his head. His feet tripped over each other, his head moved in all angles, his torso rolled like some type of feline. He was clumsy and off balance, but looked strong. Dan, on the other hand, continued circling to the left then pausing to breathe and make sure his feet weren't crossing—a huge error in fighting. (If you get hit when your feet are crossed you are going down hard, possibly becoming unconscious because your spine was already out of alignment at the time of impact. Even if you don't get hit, you are not going to be able to generate enough power to launch your own attack.) Every movement in fighting is purposeful. A fighter must be able to both defend and deliver at all times.

Despite being a relative newbie, Dan did have a wicked right cross when he planted his feet and sat down on it. To "sit down" means to be balanced in the boxing stance and to have a slight bend in the knees. When the right hand is fired, the front of the right foot pivots and the hip swivels toward the opponent. The right hand is then "turned over," meaning the knuckle on the pinky finger should face the roof and the elbow should be fully extended when fist meets jaw. When circling left against an orthodox opponent, a fighter must constantly be aware of his opponent's right hand because he is essentially moving into it. Conversely, circling to the right means moving towards the opponent's jab and left hook. The goal here is to move unpredictably, unless your opponent is known for having major power or a major lack of power in any particular punch.

Charlie's crazy movements were an attempt to be unpredictable, but even craziness has a level of predictability. He was not throwing punches and he only circled to the left. Dan needed only to cut him off, pounce into Charlie's path, plant his feet and launch the right cross. The glove landed flush on Charlie's face. Textbook. Charlie was on the ground in a heap. *Was he out cold?* I felt sick to my stomach for him. I felt good about myself.

That was the only time I saw Charlie over the next three years. School began to take precedence in my life, and I began teaching BJJ in a garage with a few friends. Then came my two years of graduate school in Arizona. Meanwhile, Charlie trained hard and began racking up wins in the amateur MMA circuit. He began beating better and better fighters, fighters known in the MMA world. He began marketing himself via Charlie-Brenneman.com. We sent emails back and forth updating each other on our lives. Part of me felt I would be the first to represent Altoona on the grand stage of the UFC.

As Charlie continued winning, I continued thinking of the time when the boxing club newcomer knocked him flat. *No way,* I'd think to myself. *I can't see it happening. I can't see Charlie ever becoming good enough to fight in the world's premier MMA organization.*

But I was wrong. I found out about Charlie's four-fight UFC deal on Sherdog.com. When I saw the article I first felt absolute happiness. There was not a guy out there who deserved it more, or who could be a better representative for Altoona and Hollidaysburg and the martial arts. Plus, he had a Master's degree. Fans would adore him. Then envy overcame me. *What about me?* I thought. *I've always felt more complete than him as a fighter. I have the Master's degree/fighter niche. Shit, I'm probably too far behind now in the fight game's constant evolution to be able to seriously make a run for it. Or am I? How the hell did he improve as much as he did? He's fighting at 170? Last I saw him I was 150 and I believe I could have smoked him. Why did I make the choices I made? Were they the right ones? I'm 24 and it's too late. I'm 24 and it's too fucking late.*

March 31, 2010. Bojangles' Coliseum. Charlotte, North Carolina. UFC Fight Night Live 21. Charlie Brenneman vs. Jason High.

Though I'd never attended a UFC event, I couldn't miss the debut of a hometown hero, so without hesitation I splurged and snagged a front row ticket. I hoped he would succeed so I could be proud of Altoona and so I'd be forced to confront my envy head on. How would watching him make me feel? I knew it would only intensify envy's burn but I wanted, needed to hurt myself.

Would this be the spark I needed to quit teaching in Charlottesville and go for broke, to see how far I could go as a combat athlete? Or would I realize I was happy with what I'd done and what I was doing? Could this experience bring closure? Could this cut me down to some level I might never recover from? I bought the ticket hoping to scratch the constant itch I had to drop everything and find out how good a fighter I could be.

I'd think about it before bed. I thought about "making a return" while having sex. I'd sit in the bathtub and wonder what weight class was best for me, where I could be most dominating. I'd studied the fields of strength and conditioning my entire life because I wanted to use the most advanced training methods to make myself the best possible fighter. I blew $1,500 (which I didn't have) to fly out to Vegas for the National Strength & Conditioning Association's annual conference solely to help advance my knowledge of training methods. I'd carved out time in my life every single day for years to research sports performance nutrition. My views have changed considerably, but at the time my reason for studying these fields had nothing to do with an interest in them or of wanting to help others. It had everything to do with living up to my own egocentric standards; me and me only.

Side note on Bojangles' Coliseum: It was once named "Independence Arena," but is now named by a brand of good ol' mass-slaughtered, deep-fried chicken. Marinate on that one.

When Bojangles' Coliseum was Independence Arena, one of the most important moments in my life and in MMA occurred: UFC 5. On April 7, 1995, Ken Shamrock fought Royce Gracie to a thirty-six-minute and six-second draw. The crowd booed frantically for action as Ken Shamrock maintained top position and defended against any offense by BJJ master and undefeated UFC fighter Royce Gracie. During their first fight two years prior, Ken had tapped-out as Royce Gracie choked him with a technique using his gi. In the interim, Royce dominated all opponents despite being outweighed. He was the sole reason BJJ went mainstream. It seemed unbeatable. Martial artists around the world who had spent years learning to punch and kick began realizing the impracticality of arts they had spent their lives mastering. They began learning this style of grappling because it proved to be the single most effective martial art when two human beings of various disciplines fought with few rules. It seemed invincible. Until this fight.

The majority of the fight took place inside the guard of Royce Gracie. Ken figured out a way to defend against BJJ attacks from the guard. He kept his face buried in Royce chest, kept Royce's back flat to the mat, kept his own elbows tight to his side to avoid Royce's armbar attempts, kept his knees wide and his base strong so Royce could not sweep him and take top position. At the fight's conclusion, the UFC commentator said: "Gracie is a mess. Shamrock looks fantastic." Side note number two: Ken looked so fantastic that several movie offers came his way after the fight.

While the legend of Royce Gracie is forever linked to the effectiveness and rise in worldwide popularity of BJJ, so should Ken Shamrock's name be forever linked as the pioneer of the "mixed" in MMA. Ken combined solid punching and wrestling with lethal leglocks and a strong and conditioned body. This made me realize that although some martial arts were clearly better than others when it comes to a fight (i.e. Muay Thai trumps taekwondo), I also came to realize that no single art is indefensible. Along with the rest of the underground MMA community, I came to see how a well-rounded approach to developing as a fighter was the best way to go. This meant studying all the martial arts proven to work inside the cage, along with studying and implementing the latest information in the fields of strength, conditioning, and nutrition.

There were clear blue skies and the sticky humidity was rising when I pulled into Bojangles' Coliseum wearing Charlie Brenneman's t-shirt. *Does Charlie know the history of this place?* I wondered. *What does it mean to him? Does it mean as much to him as it means to me? Does that matter? Why was he drinking a Pepsi during his interview a few days ago? Does he know how bad soda is for the athlete's body?* I felt guilty bringing all these thoughts and possibly their bad karma into the arena. *Why am I such an envious asshole? These feelings. They are what I came here for, right?*

I shook hands with top fighters in the sport like Dan Hardy, Spenser Fisher, and Kurt Pellegrino. I saw Eddie Bravo and Renzo Gracie—two athletes I'd worked with and studied. Lights of all colors streamed across the fans, onto the cage and into my eyes and they moved with the beat as rap and heavy metal pounded into my ears. I'm not sure if I was moving because of the music or because envy wanted to burst the hell out from inside of me.

I approached the security guard: "Excuse me sir. Excuse me."

"Yes?"

"This stadium is nearly empty, and I drove five hours just to see this one undercard fight. He's from my hometown, we're friends. Is there anyway I could sit in the front row here just for this fight?"

"I don't see why not."

So it was. Nobody had a closer seat to see Charlie Brenneman's debut UFC fight against Jason "The Kansas City Bandit" High. Heavy rock music came on. The lights dimmed. The huge television screen above the fighter's entrance read, "Charlie Brenneman, Altoona, Pennsylvania." I began a stadium-wide chant of "Span-iard, Span-iard." Charlie must have had sixty fans who had made the drive from Altoona spread throughout the crowd, all wearing his t-shirt. I tried to take pictures as he bounced in the cage to keep himself warm and focused. But I couldn't. I froze. Nerves made me forget how to take a picture or send a text message from my phone. My entire being was focused on Charlie's safety, on hoping he did well, on living vicariously through him. I could barely breathe. I sat down to catch my breath. Charlie looked over and pointed to me and I felt my envy evaporate. Every decision I'd made in my life suddenly felt validated.

At several moments throughout Charlie's fight I nearly shit myself. I felt out of my body, in his. I instinctively slipped jabs that came his way, finished the takedowns he scored by driving my hips forward. They were subtle movements, but movements intense enough and apparently frequent enough to make me feel sore the following day. Charlie controlled the fight. He secured several beautiful takedowns where he landed immediately in side control—a dominant position that the judges score favorably. He smothered Jason High with wrestling skills. He landed three solid right crosses, the same punch he'd been floored by years ago at the A.B.C. The fight went to a decision. All three judges scored the fight in Charlie's favor. He had just defeated a very game opponent. The referee raised Charlie's hand in victory and Charlie closed his eyes. He had just won his UFC debut.

The envy of seeing a local guy make it first, a local guy with even the master's degree/teacher niche carved out, the thought that it could be me backstage parting the curtains and taking the same steps Ken Shamrock did, it all disappeared. My wanting to fight again, the deep itch I couldn't reach by burying my shins into Thai pads, practicing double-leg takedowns, or deadlifting three times my bodyweight was scratched and relieved. The discontent that ruined sleep and made me feel like a worthless bum too scared to reach his potential during the day, disappeared. I no longer felt the arrogance that crept into my blood when it came to my MMA potential. I was content to watch. Content to follow. Content to cheer. Content to know I could choose a different path that, like BJJ, has its own positive principles of leverage. As Helio Gracie once riffed on Archimedes, "Give me the right leverage and I can lift the world." My leverage would be to educate and train others—be it a fifteen-year-old aspiring MMA fighter, a forty-year-old creative writer, or a ninety-year-old great-grandparent just wanting to move better. I'd help others fight obesity, diabetes, and depression. My fighting spirit would be released more against ideas than a physical opponent. I knew then that I'd spend my life going toe-to-toe with ignorance.

An hour after the fight, Charlie came down into the front row and we spoke for a few minutes. My eyes welled up from the joy of his success and from my own epiphany that I could get on with my life without feeling like a pile of shit. I didn't want to bawl in front of him.

"I'm so proud of you, Charlie," I said slapping his back. "You deserve it, brother."

"Thanks, Cameron, are you still living in Arizona doing your writing thing?"

Just then a swarm of ninety newly minted fans approached hollering, "Spaniard, can you sign my shirt?" and "Hey Charlie can I get a picture?"

Charlie tried to continue the conversation with me, but I felt the buzz of energy from all the fans closing in. I grabbed Charlie's shoulder, leaned into his ear and said, "Now is your time, man. Soak it up. Enjoy it."

"I'll try," he said through a smile spanning the length of his face.

I walked back to my seat. I looked down at my Charlie Brenneman t-shirt, looked over at him and watched as he instantly became a celebrity, looked into my camera at the pictures I'd taken of the arena prior to his entrance. At first I held the camera upside down and it hit me. I'd been looking at the whole damn situation upside down. Instead of focusing on the positive outcomes of my choices, I only thought of the what-ifs or of the positive experiences of others. *Our eyes take pictures of the world upside down*, I thought to myself. *Then our brain turns the picture the right way up and shows us what we're seeing in a way that makes sense. Is this not the point of writing?* To see things differently? *To turn established, easy untruths and turn them right side up? I've been living in the envious eyes. On the surface.*

I watched the fights for the first time in my life as an informed spectator. No more, no less. And I still feel a joy I can't reach the bottom of. When I shook hands with Charlie after his fight, I felt my cravings for the whole sport stay in his hand. The years of voices telling me I wasn't good enough faded. I literally tasted smoke. I thought about how the smoke from forest fires contain a family of chemicals that make plants hypersensitive to lower, altered light levels, how this triggers them to grow thicker, sturdier stems than they otherwise would have.

What I left in Charlie's hands were my aspirations to fight again in MMA. What he gave back was a new desire, a desire to use all the MMA and training knowledge I'd gained over the years to positively change the world. I could train fighters, but I could also train the general population and use MMA to fight the societal and health crisis in America. When I got home I enrolled to become a Certified Conditioning Coach through the Mixed Martial Arts Conditioning Association. This would pair well with the personal training certification I already had through the National Strength & Conditioning Association. My next fight would not be measured in rounds, but throughout a lifetime. It would sustain and fulfill me longer than anything in the cage could. My opponent, my fight, would be against the slipping aspects of American society.

Log 16

Thicker, sturdier bones

Wolff's Law states that bone will adapt and grow in line with resistive forces. Bones respond best to compressive forces. They require the mechanical stress that is created by physical activity. This stress must be performed on a daily basis.

Shins are more than a device for finding furniture in the dark. Bury them into Thai pads and gently tap glass bottles against them. For the body: Wear a weight-vest when walking, consistently front squat and deadlift and perform other exercises (like plyometrics) which place stress through the kinetic chain. Strong bones will prevent injury and make for a stronger body.

CHAPTER 22

Conclusion and the child, the role to be born.

I will never fight again.

It did not sting to say that. This cycle is one I want to continue for the rest of my life. By cycle I mean this: I want to fully give myself to something, then reflect deeply to extract all the juice I possibly can, then shape a story reconstituting the juice with the pulp. In this instance, I gave myself, over the course of years, to fighting, over the course of months to acting, and over the course of years to thoughts about the emotions I felt towards my father. So here I had the juice and the pulp from three different sources, and as any good nutrition enthusiast will tell you, it's much healthier to make juice with carrots, tomatoes, and apples than with just either one. They will also tell you that it's healthy to eat the pulp, it provides fiber and fiber helps us get rid of things.

Getting rid of things is how I've often felt during the completion of this book. Each time I sat down to write or to edit, I was forced to experience the past. I was forced on countless occasions, even now as I type this, to experience my father throwing my sister against the garage door, the coffee cup off the dashboard, and curse words into the air. Those moments, of course, are what seasoned writers will tell you can cause minor bouts of self-induced writer depression. I wouldn't doubt that it's the reason, after a few hours of writing, that I suddenly felt completely exhausted and reached for that extra cup of coffee.

But those are just the bad moments. I also extracted the juice from all the great moments I've had—the fights and the yoga and the acting and the training and the finding of my life partner. What happens when I relive those moments time and time again for the sake of clearer insights and hopefully equally clear yet creative prose is that they begin to dull. If you sharpen a knife all day eventually it becomes dull. So it is and has become as I finally finish this book. I've learned as much as I possibly could about the topics mentioned within these pages because I've been ultra-reflective. If I'm in a bad mood and write about a past experience I see it a little differently from when I'm in a great mood. I've purposely tried to write from all sorts of emotions so that I could, intentionally, see things from different angles.

So much of our life's most tragic and triumphant moments happen in the blink of an eye. And I fear, constantly, that I don't fully absorb those moments the way I could or should. I can say here that I've done my best. I've fought hard in the cage and I've fought equally hard, perhaps more so, on the page, trying to juice the information from these experiences. At first, it seemed like a fight was a fight, I had my hand raised and that felt good. But upon reflection I realize that that fight created a man out of me and made me believe in values that I thought only appeared in quotations and never in real life. That fight was the impetus that sparked me to write, and therefore learn, about the years of trauma brought into my life because of my father's absence.

I challenge others to join in on this cycle with me. Experience something or relive experiences in your mind then write about it. The intention need not be to publish a memoir; the intention need only be to learn. I believe that writing is the ultimate act of self-discovery. I've written this quote across every chalkboard I've ever taught on. There is something undeniably magical about sitting down and capturing all those fleeting glimmers of an experience and finding meaning. Experience something or relive an experience, write about it, drink the juice and eat the pulp, share it with others, then start over again.

I've thought about my experiences so much that I have wanted to let them go for some time now. I've had far too much juice to drink and pulp to eat. I'm full. I want to release this phase of my life into the world and therefore out of the scrutiny and reflection of my body. I want to purge it. Then, when I feel an emptiness filling me up, I want to throw myself into a new topic or experience. And I want to make juice and pulp again and taste a new flavor through the process of writing. And I want to share it with people who are willing to learn and think and drink. And I want to read works that do the same. And I think if we have this type of reciprocal relationship, one human being can have the knowledge of thousands of others by way of inhabiting their experience through well-crafted words. This is my goal until the day I die. I can ask for nothing more than for you to join me. Seriously, join me. Go to CameronConaway.com and send me a message or share your story.

Because I've reflected so much, I can point to exactly where I realized I would no longer fight again. Admitting it was a whole different matter. That occurred at the beginning of this chapter.

It was a mid-October Tucson morning in 2008. I drove from my guest-house in town to one of the highest points around: Mount Lemmon. Mount Lemmon is at the top of the Santa Catalina mountain range, a range I hike on lower elevation levels weekly. It is a little over 9,000 feet in elevation. This is about the same level that elite-caliber fighters, such as Oscar De La Hoya, train at to improve their stamina. I was thinking deeply about fighting again—which meant if this training session up in Mount Lemmon went well, that extra grain of confidence would be enough for me to have my fourth fight. A good workout would be the last sliver of fire I would need to sign up with a promoter for a fight, possibly during the semester break in December. Unlike central Tucson, it rained quite a bit in Mount Lemmon. There were no cacti. Green grass and soft soil replaced exposed brown rock. There were puddles all over the place and I walked around for quite some time. Finally, I found a perfect inclined road to run, and I reminisced about the hill I'd run in Altoona, the one where a Tastykake truck always seemed to tease me.

Tastykake Training

> Blue-hooded sweatshirt,
> black sweatpants,
> the sprint uphill
> begins. Leaves
> pitter-patter like speed-bags,
> doubling his foot speed.
> Wintry wind thrashes him
> like a Jack Russell's chew rope,
> brings mucus, blue

sleeves caked with dried
stringsnot.
Spit fades in slushroads,
he spits on the curb
where it's visible.
A Tastykake truck
rumbles in front
of him, forcing
a deep breath of exhaust. (2006)

I walked at a steady pace up the hill—a ritual I do before getting into a serious uphill run—and could feel the elevation already taking a toll on my body as I approached the top. My legs burned much sooner than usual. My heart rate was higher than usual and my lungs were working harder to get in enough air to replenish them. This hill, though no longer than the average city block, scared me because of its elevation. Scared me enough to make me smile. Smile because I knew a decision would be reached one way or the other.

After reaching the top of the hill I did some light stretching, adjusted the tongues on my shoes to the center and walked downhill to begin a series of uphill sprints and downhill walks. Hills are natures' built-in interval work-outs. I told myself I'd do three sets of three. As I reached the bottom, I placed a pencil on top of a Post-It note so I could tally each set and not forget what number I was on. I took a deep breath and took off uphill.

The burn felt good. I felt myself becoming more dangerous as a fighter. I walked down. I took off uphill again and pictured fighting in the late rounds and being full of energy while my opponent became a coward to fatigue. I walked down. Again, I went up and down. One set complete. I completed another set, though clearly I moved much slower and I became a little dizzy because I was unaccustomed to the elevation. But I finished that set and tallied it on my Post-It note.

I took off again, slower than before but giving no less effort. I labored to reach the middle of the road. The thought of stopping occurred to me, briefly. I labored hard to reach close to the top as my legs and lungs burned intensely and my mind kept telling me to quit. I reached the top and took a deep breath. I had every intention of walking back down despite the vomit I felt coming up my throat and the burn of my legs and lungs even while

I stood still for those couple seconds. In that extra second of hesitation, I looked around for a sign maybe, or maybe to see if someone was watching which could have created the impetus needed for me to continue down the hill. Whatever I was looking for, unconsciously, even if my looking around was just a stall tactic, I found meaning in it.

As I panted and felt the pain creeping into my body, the nausea in my stomach and the slight dizziness in my head, I saw a sign. Literally. The road I had been running was aptly named Retreat Road. The old me, the me driven by an incessant need to impress my absent father, the need to impress those who I fabricated to have doubted me (and those who actually did), the need to impress all those who bullied me or sized me up with a cocky grimace or badmouthed my mom, the need to impress those who beat me in other sports, or in other disciplines that make up MMA, like boxing, wrestling, and BJJ, the need to impress myself enough so that all of these insecurities could disappear, would have acted differently. The old me would have looked at that sign and thought challenge. The old me would have said fuck you and walked on down that hill. The old me wanted to look at a *Flex Magazine* and not feel depressed that a future girlfriend would much rather be with a man like that—no matter how fake—than with a man like me.

Over these years of fighting, I wanted to, in a tangible way, overcome my father's shortcomings. But now, though I wasn't ready for kids (where I'd be given the chance to prove to be a better father), I was in a great relationship for the past months that calmed my soul, that brought the stability that so often cut short the intensity of my inner-fire for fighting.

I reverted back to the past, to Stanislavsky. For years, the way I believed I could systematically do better in life was to do better than my father. Maybe my way to do this was by reaching a level of education that he didn't reach and fighting at a level that he could not have dreamed of. Now, I've completed those goals. I happened to fall in love with education and fighting as I pursued them, but I did them, in many ways, for the wrong reasons. I wonder how many people in this world, upon probing what it is that made them achieve that highest of highs in their lives, would cite pain or a close relative of pain? My greatest accomplishments grew from pain. Through writing *Caged*, I became pain-free. Now what? How could I achieve without that greatest of motivators?

The new me saw that sign—Retreat Road—and felt a more localized pain than the one where my accomplishments grew. Shortly thereafter, I said the words that had resided on the tip of my tongue for years. The words that drove me to find new obstacles, to explore new fields of interest, that provided an opposition (and therefore a victory) every morning that I woke up the second my alarm went off. The words that scared me. I said I quit.

I gasped for air. I felt the throbbing pain burn through my thighs. I felt the new me consume the old me. I thought of Antoine Lavoisier's quote from 1789 that my environmental studies instructor brought to class the week prior:

In general, respiration is nothing but a slow combustion of carbon and hydrogen, which is entirely similar to that which occurs in a lighted lamp or candle, and that, from this point of view, animals that respire are true combustible bodies that burn and consume themselves.

The new me realized I could workout to remain healthy and strong and confident with only the need to prove it to my own self rather than an audience of strangers. It was a sad ride home. But even then I could see this sadness wasn't nearly as deep as the sadness or anger I've carried with me since I was a little boy. I remembered a poem I wrote years ago.

Then and Now

Then,
a clenched fist
was mom turning
towards the stainless-steel sink,
away from dad, her back,
absorbing white knuckle
rage song.
Now,
a clenched fist
is her son, maturing
through fighting, shedding
yellow as a dandelion,
shining through rain clouds (2004)

I cried and sang the refrain of seemingly every love song I had ever heard because I missed Maggie, the woman I love who lived on the other side of the country. The woman who loves me regardless of what I achieve. The woman who brought tears to my eyes when she cradled my face, looked into my eyes and said:

Cameron, it is not what you do or have done that I love. It is you. I love you. If you decide to give up what you've worked for to be a janitor tomorrow, I will wake up each morning and make sure you have the shiniest keys in your department. I'll support you and cheer for you and shine your keys, Cameron. My love is unconditional.

When I came home there was a handwritten letter from her in my mailbox. It warmed my entire body to read her writing, to see the strokes of letters that her hands created. I sat in my house and looked at my bookshelf, poured over the writing of the many students I taught over the past couple months, listened to the hum of my refrigerator, the chirps of the pigeons and cactus wrens outside, the barks of the neighbor's dog, then the cry of my landlords' two-year-old baby boy.

As I surfed the waves of his cry, driven only by life's bare essentials, I felt my shoulders relax. I felt lighter. In that moment, I let go of everything but the essential. I let go of the negative experiences that have held me up over the years. *If this causes me to fall hard,* I said to myself, *so be it. I've learned to fall like the BJJ player, to protect the body through controlling the distribution of force by slapping the mat with hands open. With hands open. Hands open. Open. O Pen.*

CHAPTER 23

Acknowledgments

I'd like to thank a few members of the team who made this possible:

Johnny Robertson, who taught—in the only way that made sense to me at the time—this lesson: If you bust your ass, good things will happen. Johnny, I'll never forget the day I walked into the boxing club to see a newspaper article about my academic achievements hanging from the bulletin board. I knew then the importance of mind fitness.

Ken Shamrock, Lisa Hickey, Jim Arvanitis, Saulo Ribeiro, Glen Cordoza and Dinty W. Moore for blurbs that would make any writer blush.

Novelist Richard Russo, whose creative writing award at Penn State Altoona boosted my confidence and made me believe I could be a writer.

Memoirist and novelist Robert Goolrick, for telling an awestruck fan the truth and asking nothing in return.

From Penn State Altoona: my teacher and life coach, Todd Davis, whose athlete-spirit and academic advice I've relied on over the years. You were there when I crafted the very first words of the very first essay, when I had no idea it could or would lead to a book. On your shoulders I've cried, laughed, and fought for rebounds. I'm forever indebted to you. Steve Sherrill and Lee Peterson for opening the doors of your offices and home to a stressed-out student unable to make decisions and in desperate need of opinions. You helped me remain emotionally steady so I could fully realize my potential. Lee, that intro to poetry class, I can only describe what it has made of me by using the ellipses. So here....

From the University of Arizona: Ander Monson—who taught me the fine art of smashing genres. Fenton Johnson, who stressed the importance of "writing" in "creative writing." My colleague Ryan Winet, who accepted without hesitation my quirks as a friend and who read the manuscript with his poet's eye. Frances Sjoberg, who gave a hardworking small-town guy a chance to be the Poet-in-Residence at the renowned Poetry Center. Your decision opened doors that will carry me through the rest of this life.

From Poetry: Inside Out: Madeline Kiser and Guy McPherson. Madeline, you'll forever be my Tucson mom. You and your family came closer to my heart than you'll ever know. Gabo and Josh, I consider you brothers. Guy, you're often unnecessarily shrouded in some dark cloak because of the environmental topics you address, but you're one of the gentlest, warmest men I've met. You made me learn, which made my life more difficult, and for which I'll always be appreciative.

Lynn Pribus, editor extraordinaire, for smoothing out jagged edges and for teaching me how transitions in writing should be as fluid as those on the mat.

My fiancée, Maggie, for her unceasing faith in me and for the unconditional nourishment and love for which I will always reciprocate. I wake each morning with a smile because you're in my life. Maggie, you make me the strongest, happiest man I can be. I couldn't have done this without you.

My mom, who taught me through example the value of hard work, the bond of love and the dedication and devotion necessary in order to raise a child. I've applied those values in thick, sweeping layers to all the challenges I've ever tackled, and because of that, I've always walked away learning about myself.

My stepdad, Nab, for becoming a father, no, a dad to a son of which he shared no blood.

My amazing students at Ottawa University. You teach me far more than I teach you.

My band of brilliant, creative and supportive warriors on Facebook.

The number 3, for reminding me to stay humble in its three-quarter-arched, nearly-the-perfect-energy-of-an-8 way. Number 3, I use you as spaces after chapter titles, as blows into tissues, and as toe touches in the shower. You keep me grounded. You keep me striving for perfection even though I know and you know it's not impossible.

Philadelphia Volunteer Lawyers for the Arts, for even existing and for connecting me with Michael Adler.

Daryn Clark at WhatsYourFight.com for the sponsorship of a lifetime.

I'm grateful to these publications for accepting the following works in varying stages of their development:

Aethlon: The Journal of Sport Literature—Caged

Apollo's Lyre—Produce

Blue Fog Journal—Caged, Caged—Part Two, Caged—Part Three

Conceit Magazine—How the World Works

Crash—Crime and Astonishment

The Flask Review—Two Years after the Engine Shop Closed and Brief History of My Life.

Litany—Park Avenue

Memewar Magazine—Mind Margins: A Pre-Debut Prose Poem

The New Writer—A Fighter's Thoughts

Ottawa Arts Review—Caged—Part Two and Cage-Fighter

(SALit) Savannah Art and Literature—Inexact Number of Ways of Looking at a Red-Tail

The Smoking Poet—Watching Me

Stymie Magazine—Across the Middle

The Toe Tree Journal—The Patience of Varicella Zoster and Suicide Sighting

Turbulence Magazine—Eva One

Cameron writing with his sister

Cameron's first punching bag

With Renzo Gracie

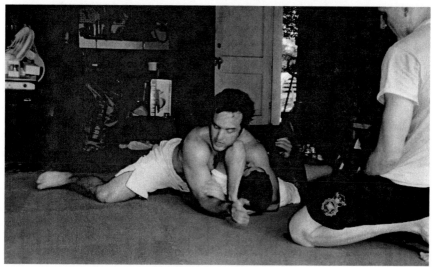

Teaching MMA out of his garage

Altoona Boxing Club

Altoona Boxing Club

Johnny Robertson   Victory two (Photo: Extreme Fighting Challenge)

Hockenberry and Conaway locked up (Photo: Extreme Fighting Challenge)

Omoplata (Photo: Extreme Fighting Challenge)　　　Medea, with Olivia Parry (Photo: Gary Baranek)

Debut victory (Photo: Extreme Fighting Challenge)

Rear naked choke
(Photo: Extreme Fighting Challenge)

Taking Hockenberry's back (Photo: Extreme Fighting Challenge)

Seconds into the debut
(Photo: Extreme Fighting Challenge)

With mom post-fight

With Nab post-fight

Chopping wood to train

Sparring at a State College park

Merging with nature at Mount Lemmon

After an outdoor sparring session

Writing poetry while
wearing Renzo Gracie
Academy t-shirt

With Pulitzer-Prize winner
Richard Russo

Author Photo